Fodor's 89
New Orleans

Fodor's Travel Publications, Inc.
New York and London

Fodor's 89 New Orleans

Editor: Jacqueline Russell
Editorial Contributors: Millie Ball, Jason Berry, Mary Gehman, Don Lee Keith, John Kemp, Lisa LeBlanc-Berry, Honey Naylor, Nancy Ries
Art Director: Fabrizio La Rocca
Cartographer: David Lindroth
Illustrator: Karl Tanner
Cover Photograph: Dennis J. Cipnic

Design: Vignelli Associates

Special Sales

Fodor's Travel Publications are available at special discounts for bulk purchases (100 copies or more) for sales promotions or premiums. Special editions, including personalized covers, excerpts of existing guides, and corporate imprints, can be created in large quantities for special needs. For more information write to Special Marketing, Fodor's Travel Publications, 201 E. 50th St., New York, NY 10022. Enquiries from the United Kingdom should be sent to Merchandise Division, Random House UK Ltd, 30-32 Bedford Square, London WC1B 3SG.

Contents

Foreword

New Orleans is a special city, often regarded as the least "American" of any in the United States. It is best known for its regional cuisine, remarkable amalgam of architectural styles, and boisterous Mardi Gras festivities, and as the birthplace of jazz music.

Our New Orleans writers have put together information on the widest possible range of activities, and within that range present you with selections of events and places that will be safe, worthwhile, and of good value. The descriptions we provide are just enough for you to make your own informed choices from among our selections.

This is an exciting time for Fodor's, as it begins a three-year program to rewrite, reformat, and redesign all 140 of its guides. Here are just a few of the exciting new features:

★ Brand-new computer-generated maps locating all the top attractions, hotels, restaurants, and shops

★ A unique system of numbers and legends to help readers move effortlessly between text and maps

★ A new star rating system for hotels and restaurants

★ Restaurant reviews by major food critics around the world

★ Stamped, self-addressed postcards, bound into every guide, give readers an opportunity to help evaluate hotels and restaurants

★ Complete page redesign for instant retrieval of information

★ FODOR'S CHOICE—Our favorite museums, beaches, cafes, romantic hideaways, festivals, and more

★ HIGHLIGHTS '89—An insider's look at the most important developments in tourism during the past year

★ TIME OUT—The best and most convenient lunch stops along the shopping and exploring routes

★ Exclusive background essays create a powerful portrait of each destination

★ A mini-journal for travelers to keep track of their own itineraries and addresses

For their help in preparing this guide, we would particularly like to thank Beverly Gianna and her staff at the Greater New Orleans Tourist and Convention Commission.

While every care has been taken to ensure the accuracy of the information in this guide, the passage of time will always bring change, and consequently, the publisher cannot accept responsibility for errors that may occur.

All prices and opening times quoted here are based on information available to us at press time. Hours and admission fees may change, however, and the prudent traveler will avoid inconvenience by calling ahead.

Fodor's wants to hear about your travel experiences, both pleasant and unpleasant. When a hotel or restaurant fails to live up to its billing, let us know and we will investigate the complaint and revise our entries where the facts warrant it.

Send your letters to the editors of Fodor's Travel Publications, 201 E. 50th Street, New York, NY 10022, or 30-32 Bedford Square, London WC1B 3SG, England.

Highlights '89 and Fodor's Choice

Highlights '89

On the hotel front there have been several renovations, some of them a result of changes in ownership. The erstwhile International on Canal Street is now a part of the Doubletree chain, and, following an expenditure of $5 million, is called the **Doubletree New Orleans.** Major changes have been made in the guest rooms and public areas, including a new restaurant and lounge. The new owners of **Le Pavilion,** at Baronne and Poydras streets, have completely redecorated the hotel and seen to the cleaning of every piece of crystal in the glittering chandeliers. The venerable **Pontchartrain Hotel** in the Garden District has also changed ownership, but any alterations will be made cautiously. (Moving the piano in the lounge a mere eight feet precipitated an avalanche of angry letters from lounge regulars.) **Howard Johnson's** has spread its umbrella to cover the former Sheraton West Bank and the Gateway in Metairie. Both hotels opened under HoJo management in the summer of 1987 following major renovations. The **Lamothe House,** on Esplanade Avenue, recently had a face-lift that catapulted the guest house into an upper-crust hostelry. The **Economy Motor Lodge Downtown,** on Tulane Avenue, laid out more than a million dollars to redo its entire facility. Finally, **Stone Manor** is an 11-room antique-filled guest house that recently opened Uptown at Peniston Street and St. Charles Avenue.

Of no less importance is news on the New Orleans dining scene. The Jackson Brewery Corporation's two new facilities, the **Millhouse** and **The Marketplace on Decatur Street,** both contain restaurants, fast-food outlets, retail shops, and boutiques. The Millhouse, adjacent to the Jax Brewery, is home to **Seb's, Birraporetti's,** and **Druscilla** restaurants; the **Hard Rock Cafe** and **Morton's Steak House** have opened their doors in the Marketplace. Over on Bourbon Street, **Felix's** has expanded to take in the former quarters of Toney's Spaghetti House next door. Recent restaurant closings include **Scruples** on Burgundy Street and **Sweet Pepper Grill** on Riverwalk.

Sports enthusiasts should note that the Canoe and Trail Shop is now **Canoe and Trail Adventures** and has moved to the Adventure Sports Store on Veterans Boulevard in Metairie. Also of interest is the new **Jack Nicklaus's English Turn Golf Course** on the West Bank, which will host the USF&G Golf Classic.

Even couch potatoes will be uprooted by the new **Riverfront Streetcar,** which at press time was scheduled to be operating by August 1988. The streetcar will roll along the Mississippi River between Esplanade Avenue and Julia Street After completion of upriver construction, the streetcar will run all the way up to the Robin Street Wharf, where the *Delta Queen* and *Mississippi Queen* put in to port. Operated by the Regional Transit Authority, the Riverfront Streetcar will have the same fare as the city buses and the St. Charles Streetcar—currently 60 cents exact fare (and five cents for a transfer). There will be 10 stops along the way—five above and five below Canal Street.

In the fall of 1990 construction should be complete on a new Riverfront Streetcar stop at the **Aquarium of the Americas and Riverfront Park.** Ground was broken for the $40 million attraction in October 1987, and work proceeds apace. Located on the

Mississippi River between the Canal Street Wharf and the Jackson Brewery, the aquarium is expected annually to attract 863,000 visitors and generate $53 million in revenue for the city. More than 4,000 different species of aquatic creatures will swim for their lives, as it were, in about a million gallons of water. The sea creatures will slosh about in four major exhibits: the Amazon (with piranhas, anacondas, and giant catfish), Caribbean Reef, Mississippi River, and Gulf Coast, the latter featuring alligators, snapping turtles, stingrays, and largemouth bass. The complex will cover 16 riverfront acres, nine acres of which will be a landscaped urban park.

Another streetcar stop will be at **Louisiana Science Centre,** which will be adjacent to Riverwalk on its upriver side. The complex is slated for a summer 1988 opening.

The Science Centre will cover 160,000 square feet and offer informative, state-of-the-art participatory exhibits. There will be exhibition galleries on two levels, a Chrysler Pavilion on the Wharf, a boat dock, laboratories, class/meeting rooms, a Math Resource Center, computer lab, food service, and an outdoor Physics Playground. Many exhibits will focus on Louisiana and Gulf Coast industries, such as natural gas, maritime, oil exploration and "water science." Hurricane season on the Gulf Coast runs from June through November. You can fulfill that lifelong dream of being in the heart of a hurricane in an exhibit that simulates everything from the stillness in the eye of the storm to 75-mile-an-hour winds and driving rain. In another exhibit you can board a man-maneuvered space vehicle and sit at the controls for a fantasy lift-off and an out-of-this-world feeling.

The Science Centre will be run by a MAPPER 5/Data Collection System donated by the Sperry Corporation. The MAPPER, which also is used to run Disney World's Epcot Center, will handle bar-code admission ticketing, exhibit monitoring, visitor evaluations, and accounting and compilation of marketing data. The MAPPER appears to have a mind of its own. (The Science Centre's phone number, incidentally, is 504/ 529$-$E $=$ MC^2, with the equation equaling 3622.)

Riverwalk and the Science Centre incorporate a portion of the 1984 World's Fair site, and plans are afoot for further utilization of that area on the riverfront. In August 1988, a 7,500-seat **Amphitheatre** will open on Erato Street, adjacent to the Science Centre facility. The first event will be the opening-night gala of the Republican National Convention. The amphitheater will be open from April through November, and developers plan to book national theatrical touring companies, dance and musical events.

Scheduled for an early 1989 opening is the 10-screen **Riverfront Movie Theatre,** which will occupy a portion of the International Pavilion of the 1984 World's Fair. First-run movies will be shown in the two-story, 2,500-seat theater, operated by the Venture International Group in association with United Artists.

There is a flurry of construction activity on Poydras Street between the Hyatt Regency Hotel and the Superdome. When the dust settles—projected for August 1988—the Central Business District will have a new mall complex. The **New Orleans Centre** will contain 600,000 square feet of space, with 150 restaurants, boutiques, and stores sprinkled throughout three levels. Among the center's tenants will be Lord & Taylor and the city's second Macy's (the first is in Kenner's Esplanade Mall).

No doubt about it, New Orleans is a party town, with a seemingly insatiable appetite for festivals. Mardi Gras, of course, is the biggest blowout of them all, but there are other festivals scheduled virtually every month of the year. Two additions to the growing fest list are the **Classical Music Festival** and the **Louis Armstrong Classic Jazz Festival** at Le Petit Théâtre du Vieux Carré on Jackson Square in the French Quarter.

The inaugural Classical Music Festival, which will be an annual January affair, coincided, not coincidentally, with the January 1988, Le Petit production of Peter Shaffer's acclaimed play *Amadeus*.

To give you an idea of what you might expect in future festivals, Mozart himself put in an appearance, along with Queen Marie Antoinette, at a young musicians' Children's Birthday Party for the music world's most famous child prodigy. A gala Austrian Dinner for Mozart's Birthday took place in the Jackson Brewery Millhouse, with music by "Amadeus and Friends" woodwind trio, and the Omni Royal Orleans Hotel hosted a Viennese Tea. A pianist, vocalist, and violinist presented an intimate peek at female concert artists in 18th-century Vienna and at the women in Mozart's life, and another program saluted classical music in 19th-century New Orleans, presenting recently discovered classical music written by "Creoles of Colour." Other events during the five-day fest included "The Voice of God: Mozart's Vocal Music," "Mozart and His Brothers: The Viennese School," Mass at St. Louis Cathedral, and, of course, a performance of *Amadeus*.

The effects of jazz on classical music will be among the symposiums during the Louis Armstrong Festival, which blasts off on July Fourth. "Satchmo," who was born in New Orleans July 4, 1900, will be saluted with a variety of jazzy doings, including riverboat cruises, jazz dances, a brass band parade, walking tours, and a big birthday bash in Louis Armstrong Park.

For information about the two festivals, write to Le Petit Théâtre du Vieux Carré, 616 St. Peter St., New Orleans, LA 70116, tel. 504/522–9958.

Prior to 1985, laid-back New Orleans was not a major convention city. Its considerable charms notwithstanding, the Crescent City lacked the facilities that major conventions require. **The New Orleans Convention Center** opened shop in 1985, and after only two years of operation has catapulted New Orleans into one of the 6 most-favored convention cities. The city hosts about 1,200 major conventions a year, for more than 800,000 delegates, who utilize about 200,000 square feet of space. The economic impact on the city hovers around $500 million.

Previously, conventions with, say, 20,000 or more delegates had to split their exhibits between the Convention Center and the Rivergate, which meant shuttle buses and a fair amount of inconvenience. But now the city is expanding its already cavernous, 381,000-square-foot convention center. The center will have 700,000 square feet of contiguous exhibit space on one level, an additional 50 meeting rooms, and a 40,000-square-foot ballroom. Ground-breaking for the expansion is set for fall 1988. January 1991 is the targeted completion date—and more than 100 conventions are already booked for the expanded facilities.

Fodor's Choice

No two people will agree on what makes a perfect vacation, but it's fun and helpful to know what others think. We hope you'll have a chance to experience some of Fodor's Choices yourself while visiting the Big Easy. For detailed information about each entry, refer to the appropriate chapters within this guidebook.

Special Moments

A rainy afternoon at the Napoleon House

Pirate's Alley in the early-morning mist

The Rex, Comus, and Zulu parades during Mardi Gras

A stroll through the Audubon Zoo

The French Quarter on Halloween

Lounging on a balcony anywhere in New Orleans

The view from the Top of the Mart

Taste Treats

Pralines at Laura's Original Fudge and Praline Shoppe

High tea at the Windsor Court

Sunday jazz brunch at Arnaud's

Bread pudding at Commander's Palace

Crawfish beignets at Clancy's

Off the Beaten Track

The Café Kafíc

Christmas Eve bonfires in St. James Parish along the Mississippi River

The Milton H. Latter Memorial Library

After Hours

The Blue Room at the Fairmont

Dancing on the sidewalk in front of the Maple Leaf Bar

A night parade at Mardi Gras

Café du Monde

Tipitina's

Traditional jazz at Preservation Hall

Hotels

La Mothe House *(Very Expensive)*

Hotel Maison De Ville *(Very Expensive)*

The Pontchartrain Hotel *(Very Expensive)*

The Windsor Court *(Very Expensive)*

The Josephine Guest House *(Moderate)*

Le Richelieu in the French Quater *(Moderate)*

French Quarter Maisonnettes *(Inexpensive)*

Restaurants

Antoine's *(Very Expensive)*

Brennan's *(Very Expensive)*

The Grill Room at the Windsor Court *(Very Expensive)*

Patout's *(Expensive)*

Constantin's *(Moderate)*

Galatoire's *(Moderate)*

L'Eagles Bar and Grill *(Moderate)*

Camellia Grill *(Inexpensive)*

Central Grocery and Deli *(Inexpensive)*

Popeye's Famous Fried Chicken *(Inexpensive)*

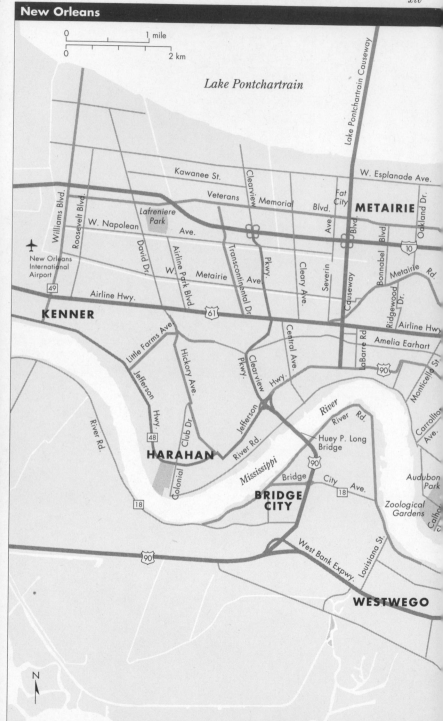

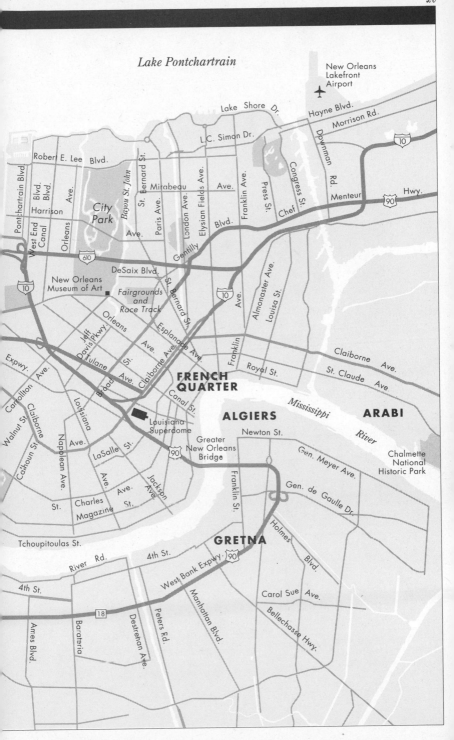

International Date Line

MONDAY
SUNDAY

+12 +13 -9

-3

-4

-10

3

7

-5 -4

4

-7

14 15

5 -8 8

13

9

6

10

17 16

11

-6

18

12

22

19

-5 -4 -3

20

23

-3

21 24

+11

+12

-11

-10

-9

-8

-7

-6

-5

-4

-3

-2

Numbers below vertical bands relate each zone to Greenwich Mean Time (0 hrs.).
Local times frequently differ from these general indications,
as indicated by light-face numbers on map.

Auckland, **1**
Honolulu, **2**
Anchorage, **3**
Vancouver, **4**
San Francisco, **5**
Los Angeles, **6**
Edmonton, **7**

Denver, **8**
Chicago, **9**
Dallas, **10**
New Orleans, **11**
Mexico City, **12**
Toronto, **13**
Ottawa, **14**
Montreal, **15**

New York City, **16**
Washington, DC, **17**
Miami, **18**
Bogotá, **19**
Lima, **20**
Santiago, **21**
Caracas, **22**

Rio de Janeiro, **23**
Buenos Aires, **24**
Reykjavik, **25**
Dublin, **26**
London (Greenwich), **27**
Lisbon, **28**
Algiers, **29**
Paris, **30**
Zürich, **31**

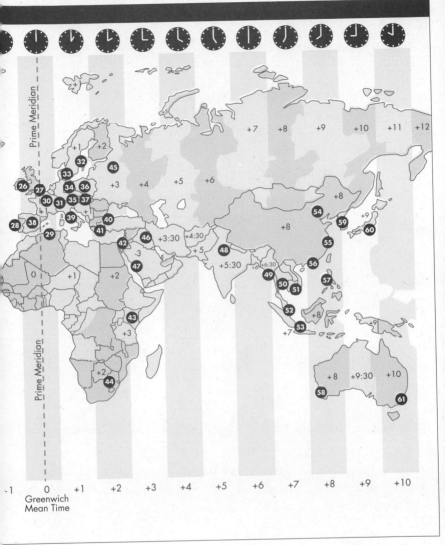

Introduction

by Don Lee Keith

The author of this essay is a writer, editor, and critic in New Orleans.

When the sun rises over New Orleans's French Quarter, it sends the waterfront rats scurrying for wharf cover. Next, it shakes awake the vagabonds whose eyes and memories have failed in the night; before long, that lost society must also retreat to some other darkness.

But day is never the real victor in the capricious 108 square blocks that cling to the crescent banks of the Mississippi. Even at noon the French Quarter is seldom fully awake. In its dreams are still splendid riverboats, passionate romance, and pistol duels beneath moss-draped oaks, undisturbed by the more modern sounds of delivery trucks and commercial barges. For more than two and a half centuries New Orleans has dreamed those dreams, and perhaps through them has managed to survive the ravages of plagues and fires and storms that would have laid to waste far less vulnerable cities.

By mid-morning the Vieux Carré (or Old Square) is forced by business schedules to yawn a bit here, stretch a bit there. Up go the umbrellas of the artists near the Place d'Armes, with its narcotic view of St. Louis Cathedral. Early tourists wander along the cracked and uneven sidewalks, pausing occasionally to examine the lacy, foreign-looking ferns that sprout from crevices. Canvas awnings on little shop fronts are unfurled. Stuffed "mammies" appear outside candy stores. And bag after bag of ice crunches its way from truck beds to the shoulders of deliverymen and finally into a saloon where it will be served in rum-based drinks called Hurricanes.

By lunchtime, a perfume boutique can be sensed a half block off, its flowery scents mingling with the aromas of rich coffee and red beans and rice from small restaurants.

As afternoon progresses, jazz tunes float from the open doors of musty buildings. A black boy in a ragged tuxedo tapdances near the curb, holding out his baseball cap for coins. At the corner an art student squats against a lamppost and sketches a house with a wraparound, wrought-iron balcony and a faded sign painted big on the side: "Uneeda Biscuits."

Ruthie the Duck Girl stops an acquaintance to bum a cigarette. She takes two, "one for now and one for later." Ruthie is wearing a new dress, as always, from the Goodwill; it is vintage 1958: net bodice with sweetheart neckline and a full ballerina-length skirt. Ruthie is walking her new duck; she yanks it along on its string, alternately prodding and shouting for the duck to behave.

A leftover hippie on the steps of a T-shirt emporium gets surprisingly few frowns as he methodically and peacefully plaits strips of leather. In the French Quarter he has found his niche, and shares a sense of freedom with others whose lifestyles demand a degree of tolerance not afforded in other sections of the city.

It is difficult to conceive of Ruthie or the hippie "belonging" outside the French Quarter, although many native Orleanians have stopped recoiling at the sight of them. In most cases, it is just as difficult to conceive of native Orleanians "belonging" elsewhere. The giveaway is the very identifiable quality of their speech, which puts a homemade label on inflections. It's also what they say, not just how they say it: The median strip that divides a wide street is a "neutral ground"; when a grocer or shop owner includes a little something extra in a customer's order, it's "lagniappe"; a sidewalk is a "banquette."

When you ask for directions, you're not likely to hear the words north or south, east or west. Rather, it'll be Riverside, Lakeside, Uptown, Downtown. That's New Orleans talking, and talking is something its people do a lot of. Only the tones differ with the neighborhoods.

For instance, Uptown (anything on the other side of Canal Street from the French Quarter) is where the tone of New Orleans is generally thought to be somewhat gentler. And indeed, Uptown—with its fabled St. Charles Avenue, having rounded Lee Circle and set its course toward meeting the river some 75 blocks away—often thinks of itself as *being* gentler.

Such a claim would have been hastily challenged in the early 1800s, when the Louisiana Purchase paved the way for Americans to settle Uptown. Creoles, the original settlers whose roots were very much Downtown, considered the interloping Americans to be vulgar, barbaric, and thoroughly unsavory. By 1820, however, the Americans outnumbered the Creoles three to one, and the newer Orleanians would soon be far less concerned about what Creoles thought than about their own neoclassical existence in their Uptown utopia. That residential area was to be known eventually as the Garden District, and even now, it is a neighborhood that inspires as much awe as any in the world.

Many of the gigantic antebellum mansions, with their vast lawns, look exactly as they looked more than a century ago; a few are still in the same families. There is less activity on these streets than in Downtown neighborhoods, fewer people on the sidewalks. A sort of imposed quiet prevails. Perhaps it was that aspect of the Garden District that prompted writer Oliver Evans to propose that the area is like "an elegant corpse."

Despite a gracious familiarity sometimes ascribed to Uptown living, there is a definite laissez faire—often expected, occasionally demanded—in the Garden District. A matron returning from her weekly luncheon engagement may have been waving for years to another woman tending her roses in the next block, yet the two may never have known each other's name—nor cared to. Families in duplex cottages may share nothing save the light from a common street lamp.

Life in the large houses is not markedly dissimilar from life in the smaller cottages. Newspapers are delivered, ferns are watered, kids are shuffled off to day camp. It is only the trappings that form the difference, and the size of the trappings of the big houses seems to make that difference significant.

On the Riverside end of the Garden District, and extending several blocks closer to Canal Street, is the Irish Channel, a blue-collar neighborhood that is considerably nearer in feeling to Downtown. Here attitudes seem more relaxed, less formal, and pleasures are simpler.

Uptown from the Garden District, the University Section spreads toward the lake. A turn of streetcar tracks signals the end of St. Charles Avenue and the beginning of Carrollton Avenue. Soon, Carrollton Avenue will lead through portions of Mid-City, along the periphery of City Park, and eventually to the lakefront. Any traveler who has reached that final point has crossed over into the realm of *déjà vu* realty. The expensive surroundings and manicured lawns of green are mute reminders that seldom, if ever, has New Orleans's peculiar potion of charm employed predictability as a vital ingredient.

The components of that charm remain a mystery that ranks with the location of the buried loot of the pirate Jean Lafitte.

Several years ago, a group of urban anthropologists, armed with the sacrosanct premise that New Orleans's distinctive appeal merely reflects the distinctive nature of its people, set out to define that nature and to determine what made it distinctive. Questions were posed and answers were recorded, and once the city had been sampled as randomly as credibility required, a computer spat out the survey's findings.

Among the revelations were certain disclosures about one deeply Downtown neighborhood that lies immediately below the French Quarter. The survey indicated that a higher percentage of residents in that section do 10 specific things that just might be considered heavy with the flavor of New Orleans:

1) More residents there go to early mass on Ash Wednesday, the day following Mardi Gras;
2) More people won't drink coffee unless it's brewed with chickory;
3) More people can name at least one hit record by New Orleans–born Fats Domino;
4) More have actually seen mirlitons (vegetables grown locally and usually stuffed like bell peppers) growing on the vine;
5) More live in a house that has a Zulu coconut somewhere on the premises (these coconuts are tossed to crowds during the black Zulu parade on Mardi Gras);
6) More are related to (or know someone who is related to) a girl named Darlene;
7) More shop at Schwegmann's, a locally owned supermarket chain, at least once a week;
8) More know what number is worn by the Saints' star quarterback;
9) More consider a po-boy (an overstuffed sandwich on French bread said to have originated in New Orleans) to be the ideal lunch for a working day; and
10) More say "N'Awlins."

A good many residents of that neighborhood, like those of several other sections, admitted in the questionnaire that a favorite time of day is late afternoon, when they sit on the stoops in front of their houses, chatting with neighbors and "unwinding."

Dusk, that hour of approaching sundown, is when the muscle of the French Quarter begins to flex. Softly lit by glowing gas lanterns, the Vieux Carré wears darkness well. Imperfections seem less distracting, almost appealing; no wonder the sun shines shyly—in New Orleans, night is brighter. A background fugue seems to play as an aura of the past hovers, its magic empowered by the proximity of the buildings and the close, narrow streets.

In the beginning those streets were little more than open gutters, and early residents lived with the dangers of malaria, floods, snakes, and cannibalistic Indians. Ownership of the colony kept switching—French, then Spanish, then French again, and finally American. Still, the changing of flags did not affect its settlers' allegiance in establishing themselves as individuals in a city that was already individual itself.

Somewhere along the early way, the city had also developed a peculiar pride that would turn treacherously malignant. It would distort the city's values during the suffocating occupation by the Union's Yankee soldiers, turn the city's back on the politically frenzied Reconstruction, and fuel an attitude of aloofness during the strangling Depression. New Orleans somehow figured that to dismiss the enemy was to disarm the enemy; the result of this refusal to recognize reality was a crippling scar on the city's progress. Only within the last dozen or so years has New Orleans begun to live because of itself rather than despite itself.

Ironically, the French Quarter—by tradition the most decadent area of the city—has emerged as particularly progressive. Significant buildings are constantly being carefully restored, pedestrian malls have been designated for parts of Bourbon and Royal Streets, and Jackson Square is newly landscaped. The riverfront adjacent to the square is at its liveliest since antebellum days. The historic French Market, where Indians once swapped their goods, has been modernized for increased public use. And young professionals, many of them native to the city, are moving into the Vieux Carré and finding their way into the life of the section.

Residents of the French Quarter are primarily concerned with, and fiercely protective of, their right to live as they please. Up-and-coming yuppies live alongside the likes of Ruthie the Duck Girl, clear evidence of the more eccentric nature of this neighborhood. New Orleans's nickname, the Big Easy, seems perfectly apropos in the Vieux Carré, a neighborhood that perfectly reflects the flavor of New Orleans.

1 Planning Your Trip

Before You Go

Visitor Information

For free brochures and additional information contact the **Greater New Orleans Tourist and Convention Commission,** 1520 Sugar Bowl Dr., New Orleans, LA 70112, tel. 504/566–5011 or 504/566–5031.

Another source of information is the **Louisiana Department of Tourism,** 666 North Foster, Box 94291, Baton Rouge, LA 70804, tel. 504/925–3800 or 800/342–8100.

Tour Groups

Although you will have to march to the beat of a tour guide's drum rather than your own, taking a package tour is likely to save you money on airfare, hotels, and ground transportation. For the more experienced or adventurous traveler, a variety of special-interest and independent packages are available. Listed below is a sampling of available options. Check with your travel agent or the Greater New Orleans Tourist and Convention Commission (tel. 504/566–5011) for additional resources.

When considering a tour, be sure to find out (1) exactly what expenses are included (particularly tips, taxes, side trips, additional meals and entertainment); (2) ratings of all hotels on the itinerary and the facilities they offer; (3) cancellation policies for both you and the tour operator; and (4) if you are traveling alone, what the single supplement is. Most tour operators request that bookings be made through a travel agent—there is no additional charge for doing so.

General-Interest Tours
American Express Vacations (Box 5014, Atlanta, GA 30302, tel. 800/241–1700 or in GA, 800/282–0800) offers the "Dixielander," which begins and ends in New Orleans, with stops in Baton Rouge, Natchez, and Vicksburg along the way.
Cosmos/Globus Gateway (150 S. Los Robles Ave., Suite 860, Pasadena, CA 91101, tel. 818/449–0919 or 800/556–5454) has a "Heritage of the Deep South" tour that explores the history of the city and its neighbors in Mississippi and Alabama.
Domenico Tours (751 Broadway, Bayonne, NJ 07002, tel. 800/554–TOUR) offers New Orleans for five days and a New Orleans/Memphis/Nashville package.

Special-Interest Tours
Mardi Gras: *Maupintour* (Box 807, Lawrence, KS 66044, tel. 913/843–1211 or 800/255–4266) takes you to the country's biggest annual party. *Tours by Andrea* (826 Perdido St., Suite 100, New Orleans, LA 70112, tel. 504/524–8521) celebrates Mardi Gras with a package featuring a Mardi Gras Ball complete with gourmet dinner and 11-piece orchestra.
Cuisine: *Tours by Andrea* offers a "Gourmet Delight" tour of popular New Orleans restaurants. *Travel New Orleans* (434 Dauphine St., New Orleans, LA 70112, tel. 504/561–8747) offers a tour called "New Orleans with a Dash of Tabasco" that combines the sights and tastes of Cajun country.
Music: *Travel New Orleans* offers "Jazz Around Louisiana," with four days' admission to the Jazz and Heritage Festival

(last week in Apr. and first week in May) and stops in Baton Rouge and Lafayette. A more basic three-day tour, with two days' admission to the festival, is also available. *Tours by Andrea's* "Rhythm of New Orleans" tour seeks out the New Orleans sound in its hopping nightclubs.

Package Deals for Independent Travelers

American Fly AAway Vacations (tel. 800/433–7300 or 817/355–1234) offers city packages with discounts on hotels and car rental. Also check with **Delta Air Lines** (tel. 800/241–6108 or 404/765–2952) and **Continental Airlines** (tel. 713/821–2100) for packages. **American Express** has similar city packages, with half-day sightseeing tours. **Travel New Orleans** (*see* Special-Interest Tours) has three year-round packages: "Sights and Sounds of New Orleans," "Escape to New Orleans," and "New Orleans Combo." **Tours by Andrea** (*see* Special-Interest Tours) offers a "New Orleans Quickie," with a choice of 22 hotels for a two-night stay, and "New Orleans Experience."

Tips for British Travelers

Government Tourist Offices Contact the **United States Travel and Tourism Administration** (22 Sackville St., London W1X 2EA, tel. 01/439–7433) for a wealth of useful tourist information.

Passports and Visas You will need a valid, 10-year passport and a U.S. Visitor's Visa. Apply for your passport either through your travel agent or on special forms available from your local post office. The passport will cost £15 and you should allow at least six weeks for it to be processed.

Get your U.S. Visitor's Visa (which can only be put in a 10-year passport) either through your travel agent or directly from the **United States Embassy, Visa and Immigration Department** (5 Upper Grosvenor St., London W1A 2JB, tel. 01/499–3443). Visas can only be applied for by post; the Embassy no longer accepts applications made in person.

Vaccinations are not necessary to enter the United States.

Customs and Duties If you are over 21, you can take into the United States: 200 cigarettes, or 50 cigars, or two kilos of tobacco, and one U.S. quart of alcohol. Everyone is entitled to take into the United States duty-free gifts up to the value of $100. Don't take in meat or meat products, seeds, plants, fruit, etc., and avoid illegal drugs like the plague.

Returning to the UK, you may take home, if you are 17 and over: (1) 200 cigarettes or 100 cigarillos or 50 cigars or 250 grams of tobacco; (2) two liters of table wine and (a) one liter of alcohol over 22% by volume (most spirits), (b) two liters of alcohol under 22% by volume (fortified or sparkling wine), or (c) two more liters of table wine; (3) 50 grams of perfume and 1/4 liter of toilet water, and (4) other goods up to a value of £32.

Insurance We strongly recommend that you insure yourself to cover health and motoring mishaps. **Europ Assistance** (252 High St., Croydon CRO 1NF, tel. 01/680–1234) offers an excellent service, all the more valuable when you consider the possible costs of health care in the United States.

It is also wise to take out insurance to cover loss of luggage (though check that this isn't already covered in any existing home-owner's policies you may have). Trip-cancellation insurance is a wise buy. **The Association of British Insurers** (Aldermary House, Queen St., London EC4N 1TT, tel. 01/248–4477) will give comprehensive advice on all aspects of vacation insurance.

Tour Operators **Albany Travel (Manchester) Ltd.** (190 Deansgate, Manchester M3 3WD, tel. 061/833–0202) offers an eight-day tour of the Deep South, which starts from the "Heart of Dixie" and takes in Baton Rouge, Natchez, Vickburg, and Jackson and then heads back to New Orleans along the coast. Prices start from £529 per person.

American Airplan (Marlborough House, Churchfield Rd., Walton-on-Thames, Surrey KT12 2TJ, tel. 0932/246166) offers seven-day "Dixieland" tours. Prices start at £479 per person and includes a week's car rental.

Jetways (93 Newman St., London W1P 3LE, tel. 01/637–5444) offers a wide range of flights only (from £411), city breaks, and motor-home vacations.

Thomas Cook (45 Berkeley St., London W1A 1EB, tel. 01/629–0999) offers a 17-day escorted tour called "Confederate Trail from New Orleans," which includes stops at New Orleans, Stone Mountain, Charlestown, Richmond, and Washington. Price range from £1,345 to £1,375, depending on season.

Airfares If you want to get to New Orleans on your own, then you'll probably be looking for a low-price air ticket. The best places to look are in the ads of daily and Sunday newspapers and in magazines like *Time Out*. Be prepared to be flexible—you'll be extremely lucky to find a flight on the exact day and time you want to travel—and start looking well in advance as cheap airfares disappear remarkably quickly. However, with perseverance you should be rewarded with an affordable ticket. As we went to press, a round-trip ticket to New Orleans cost about £329. APEX fares offered by the major airlines are also worth checking out; prices as we went to press started at £394.

Car Rental There are branches of most of the well-known car-rental companies in New Orleans, including **Avis, Budget, Hertz,** and **National.** You can make your arrangements either before you leave or when you have reached your destination.

Avis (Hayes Gate House, Uxbridge Rd., Hayes, Middlesex, tel. 01/848–8733) operates the SuperValue scheme. Seven days' rental of, say, a Chevette costs about £98, and £24 per day for extra days. Another excellent scheme is Avis's Drive Away Checks. They are available in three denominations—£15, £23, and £31—and cover the cost of one days' car rental (depending on type of car). Buy them before you leave and pick your car on arrival; booking isn't necessary but cars are subject to availability. If you don't use all your checks, your money will be fully refunded when you get home.

Hertz (Radnor House, 1272 London Rd., London SW16 4XW, tel. 01/679–1777) operates the Affordable World Scheme. Seven days' rental of, say, a Ford Escort will cost about £64, extra days cost about £15 per day.

Most rental schemes include unlimited mileage and some form of insurance, but don't forget to budget for the price of gas and local taxes.

When to Go

In New Orleans, like most of the South, June through September is hot and humid. Just mustering the energy to raise a mint julep to your lips may cause malaise. During these infamous long, hot summers the sun shines for as long as 11 hours each day, which may explain why things are less hurried down here—there's lots of time and it's so hard to stay cool! If you must visit New Orleans during these sticky months, you'll find that all hotels and restaurants are air-conditioned.

June through November are the months to watch for torrential rains, twisters, and even hurricanes in New Orleans. These conditions occur mainly with quick changes in temperature that accompany cold fronts.

October to March can be plagued with heavy fogs. Although winters are mild here compared to northern climes, the high humidity can really put a chill in the air. Don't be surprised to see women wearing fur coats in many of the city's finer establishments.

Perhaps the best time to visit the city is early spring. Days are pleasant, except for seasonal cloudbursts, and nights are cool. The azaleas are in full bloom while the city bustles from one outdoor festival to the next.

Climate　The following are average daily maximum and minimum temperatures for New Orleans.

Jan.	62F	17C	May	83F	28C	Sept.	86F	30C
	47	8		68	20		73	23
Feb.	65	18	June	88	31	Oct.	79	26
	50	10		74	23		64	18
Mar.	71	22	July	90	32	Nov.	70	·21
	55	13		76	24		55	13
Apr.	77	25	Aug.	90	32	Dec.	64	18
	61	16		76	24		48	9

Current weather information on 235 cities around the world—180 of them in the U.S.—is only a phone call away. To obtain the Weather Trak telephone number for your area, call 800/247-3282. The local number plays a taped message that tells you to dial the three-digit access code for the destination you're interested in. The code is either the area code (in the U.S.) or the first three letters of the foreign city. For a list of all access codes, send a stamped, self-addressed envelope to Cities, Box 7000, Dallas TX 75209. For further information, phone 214/869-3035 or 800/247-3282.

Festivals and Seasonal Events

Top seasonal events in New Orleans include the Sugar Bowl on New Year's Day, Mardi Gras celebrations, the Spring Fiesta in April, and Creole Christmas celebrations throughout the month of December. For exact dates and further information, contact the **Greater New Orleans Tourist and Convention Commission,** 1520 Sugar Bowl Dr., New Orleans, LA 70112, tel. 504/566-5011.

Jan. 1: Sugar Bowl Classic, the city's oldest annual sporting event, includes not only one of the biggest college football games of the year, but also tennis, basketball, sailing, running, and flag football championship events. 1500 Sugar Bowl Dr., New Orleans, LA 70112, tel. 504/525–8573.

Late Jan.: The New Orleans Classical Music Festival offers a blend of musical entertainment and winter festivities. Contact Le Petit Théâtre du Vieux Carré, 616 St. Peter St., New Orleans, LA 70116, tel. 504/522–9958 (*see* Highlights).

Mid-Feb.: Lundi Gras (Fat Monday, the day before Mardi Gras), a recent addition to Carnival, includes a parade, fireworks, and a masked ball, all at the Spanish Plaza, adjacent to Riverwalk.

Early Feb. or Mid-Mar.: Mardi Gras is rollicking, raucous, and ritualistic. It's street celebrations, parades, and formal masked balls (*see* Carnival in Portraits in New Orleans).

Late Feb.: Black Heritage Festival includes gospel and jazz performances, art exhibits, and a mock jazz funeral, at several city locations. Information: Audubon Zoo, Box 4327, New Orleans, LA 70178, tel. 504/861–2537.

Mid-Mar.: St. Patrick's Day Parade begins at Molly's at the Market Pub and covers the French Quarter. Information: Molly's Pub, 1107 Decatur St., New Orleans, LA 70116, tel. 504/525–5169.

Late Mar.: Tennessee Williams—New Orleans Literary Festival features performances of the author's plays and tours of his favorite French Quarter haunts. Tel. 504/524–1536.

Early to mid-Apr.: French Quarter Festival includes fireworks, 100 hours of free entertainment, and the world's largest jazz brunch. Tel. 504/522–5730.

Early to mid-Apr.: Spring Fiesta spotlights the French Quarter's historic homes and includes a parade and the coronation of a queen. Tel. 504/581–1367.

Mid-Apr.: Crescent City Classic is a very popular 10-km road race that culminates in a huge party in Audubon Park. Classic, 8200 Hampson St., Suite 409, New Orleans, LA 70118, tel. 504/861–8686.

Late Apr.: New Orleans Jazz and Heritage Festival involves more than 4,000 musicians. Held at the Fairgrounds. Tel. 504/522–4786.

Early May: Zoo-to-Do is a 100-hour fund-raiser for the Audubon Zoo. Box 4327, New Orleans, LA 70170, tel. 504/861–2537.

Early June: The Great French Market Tomato Festival includes cooking demonstrations and tastings at the French Market. Tel. 504/522–2621.

Early July: New Orleans Food Festival is held in downtown New Orleans in the Rivergate Exhibition Center, 4 Canal St., New Orleans, LA 70130, tel. 504/529–2861.

July 4 weekend: The Louis Armstrong Festival is jazzin'. Le Petit Théâtre du Vieux Carré, 616 St. Peter St., New Orleans, LA 70116, tel. 504/522–9958 (*see* Highlights).

Early to mid-July: La Fête is the National Festival of Food and Cookery, at various locations throughout the city. Tel. 504/525–4143.

Early Sept.: Mississippi River Challenge Cup Race is a powerboat competition that stretches from New Orleans to St. Louis. Tel. 314/367–3062.

Late Sept.–early Oct.: Virginia Slims Tennis Tournament is held annually at the University of New Orleans's Lakefront

Arena, 6801 Franklin Ave., New Orleans, LA 70122, tel. 504/286–7222.

Early Oct.: Festa d'Italia is a three-day affair featuring Italian food and music. Tel. 504/891–1904.

Early Oct. Swamp Festival means Cajun food, music, and crafts at Audubon Zoo. Tel. 504/861–2537.

Oct. 31.: Halloween is celebrated with enthusiasm in this city of voodoo and legends.

Late Nov.: Bayou Classic is the traditional end-of-season football game between Southern University and Grambling University at the Louisiana Superdome. Ticket Office, Box 50488, New Orleans, LA 70150, tel. 504/587–3663.

Dec.: A Creole Christmas includes tree-lighting, teas, caroling, parades, and open houses all month long. The French Quarter Festival, 1008 N. Peters St., New Orleans, LA 70116, tel. 504/522–5730.

Dec. 31: Countdown is a huge, televised New Year's Eve celebration in Jackson Square, similar to the one in New York's Times Square.

What to Pack

Luggage allowances on domestic flights vary slightly from airline to airline. Most allow three checked pieces and one carry-on. Some give you the option of two checked and two carry-on bags. In all cases, bags that you check in cannot weigh more than 70 pounds each or be larger than 62 inches (length + width + height). Carry-on luggage cannot be larger than 45 inches (length + width + height) and must fit under the seat or in the overhead luggage compartment.

In the summer, pack for hot, sticky weather but be prepared for air-conditioning bordering on the glacial. Winters are mild but damp. You'll want a coat, or warm jacket, especially for evenings, which can be downright cold. New Orleans is casual during the day, and casual to slightly dressy at night. Many restaurants in the French Quarter require men to wear a jacket and tie. For sightseeing, pack walking shorts, sundresses, cotton slacks or jeans, and T-shirts. Pack an umbrella for sudden thunderstorms during the summer, but leave the plastic raincoats behind (they're extremely uncomfortable in the high humidity). In the summer you'll want a sun hat and plenty of sunscreen lotion, even for strolls in the city, because the sun can be fierce. Mosquitoes come out in full force after sunset in the hot weather, so take insect repellent if you plan to be outdoors in the evenings or to dine alfresco.

Cash Machines

Virtually all U.S. banks belong to a network of ATMs (Automatic Teller Machines), which dispense cash 24 hours a day in cities throughout the country. There are some eight major networks in the United States, the largest of which are Cirrus, owned by MasterCard, and Plus, affiliated with Visa. Some banks belong to more than one network. These cards are not automatically issued; you have to apply for them. Cards issued by Visa and MasterCard also may be used in the ATMs, but the fees are usually higher than the fees on bank cards. There is also a daily interest charge on credit card "loans," even if monthly bills are paid on time. Each network has a toll-free number you can call to locate machines in a given city. The Cirrus number is 800/4–CIRRUS; the Plus number is 800/THE–PLUS. Check with your bank for information on fees and on the amount of cash you can withdraw on any given day.

Traveling with Film

If your camera is new, shoot and develop a few rolls of film before leaving home. Pack some lens tissue and an extra battery for your built-in light meter. Invest about $10 in a skylight filter and screw it onto the front of your lens. It will protect the lens and also reduce haze.

Film doesn't like hot weather. If you're driving in summer, don't store film in the glove compartment or on the shelf under the rear window. Put it behind the front seat on the floor, on the side opposite the exhaust pipe.

On a plane trip, never pack unprocessed film in check-in luggage; if your bags get X-rayed, you can say goodbye to your pictures. Always carry undeveloped film with you through security and ask to have it inspected by hand. (It helps to isolate your film in a plastic bag, ready for quick inspection.) Inspectors at American airports are required by law to honor requests for hand inspection; abroad, you'll have to depend on the kindness of strangers.

The old airport scanning machines—still in use in some Third World countries—use heavy doses of radiation that can turn a family portrait into an early-morning fog. The newer models— used in all U.S. airports—are safe for anything from five to 500 scans, depending on the speed of your film. The effects are cumulative; you can put the same roll of film through several scans without worry. After five scans, though, you're asking for trouble.

If your film gets fogged and you want an explanation, send it to the National Association of Photographic Manufacturers, 600 Mamaroneck Ave., Harrison, NY 10528. They will try to determine what went wrong. The service is free.

Car Rentals

Having a car in New Orleans is no problem—except when you're likeliest to be there, at Mardi Gras. Then the whole French Quarter is closed to traffic and cars parked on parade routes get whisked away. Streetcars and a good bus system are adequate for central New Orleans; cars are advisable for excursions to surrounding areas. **Hertz** (tel. 800/654–3131), **Avis** (tel. 800/331–1212), **National** (tel. 800/328–4567), **Budget** (tel. 800/527–0700), and other major companies have airport and downtown locations. Keep in mind that some companies charge more at their French Quarter locations than at the airport and that it's an $18 cab fare between the airport and the French Quarter. **Alamo** (tel. 800/327–9633) and **Enterprise Leasing** (tel. 504/464–6171) are both good budget firms.

It is essential to reserve a rental car well in advance for New Orleans during Mardi Gras. Get a reservation number, and find out in advance what the collision damage waiver covers and whether your own personal, corporate, or supplemental policy doesn't already cover damage to a rental car. Find out if you must pay for a full tank of gas, whether you use it or not, and ask about promotional, weekend, and 14-day-advance-reservation rates.

Traveling with Children

Publications *Family Travel Times* is an 8- to 12-page newsletter published 10 times a year by TWYCH (Travel with Your Children), 80 Eighth Ave., New York, NY 10011, tel. 212/206–0688. Subscription includes access to back issues and twice-weekly opportunities to call in for specific advice.

Great Vacations with Your Kids: The Complete Guide to Family Vacations in the U.S., by Dorothy Ann Jordon and Marjorie Adoff Cohen (E.P. Dutton, 2 Park Ave., New York, NY 10016; $9.95), details everything from city vacations to outdoor adventures and child-care resources.

New Orleans for Kids is an "activity book and tour guide" published by and available free from the Greater New Orleans Tourist and Convention Commission, Louisiana Superdome, Sugar Bowl Dr., New Orleans, LA 70112, tel. 504/566–5011.

Hotels **The Windsor Court** (300 Gravier St., New Orleans, LA 70140, tel. 504/523–6000) has more suites than rooms and allows children under 16 to stay free with parents. **Sheraton New Orleans** (500 Canal St., New Orleans, LA 70130, tel. 504/525–2500 or 800/325–3535) welcomes families, as does the **Royal Sonesta Hotel** (300 Bourbon St., New Orleans, LA 70104, tel. 504/586–0300 or 800/343–7170), which has a children's menu and pool. Most **Days Inn** hotels (tel. 800/325–2525) charge only a nominal fee for children under 18 and allow children age 12 and under to eat free. The **Olivier House** (828 Toulouse St., tel. 504/525–8456) welcomes children and pets.

Home Exchange See *Home Exchanging: A Complete Sourcebook for Travelers at Home or Abroad*, by James Dearing (Globe Pequot Press, Box Q, Chester, CT 06412, tel. 800/243–0495 or in CT 800/962–0973).

Getting There On domestic flights, children under two not occupying a seat travel free. Various discounts apply to children two–12. Reserve a seat behind the bulkhead of the plane, which offers more legroom and can usually fit a bassinet (supplied by the airline). At the same time, inquire about special children's meals or snacks, offered by most airlines. (See "TWYCH's Airline Guide," in the February 1988 issue of *Family Travel Times*, for a rundown on the services offered by 46 airlines.) Ask in advance if you can bring aboard your child's car seat. For the booklet, "Child/Infant Safety Seats Acceptable for Use in Aircraft," write Community and Consumer Liaison Division, APA-400 Federal Aviation Administration, Washington, D.C. 20591, tel. 202/267–3479.

Baby-sitting Services Make child-care arrangements with the hotel concierge or housekeeper.

Hints for Disabled Travelers

An organization of travel agents called **TAGNO** (Travel Agents of Greater New Orleans) specializes in providing services to disabled travelers. Contact TAGNO at Destinations Unlimited, 7240 Crowder Blvd., Suite 100, New Orleans, LA 70127, tel. 504/241–7997.

The Information Center for Individuals with Disabilities (20 Park Plaza, Room 330, Boston, MA 02116, tel. 617/727–5540) offers useful problem-solving assistance, including lists of travel agents that specialize in tours for the disabled.

Moss Rehabilitation Hospital Travel Information Service (12th St. and Taber Rd., Philadelphia, PA 19141, tel. 215/329–5715) provides information on tourist sights, transportation, and accommodations in destinations around the world. The fee is $5 for each destination. Allow one month for delivery.

Travel Industry and Disabled Exchange (TIDE, 5435 Donna Ave., Tarzana, CA 91356, tel. 818/343–6339) is an industry-based organization with a $15 per person annual membership fee. Members receive a quarterly newsletter and information on travel agencies and tours.

Mobility International (Box 3551, Eugene, OR 97403, tel. 503/343–1284) has information on accommodations, organized study, etc., around the world.

The Society for the Advancement of Travel for the Handicapped (26 Court St., Penthouse Suite, Brooklyn, NY 11242, tel. 718/858–5483) offers access information. Annual membership costs $40, or $25 for senior travelers and students. Send $1 and a stamped, self-addressed envelope.

Greyhound (tel. 800/531–5332) will carry a disabled person and companion for the price of a single fare. **Amtrak** (tel. 800/USA–RAIL) requests 24-hour notice to provide redcap service, special seats, and a 25% discount.

The Itinerary (Box 1084, Bayonne, NJ 07002, tel. 201/858–3400) is a bimonthly travel magazine for the disabled.

Access to the World: A Travel Guide for the Handicapped by Louise Weiss is useful but out of date. Available from Facts on File (460 Park Ave. South, New York, NY 10016, tel. 212/683–2244).

Frommer's Guide for Disabled Travelers is also useful but dated.

Hints for Older Travelers

The **American Association for Retired Persons** (AARP, 1909 K St. NW, Washington, D.C. 20049, tel. 202/662–4850) has two programs for independent travelers: (1) *The Purchase Privilege Program*, which offers discounts on hotels, airfare, car rentals, and sightseeing; and (2) the *AARP Motoring Plan*, which offers emergency aid and trip routing information for an annual fee of $29.95 per couple. AARP members must be 50 or older. Annual dues are $5 per person or couple.

When using an AARP or other identification card, ask for a reduced hotel rate when you make your reservation, not when you check out. At restaurants, show your card to the maître d' before you are seated, since discounts may be limited to certain set menus, days, or hours. When renting a car, remember that economy cars, priced at promotional rates, may cost less than cars that are available with your ID card.

Elderhostel (80 Boylston St., Suite 400, Boston, MA 02116, tel. 617/426–7788) is an innovative 13-year-old program for people 60 and older. Participants live in dorms on some 1,200 campuses around the world. Mornings are devoted to lectures and seminars; afternoons, to sightseeing and field trips. The all-inclusive fee for two to three-week trips, including room, board, tuition, and round-trip transportation, is $1,700–$3,200.

Travel Industry and Disabled Exchange (TIDE, 5435 Donna Ave., Tarzana, CA 91356, tel. 818/343–6339) is an industry-based organization with a $15 per person annual membership fee. Members receive a quarterly newsletter and information on travel agencies and tours.

National Council of Senior Citizens (925 15th St. NW, Washington, DC 20005, tel. 202/347–8800) is a nonprofit advocacy group with some 4,000 local clubs across the country. Annual membership is $10 per person or $14 per couple. Members receive a monthly newspaper with travel information and an ID card for reduced rates on hotels and car rentals.

Mature Outlook (Box 1205, Glenview, IL 60025, tel. 800/336–6330), a subsidiary of Sears, Roebuck & Co., is a travel club for people over 50, with hotel and motel discounts and a bimonthly newsletter. Annual membership is $7.50 per couple. Instant membership is available at participating Holiday Inns. "Travel Tips for Senior Citizens" (U.S. Dept. of State Publications 8970, revised Sept. 1987) is available for $1 from the Superintendent of Documents, U.S. Government Printing Office, Washington, DC 20402.

Golden Age Passport is a free lifetime pass to all parks, monuments, and recreation areas run by the federal government. People over 62 should pick them up in person at any national park that charges admission. A driver's license or other proof of age is required.

Further Reading

For a good mixture of romance and adventure with an eccentric cast of characters, pick up *Bandits* by Elmore Leonard. Frances Parkinson Keyes's *Dinner at Antoine's* is a charming murder mystery set in a famous New Orleans restaurant. *Black Sunday*, by Thomas Harris, is a novel about a plot to blow up the Superdome.

Edna Ferber's *Saratoga Trunk* is a historical adventure novel set in New Orleans. *A Feast of All Saints*, by Anne Rice, describes the lives of the "free people of color" (a localism for blacks who were not enslaved prior to Emancipation) in pre-Civil War New Orleans.

Other novels set in the city include: *Lives of the Saints*, by Nancy Lemann, a fun novel about a wacky New Orleans family; Kate Chopin's *The Awakening*, about the life of one New Orleans woman in the mid-1800s; *The Moviegoer*, by Walker Percy, full of details about the city as it follows a charming, neurotic native of New Orleans; and *A Confederacy of Dunces*, by John Kennedy Toole, a Pulitzer-prize-winning story set in New Orleans.

Women and New Orleans, by Mary Gehman with photos by Nancy Ries, traces the history of the city's women from 1718 to the present. For an interesting history of the city—through an explanation of New Orleans street names—read *Frenchmen Desire Good Children*, by John Chase. Al Rose's *Storyville* gives a good account of the origins of jazz and New Orleans's once infamous red-light district, Storyville.

Getting to New Orleans

By Plane

Be sure to distinguish among nonstop flights—no changes, no stops; direct flights—no changes but one or more stops; and connecting flights—two or more planes, two or more stops.

New Orleans's Moisant International Airport, located in Kenner, is 15 miles west of the city. It is served by **American** (tel. 800/433–7300), **Continental** (tel. 800/525–0280), **Delta** (tel. 800/221–1212), **Eastern** (tel. 800/327–8376), **Lacsa** (tel. 800/225–2272), **Midway** (tel. 800/621–2272), **Northwest** (tel. 800/225–2525), **Piedmont** (tel. 800/334–0429), **Royale** (tel. 800/282–3125), **Sasha** (tel. 800/327–1225), **Southwest** (tel. 504/523–5683), **Taca** (tel. 800/535–8780), **TWA** (tel. 800/221–2000), **United** (tel. 800/241–6522), and **USAir** (tel. 800/231–3131).

Luggage Regulations **Carry-on Luggage.** New rules have been in effect since January 1, 1988, on U.S. airlines in regards to carry-on luggage. The model for these new rules was agreed to by the airlines in December 1987 and then circulated by the Air Transport Association with the understanding that each airline would present its own version.

Under the model, passengers are limited to two carry-on bags. For a bag you wish to store under the seat, the maximum dimensions are 9″ × 14″ × 22″, a total of 45″. For bags that can be hung in a closet or on a luggage rack, the maximum dimensions are 4″ × 23″ × 45″, a total of 72″. For bags you wish to store in an overhead bin, the maximum dimensions are 10″ × 14″ × 36″, a total of 60″. Your two carry-ons must each fit one of these sets of dimensions, and any item that exceeds the specified dimensions will generally be rejected as a carry-on, and handled as checked baggage. Keep in mind that an airline can adapt these rules to circumstances, so on an especially crowded flight don't be surprised if you are only allowed one carry-on bag.

In addition to the two carry-ons, the rules list eight items that may also be brought aboard: a handbag (pocketbook or purse); an overcoat or wrap; an umbrella; a camera; a reasonable amount of reading material; an infant bag; crutches, cane, braces, or other prosthetic device upon which the passenger is dependent; and an infant/child safety seat.

Note that these regulations are for U.S. airlines only. Foreign airlines generally allow one piece of carry-on luggage in tourist class, in addition to handbags and bags filled with duty-free goods. Passengers in first- and business-class seats are also allowed to carry on one garment bag. It is best to check with your airline ahead of time to find out what their exact rules are regarding carry-on luggage.

Checked Luggage. U.S. airlines allow passengers to check in two suitcases whose total dimensions (length + width + height) do not exceed 60". There are no weight restrictions on these bags.

Rules governing foreign airlines vary from airline to airline, so check with your travel agent or the airline itself before you go. All the airlines allow passengers to check in two bags. In general, expect the weight restriction on the two bags to be not more than 70 pounds each, and the size restriction on the first bag to be 62" total dimensions, and on the second bag, 55" total dimensions.

Luggage Insurance Airlines are responsible for lost or damaged property only up to $1,250 per passenger on domestic flights, and $9.07 per pound (or $20 per kilo) for checked baggage on international flights, and up to $400 per passenger for unchecked baggage on international flights. If you're carrying valuables, either take them with you on the airplane or purchase additional insurance for lost luggage. Some airlines will issue additional luggage insurance when you check in, but many do not. One that does is American Airlines. Its additional insurance is only for domestic flights or flights to Canada. Rates are $1 for every $100 valuation, with a maximum of $400 valuation per passenger. Hand luggage is not included. Insurance for lost, damaged, or stolen luggage is available through travel agents or directly through various insurance companies. Two that issue luggage insurance are **Tele-Trip** (tel. 800/228–9792), a subsidiary of Mutual of Omaha, and **The Travelers Insurance Co.** Tele-Trip operates sales booths at airports, and also issues insurance through travel agents. Tele-Trip will insure checked luggage for up to 180 days and for $500 to $3,000 valuation. For one to three days, the rate for a $500 valuation is $8.25; for 180 days, $100. The Travelers Insurance Co. will insure checked or hand luggage for $500 to $2,000 valuation per person, and also for a maximum of 180 days. Rates for one to five days for $500 valuation are $10; for 180 days, $85. For more information, write The Travelers Insurance Co. (Ticket and Travel Dept., 1 Tower Sq., Hartford, CT 06183). Both companies offer the same rates on domestic and international flights. Check the travel pages of your Sunday newpaper for the names of other companies that insure luggage. Before you go, itemize the contents of each bag in case you need to file an insurance claim. Be certain to put your home address on each piece of luggage, including carry-on bags. If your luggage is stolen and later recovered, the airline must deliver the luggage to your home free of charge.

Smoking If smoking bothers you, ask for a seat in the nonsmoking section. If the airline tells you there are no nonsmoking seats, insist on one: FAA regulations require U.S. airlines to find seats for all nonsmokers.

Between the Airport and City Center Shuttle bus service to and from the airport and downtown hotels is available through **Airport Rhodes** (tel. 504/469–4555 or 504/464–0611). Buses leave regularly from the ground floor level near the baggage claim. To return to the airport, call at least two hours in advance of flight time. One-way cost is $7 a person and the trip takes about 40 minutes. **Louisiana Transit** (tel. 504/737–9611) also runs a bus from the airport to the Central Business District. The trip costs $1.10 in exact change and takes about 45 minutes.

Taxis cut about 15 minutes from the trip but cost $18 for the first three people and $6 for each additional person after that.

By Car

I-10 runs from Florida to California and passes directly through the city. To get to the CBD, exit at Poydras Street near the Louisiana Superdome. For the French Quarter, look for the Vieux Carré exit.

By Train

Three major Amtrak lines arrive at and depart from New Orleans's Union Passenger Terminal (1001 Loyola Ave., tel. 504/528–1600 or 800/USA–RAIL), in the heart of the Central Business District. The *Crescent* makes daily runs from New York to New Orleans by way of Washington, DC. The *City of New Orleans* runs daily between New Orleans and Chicago. The *Sunset Limited* makes the two-day trip between New Orleans and Los Angeles. It departs New Orleans on Monday, Wednesday, and Sunday, and leaves Los Angeles on Saturday, Wednesday, and Friday.

By Bus

Greyhound Bus Lines (1001 Loyola Ave.) has only one terminal in the city. It is located in the CBD in the Union Passenger Terminal. Ask about special travel passes. Check with your local Greyhound ticket office for prices and schedules.

2 Portraits of New Orleans

New Orleans: A History

by John R. Kemp

A columnist for New Orleans Magazine, John R. Kemp has written several books about the city, including New Orleans: An Illustrated History.

Known to generations as the Crescent City and more recently as the "Big Easy," New Orleans is a city whose magical names conjure up images of a Gallic-Hispanic and Caribbean heritage in a predominantly Anglo-Saxon culture, an amalgamation that forms a unique city and people. It was founded by the French on the banks of the Mississippi River in 1718, taken over by the Spanish in 1762, regained by Napoleon in 1800, and sold to the United States in 1803.

During most of its 271 years of history, New Orleans has survived yellow fever and cholera epidemics, Indian wars, slave uprisings, economic depressions, revolts, conspiracies, hurricanes, floods, the American and French revolutions, the Civil War and Reconstruction, racial riots, and political corruption. Today its jazz, Vieux Carré (the French Quarter), cuisine, Mardi Gras, and port are known worldwide.

New Orleans is a city whose mystique has captured the imaginations of generations of writers and motion picture and television producers, a city of tourists, beignets (French doughnuts), Creoles, aboveground cemetery tombs, William Faulkner's French Quarter, Tennessee Williams's *A Streetcar Named Desire*, Walker Percy's *The Moviegoer*, and John Kennedy Toole's *A Confederacy of Dunces*. It stands like a curious island of Roman Catholicism (of the Mediterranean variety) in a southern sea of hard-shell Protestantism that looks upon New Orleans as "Sin City." Novelist Walker Percy, who lives just outside the city, once wrote that to reach New Orleans the traveler must penetrate "the depths of the Bible Belt, running the gauntlet of Klan territory, the pine barrens of south Mississippi, Bogalusa, and the Florida Parishes of Louisiana. Out over a watery waste and there it is, a proper enough American city, and yet within the next few hours, the tourist is apt to see more nuns and naked women than he ever saw before."

As San Francisco is often called the most Asian of Occidental cities, New Orleans could be considered the most northern Caribbean city. Perhaps journalist A.J. Liebling best characterized it when he described New Orleans as a cross between Port-au-Prince, Haiti, and Paterson, New Jersey, with a culture not unlike that of Genoa, Marseilles, Beirut, or Egyptian Alexandria. Colonial New Orleans was very much a part of the economic, political, and social milieu of the French and Spanish Caribbean; its earliest population consisted of lesser French and Spanish gentry, tradesmen, merchants, prostitutes, criminals, clergy, farmers from the fields of France and Germany, Acadians from Canada, Canary Islanders, Indians, Africans, Englishmen, Irishmen, and English-Americans. Later came the Italians, Greeks, Cubans, Vietnamese, and others from the Earth's four corners, who have made New Orleans one of the nation's most cosmopolitan cities.

Because of the large Irish, German, and Yankee immigration into this river-port city in the middle of the last century, visitors are likely to hear a Brooklyn-style accent spoken in one section of the city, while hearing an interesting blend of New England and southern accents in another part of town. Tune your ear for the familiar "choich" for church and "zink" for sink, and particularly for the "downtown" greeting, "Where y'at!" New Orleans's southern accent has a lot less magnolia and mint julep than a Mississippi or Georgia accent.

It all began on Mardi Gras day in 1699 when a small French-Canadian expedition dropped anchor near the mouth of the Mississippi to explore and colonize "La Louisiane." For the next few years the expedition built a series of posts and fortifications along the river and the Gulf Coast, including what is today Mobile, Alabama, and Biloxi, Mississippi. By 1718, a permanent settlement was deemed necessary to hold France's claim to the Mississippi; the British and Spanish had their eyes on the vast Mississippi Valley. When French-Canadian Jean Baptiste, Sieur d'Bienville, established that settlement, it must have seemed only natural (and politically wise) to name it after Philippe, Duc d'Orleans, who was ruling France as regent for young Louis XV. Local legend has it that Bienville gave the settlement the feminine form of the adjective "new" and called it "Nouvelle Orleans" because the duke, who was a little effeminate, preferred to wear women's clothes.

New Orleans has had its glories and problems over the years, with two major standouts—hurricanes and politics. Contrary to orders from France, Bienville insisted upon building his settlement where New Orleans still stands today. He claimed the site was high and dry and protected from hurricanes, but during its first four years, the little village was wiped out four times by hurricanes. Politics have been an equally stormy art form here since the city's beginning; even the naming of the first city streets was a stroke of diplomatic genius. As historian John Chase notes in his delightful book on the origins of New Orleans street names, *Frenchmen Desire Good Children* (each name in the title is a street name), Bourbon, Orleans, Burgundy, and Royal streets were so named in honor of the royal families of France. Also honored were the Conti, Chartres, and Conde families, cousins to the Bourbons and Orleanses. (Conde Street was once a section of Chartres Street from Jackson Square to Esplanade Avenue before the name was dropped in 1865; Chartres now extends from Canal Street to Esplanade.) St. Peter Street was named for an ancestor of the Bourbon family; Louis IX, the Saint-King, was honored with St. Louis Street; Louis XIII's widowed Queen Ann got St. Ann Street; and Toulouse and Dumaine streets were named for Louis XIV's politically powerful royal bastard children.

The best place to get a real feel for the city's unique history is Jackson Square, the heart of the French Quarter, where you are surrounded by the river, St. Louis Cathedral, the colonial Cabildo and Presbytere, and the Pontalba Apartments. Called the Place d'Armes by the French and Plaza de Armas by the Spanish, this was the town square where the militia drilled and townsfolk met. It also was where public hangings, beheadings, "breakings at the wheel," and brandings were carried out. Of the countless stories of public executions and floggings, perhaps the most bizarre case concerned the 1754 mutiny of several Swiss soldiers stationed on Cat Island (just off today's Mississippi Gulf Coast), who killed their oppressive and sadistic commander. The soldiers were captured and executed in the Place d'Armes; two were broken at the wheel with sledgehammers, and a third, a Swiss soldier, was nailed alive in a coffin and then sawed in half.

The Place d'Armes, site in 1803 of the Louisiana Purchase ceremony, was renamed Jackson Square in the 1850s in honor of Andrew Jackson, the hero of the Battle of New Orleans in the War of 1812 and later president of the United States. In the center of the square is an equestrian statue of Jackson erected in 1856, one of three cast: A second stands in Lafayette Park in front of the White House in Washington, D.C., and a third, in Nashville, Tennessee, Jackson's hometown. Today Jackson Square springs to life each day with artists, street musicians, jugglers, and a host of wandering minstrels who follow the sun and tourist trade.

The old city, fanning out from the square, is filled with the legends and romances of an ever-changing people. Although the French Quarter is a living city and not a re-created fantasy world, history and time hang over the Vieux Carré like the thick, damp fogs that roll in from the river. You see the past everywhere—through the wrought iron gates and down the ancient alleys, in the steamy courtyards tucked out of sight, in the graceful colonial dwellings that hang over narrow streets. You find it in museums and the old stories about Madame Lalaurie's tortured slaves, the romantic drama surrounding the Baroness Pontalba, Pere Antoine, pirate Jean Lafitte, voodoo and its queen, Marie Laveau, revolutions, the Civil War, and yellow fever.

The history of New Orleans is inseparable from the port of New Orleans. The port is why the city was founded and why it survived. France wanted to colonize Louisiana, and built New Orleans to reap imagined riches from the vast interior of North America. Despite the expectations of the first explorers and the French crown, gold and silver did not come pouring out of the North American wilderness; different treasures waited. Quantities of tobacco, lumber, indigo, animal hides, and other indigenous products were floated downriver on flatboats to the new city, where ships from France, Spanish Florida, the West Indies, and the British colonies waited to trade for them with spices, cloth, cutlery, wine, utensils, foods, and other such goods. New Orleans became a commercial center, connecting Europe and the West Indies with the back country and upper regions of the Mississippi.

Trade was not without its difficulties. Storms, poorly built ships, privateers, colonial wars, and financially shaky entrepreneurs all added risks to commerce. There were other troubles as well; by the mid-18th century, serious international problems were brewing.

In 1754 the long-running dispute between France and England over who owned what in America erupted into war. Dubbed the "Seven Years' War" in Europe and the "French and Indian War" in the British colonies along the Atlantic seaboard (a war begun by British militiaman George Washington), it ultimately eliminated France as a colonial power in America. Despite an alliance with Spain (organized in the war's last years) France was defeated, and in 1763 it ceded to England all French territory east of the Mississippi River, keeping for itself just two small islands in the St. Lawrence Seaway.

Not included in the package, however, was New Orleans. Along with all the Louisiana territory west of the Mississippi River, the port had been signed over to Louis XV's cousin, King Carlos III of Spain, in the secret Treaty of Fontainebleau in 1762. (Perhaps that's where the long tradition of back-room deals got its start in Louisiana.) Louis gladly turned Louisiana over to his Spanish cousin. The colony was costing him his royal shirt, and the merchant class in France wanted nothing more to do with it. Carlos III, on his part, accepted the unprofitable holding as a buffer to keep the British away from nearby Mexico.

L ouisiana Frenchmen, however, generally opposed the change to Spanish rule. When the first Spanish governor, Don Antonio de Ulloa, arrived, he did little to court their favor. After a few breaches in local etiquette and several commercial edicts that hurt the colony's already sagging economy, the settlers drove Ulloa out of Louisiana in a bloodless coup in October 1768. (Local historians, trying to upstage the British colonies along the Atlantic, claim this was the first revolution on American soil against a foreign monarch.)

Retaliation from the mother country was quick and complete. In July 1769, the Spanish fleet dropped anchor at the mouth of the Mississippi, with 2,600 Spanish soldiers under the command of Gen. Alexander O'Reilly, an Irishman in Spanish service. O'Reilly quashed the short-lived rebellion, set up a new government in the colony, and executed the ringleaders of the rebellion.

The American Revolution afforded two of O'Reilly's successors, Unzaga and Galvez, the opportunity to attack their British colonial rival. Through the Louisiana colony, the Spanish sent supplies and munitions to the American rebels and allowed American raiding parties to launch forays into British West Florida. Galvez attacked and captured the British forts at Pensacola, Mobile, and Baton Rouge; and while the British were kept busy with the rebellious colonies, the Spanish took the opportunity to regain West Florida, which they had lost to the British during the French and Indian War.

The Spanish governors of Louisiana opened New Orleans's gates to a great variety of peoples by establishing an open-minded immigration policy that welcomed British-Americans escaping the Revolution as well as Acadians (whose descendants are Louisiana's famous Cajuns) fleeing the British in Canada. (The Cajuns later moved on to south-central and southwest Louisiana.) Canary Islanders came and settled just below New Orleans, where their descendants still live and speak their ancient language today.

Spanish New Orleans weathered several storms during the last decades of the 18th century, including the French Revolution. Mobs roamed the streets calling New Orleans Governor Carondelet a *cochon de lait* (suckling pig) and shouting "Liberty, Equality, and Fraternity." Carondelet brought in troops and outlawed publications concerning the Revolution in France. Diplomatically, he also gave refuge to French aristocrats fleeing the carnage, which won him back some favor with the Louisiana French.

Carondelet also had problems upriver with the westward-expanding Americans (usually Kentuckians, called "Kaintocks"). During the American Revolution, the rebels had assured the Spanish that they had no designs on Louisiana. But by the 1790s their assurances began to carry less weight; Americans' use of the river had grown, and so, too, had American desire for free navigation along its length.

As time passed, the situation worsened. Spanish officials in New Orleans occasionally seized American flatboats; the Americans responded by rattling sabers, urged on by the "Kaintocks," who called for an invasion of the Louisiana colony. War between the United States and Spain over Louisiana was narrowly averted in 1795 upon the signing of the Pinckney Treaty.

By the end of the 18th century, New Orleans had become a major North American port handling cargo from all over the world, with a population close to 10,000 and a well-earned reputation as a gay and colorful city. Mardi Gras was celebrated regularly (though it wasn't yet the extravagant carnival of parades seen today), and Creole food—that unique combination of French, Spanish, West Indian, and African cuisines for which New Orleans is so famous—had found its place on local palates. Unfortunately, much of the old colonial city was destroyed in three fires during the 1790s, but each time it was quickly rebuilt; most of the French Quarter of today was constructed during the Spanish colonial days and after the Louisiana Purchase in 1803. The oldest building in the French Quarter, and the only one remaining from French colonial years, is the former Ursuline Convent on Chartres Street, constructed in the mid-1750s.

For all the changes of the 18th century, the opening of the 19th was to bring even more. In France, Napoleon had taken power, and had reestablished the country as a formidable military force on the Continent. In 1800 he forced Spain to retrocede Louisiana to the French; New Orleans was back in the hands of its first colonial parent, though Spanish officials continued to run the colony for the next three years.

This news sat poorly with U.S. President Thomas Jefferson, who feared that war with France had become inevitable. The issue that concerned him was free navigation along the Mississippi River. To solve the problem, he resolved to buy New Orleans and a portion of West Florida bordering the Mississippi, including Baton Rouge. Napoleon, anxious for money to finance his imminent war against England (and reasonably sure that he would lose the land to England or the United States when war came), went Jefferson one better; he offered to sell the entire Louisiana colony.

On April 29, 1803, American emissaries agreed to pay $11,250,000 for Louisiana and, at the same time, to write off $3,750,000 in French debts, setting the territory's cost at $15 million. Short on cash, the United States borrowed the money to buy the territory from banking houses in London and Amsterdam. After the sale, Napoleon commented: "This accession of territory affirms forever the power of the United States, and I have just given England a maritime rival that sooner or later will lay low her pride."

The "Americanization" of New Orleans moved quickly during the first decade of the 19th century. The city's first suburb,

Faubourg St. Mary (today's Central Business District), sprang up and bustled with construction and commerce; this was the American Section. Mississippi flatboatmen by the thousands made their way downriver from the Missouri and Ohio rivers to sell their cargoes in New Orleans, then made their way home overland along the Natchez Trace.

The year 1812 brought statehood to Louisiana, and, almost equally important, the arrival of the first steamboat, the *New Orleans*, captained by Nicholas Roosevelt, ancestral kinsman of the two presidents. Eighteen twelve also brought war against Britain. Though its first effects on New Orleans were slight, the War of 1812 eventually came hard to the city. In 1815, Andrew Jackson, with a ragged army of Louisianans and helped by Jean Lafitte, Lafitte's Baratarian pirates, and Tennessee and Kentucky volunteers, fought the British and stopped them in a bloody battle at Chalmette Plantation, a few miles downriver from the city. Although casualty estimates for the Battle of New Orleans conflict somewhat, reports placed American losses at 13 killed and 39 wounded, and British losses at 858 killed and 2,468 wounded. Ironically, the battle took place two weeks after the United States and Britain signed a treaty ending the war. Every January 8th local historical groups reenact the victory at Chalmette Battlefield, which is now a national park.

The years between the Battle of New Orleans and the Civil War have been described as the city's golden era. By 1820 the population had reached 25,000; during the next 10 years it doubled. By 1840 it had doubled again, with a census count of 102,000 people within New Orleans; about half were black, both free and slave. The burgeoning port was choked with seagoing ships and riverboats laden with sugar, molasses, cotton, raw materials from upriver, and refined goods from Europe and the Northeast.

The golden age also gave birth to one of New Orleans's most famous pastimes: the Mardi Gras parade. Mardi Gras had been celebrated on the European continent, one way or another, for centuries. The parades, however, originated in Mobile, Alabama, but later moved to New Orleans, where the custom flourished. Begun in the 1820s when bands of maskers marched through the streets throwing confetti and flour (and sometimes lye) in the faces of onlookers, the parades were first staged by Americans in the American Sector, and not by the French or Spanish populace, who preferred their gala balls. Vehicles were first used in 1839, and the first carnival organization, the Mistick Krewe of Comus, was formed in 1857.

Through the years of prosperity and celebration, disease continued to stalk the city. The almost yearly visits of yellow fever, cholera, and typhus—encouraged by widespread poverty—took thousands of lives; 8,000 fell to yellow fever in 1853, and another 2,700 in 1856. In that same year cholera claimed the lives of over 1,000 people, and tuberculosis killed 650. Despite its other qualities, New Orleans was known as one of the unhealthiest cities in the northern hemisphere.

If the 18th century can be seen as New Orleans's childhood, then the antebellum period was its adolescence and young adulthood; by its end, the city had reached full maturity. Prosperous and growing, it possessed an international personality that distinguished it from every other city on the North American continent.

But the Civil War was to change that. On January 26, 1861, Louisiana seceded from the Union. It was a difficult choice for New Orleanians, many of whom had strong commercial and family ties with the Northeast and Midwest. Less than three months after secession, the war began when Southern troops, under the command of New Orleans's own General Pierre Gustave Toutant Beauregard, opened fire on Fort Sumter in Charleston harbor. A month later a Union fleet blockaded the mouth of the Mississippi River, causing severe economic hardship in the city.

The Confederate flag waved barely a year over New Orleans before it fell to Union forces under the command of "damn the torpedoes" Adm. David Glasgow Farragut in April 1862. When the Union fleet arrived and trained its guns on a panicked city, the mayor refused to surrender; Farragut threatened to bombard the city, but backed down. After a brief standoff, a naval squad went ashore and lowered the Confederate flag. New Orleans, the Confederacy's largest city, had fallen, and Reconstruction had begun.

New Orleans had the dubious distinction of being under Reconstruction longer than any other place in the Confederacy—from May 1862 to April 1877. The city's port and nearby fertile plantations were sources of immense profits for corrupt politicians under Reconstruction; the social and political upheaval it brought on was often violent, with bloody street battles between New Orleans natives and factions of the military-backed Reconstruction government. Withdrawal of federal troops in April 1877 brought an end to 15 years of Reconstruction; it also ended a flicker of hope that blacks in New Orleans would enjoy the same constitutional rights and protections as whites. With the end of Reconstruction came home rule and New Orleans's Gilded Age.

The last two decades of the century saw an era of conscious boosterism, economic booms and busts, corruption and reform, labor unrest and racial retrenchment. With a population of more than 216,000, New Orleans was still the largest city in the South. Large and elaborate Victorian homes, decorated with mass-produced gingerbread frills, sprang up along major avenues and thoroughfares.

New Orleans entered the 20th century with an air of optimism. North and South put aside their differences to defeat the Spanish in the Spanish-American War in 1898. Uptown continued to grow with new mansions along St. Charles Avenue, and skyscrapers in the Central Business District hovered over the early 19th-century buildings of the old American Sector. The New Orleans World Cotton Exposition of 1884 clearly forecast a new century of new promises and new hopes.

The prosperity continued until the Great Depression of the 1930s, as skyscrapers towered even higher above the old city. World War II, however, was a turning point in New Orleans's history. Although the city prospered during the war years, its population began to fall behind that of other American and Southern cities. By 1950 it was no longer the South's largest city, falling to second place behind Houston. By 1970 the Crescent City had dropped to fifth place in the South, and the 1980 census showed it slipping even further behind.

Census returns that year also showed a decline in the urban population, while surrounding suburbs grew dramatically. Since the early 1960s, tens of thousands of middle-class white and black families have moved to the sprawling suburban communities surrounding the city; thousands of acres of soupy marshlands have given way to tract housing and shopping centers. Unfortunately, the flight to suburbia has destroyed most of New Orleans's old neighborhoods.

Many New Orleanians, however, especially young and affluent couples, have refused to abandon the city, preferring to stay behind to buy and renovate old homes in the declining Victorian neighborhoods. Their work, courage, and good taste have revitalized entire sections of the city. The restoration craze has even spread to the Central Business District, which is experiencing its biggest construction boom since the 1850s. During the 1960s and 1970s, developers thought everything old had to be razed to make way for the new; scores of buildings dating from the 1850s and earlier gave way to the wrecker's ball. In more recent years, however, developers have found it profitable and desirable to adapt pre-Civil War buildings and warehouses to modern use, with magnificent results, especially in what has become known as the Warehouse District.

The construction of the Louisiana Superdome in the early 1970s and the 1984 New Orleans World's Fair also had considerable impact on the Central Business District. One glance at the city's skyline quickly reveals that the Central Business District is taking on all the trappings of a Sun Belt city. During the last decade the district has experienced phenomenal growth, despite the downturn in the region's oil and gas industries, with more than a dozen new skyscrapers rising above New Orleans's 18th-century suburb. Major oil companies have built regional corporate offices here, and big-name hotel chains, including Hyatt-Regency, Hilton, Marriott, Westin, Meridien, and Sheraton, have constructed luxurious high-rise hotels in the district.

More than 270 years have passed since Bienville's engineers and work crews built the first palmetto huts at the crescent in the Mississippi River. Today New Orleans, the Crescent City, the Big Easy, is scarred and somewhat decayed, but it can be the most beautiful and charming of hostesses. Its people, history, cuisine, and its alluring 19th-century mystique and Caribbean-like culture make it like no other city in the nation.

Voodoo and the Life of Spirits in New Orleans

by Jason Berry

The author of Amazing Grace: With Charles Evers in Mississippi and co-author of Up From the Cradle of Jazz: New Orleans Music Since World War II, Jason Berry also writes for numerous publications.

Imagine New Orleans in the colonial era. Rain-sodden, prone to yellow fever epidemics, it is a remote port whose plantation economy turns on the toil of African slaves. Indian communities dot swampy woodlands that are well removed from the great estates where Creole aristocrats, their society welded to interests of the Church, eat sumptuously and party well.

Voodoo charges the territory with powerful impulses, bewildering planter and priest. Away from the plantation house, in the secluded woods near river and bayou, booming drums summon slaves to torchlit ceremonies in the night. Men and women gyrate to the percussive rhythms as a cult priest chants. Slap goes his knife, slicing through a chicken's neck—up gushes the blood, covering his hands. Around and around the worshipers dance, shouting in response to the priest's African chants.

Voices pulsate to the beat of hands and sticks on drums, pulsating on and on until the spirit hits and a woman is possessed by a current of psychic energy. Her shoulders shake, her body twists, her tongue speaks words no white man understands. The cultists gather round, calming her till the possession passes and she is released from her spell. Now the drum beats become more insistent and the ceremony resumes.

In the nearby mansion, a Creole planter does not like what he hears; he tells himself he treats his slaves well. But what do those cries mean? A foreboding seeps into his night.

In the 18th century, voodoo was the most dramatic symbol of division between master and slave, and it loomed as a sinister threat to the ruling class. In 1782, the governor of Louisiana, fearing rebellious uprisings of the cults, put a clamp on voodoo-worshiping slaves imported from the Caribbean island of Martinique. But by then it was too late—voodoo had taken root.

Voodoo was a religion that had journeyed to the New World in the hearts and minds of African slaves uprooted from the animist culture of their homeland. Its origins lay in West Africa, particularly in the ancient kingdom of Dahomey (today the People's Republic of Benin) and in neighboring Yorubaland (what is now Nigeria).

In the 1720s, millions of Africans were captured by West African kings and sold as slaves to foreign merchants. Chained and hungry, the hostages were shipped in the holds of large ships that crossed the ocean. The Africans, as beheld by Caribbean and Southern planters, were people without religion, redeemed from the savage world they had left behind.

In reality, they came from large, extended families. Their African culture revolved around communal ceremonies that honored the spirits of departed ancestors. Music and dance rituals recognized the dead as existential presences; devotees wore masks to embody ancestral figures, deities, animals, and forces of nature.

The Yoruba believed that existence consists of three interconnected zones: the living, the dead, and the unborn. In rituals (still performed today) masked figures danced to percussive rhythms that evoked the ancients, or orisas.

The tone of the "talking drums" communicated the tribal vocabulary. The drum voice and dancer's mask formed a continuum—one gave language through music, and the other an image of the spirit. Voodoo was the faith, the center of gravity for the tribe, and it, along with its followers, crossed the Atlantic Ocean in the overloaded slaveholds. However, the masks would now lie buried in the savannas of the mind: Communications with the orisas in the white man's land would be dangerous and difficult.

The deepest implanting of voodoo occurred on the island of Saint-Domingue, as Haiti was known before 1804. The Fon, natives of Dahomey, cast a large influence over the island's slave communities. Just as the Yoruba evoked their orisas, the Fon summoned their spirits, called loa. To the Fon, "vodun" meant "god" or "protective spirit."

Indoctrinated as Catholics, slaves on Haiti used the Mass in melding African spirits with visages of Christian saints. The Mass provided a New World ritual for voodoo's elastic reach; cultists could forsake the knife from chicken or goat and transform their worship in a less bloody rite while maintaining its inner core complete with sacrificial gods and drumbeats.

On the night of August 22, 1791, while a storm raged through Saint-Domingue, a cult priest named Boukman led a voodoo incantation, drank blood from a pig, and, as reported by historian C.L.R. James, told his followers: "The gods of the white man inspire him with crime. . . . Our god who is good to us orders us to revenge our wrongs." Boukman was killed, but his revolt was one in a succession of slave rebellions culminating with the overthrow of French forces in 1804 and the founding of the Republic of Haiti.

Over the next decade waves of planters, free Creoles of color, and slaves reached New Orleans, many via Cuba, scattering seeds that sprouted new voodoo cults. By then nearly a century had passed since the first slaves had arrived in Louisiana; the vocabulary of African drum voices had been effectively erased, but the religious sensibility had found a new cultural passageway.

In the early 1800s, land along ramparts of New Orleans (what is now Louis Armstrong Park) became known as Place Congo, or Congo Square. On Sundays, slaves gravitated there for massive drum-and-dance convocations. They were not actual voodoo ceremonies, though the underlying impulse was similar, and white planters and their wives gawked at these spectacles performed in the open sunlight. Congo Square was outlawed about 1835; however, the sustained impact of tribal drums and dancing created for the slaves a link to their African past.

New Orleans was fast becoming a culture métissage—a mixture of bloodlines. Segregation was the law, but social intercourse was fluid among the peoples, especially between Creole planters and mistresses they found among the mulatto women. As the antebellum era wore on, the voodoo sensibility

—adaptive to the culture in which it found itself—worked its way into the thoughts and culture of aristocratic white society.

In the 1820s, voodoo queen Marie Laveau (believed to have been of Negro, Indian, and white blood) worked as a hairdresser in white homes, where she gathered secrets of the Creole elite by utilizing domestic servants to spy on whites, many of whom sought her advice as a spiritual counselor. A practicing Catholic, she nevertheless frequently prescribed the sticking of a pin into a voodoo doll to provoke trouble for someone's nemesis or magical gris-gris dust (spell-casting powder) as a curative or protective hex. Her influence with blacks was greater by virtue of her sway over whites.

Marie made quite a living as a spiritual guide, selling her hexes and charms; she also made regular visits to the local prison. She groomed her daughter Marie to carry on the voodoo tradition; it was the second Marie whose exotic ceremonies of the night became legendary. Sex orgies reportedly occurred during voodoo rites of the late 19th century.

Dr. John, another important voodoo legend, was a towering black man (reputed to be a Senegalese prince in his former life) who owned slaves and was apparently a polygamist. He cultivated his own network of informants among slaves and servants who worked for whites. Aristocrats are said to have sought his advice, making him a legendary figure to blacks, but an outright cult priest he apparently was not.

In New Orleans today, voodoo is a bare whisper of its former self, a shadow along the margins of a different spirit world, grounded in the folkways of black Christian churches. As voodoo waned with early 20th-century urbanization, spiritualistic religions took root in New Orleans's churches. In these mostly small chapels, blacks honored the presence of St. Michael the Archangel, Black Hawk the Indian, Leith Anderson, Mother Catherine, and other benevolent figures. While the base religion was Christianity, Haitian voodoo had turned African deities into images of Catholic saints; the spiritualistic churches transformed the faces once again, finding North American spirits to fit the visages of the new pantheon. Spirits may change as culture goes through upheavals, but the coil of memory springs the imagination, triggering messages in music and dance, myth and symbol.

American Indian tribes shared this imaginative process. Black Hawk was a powerful Sauk chief in Illinois who died in 1838. As Yoruba and Fon spirits resurfaced in Haiti, so the spirit of Black Hawk coursed through the mental chambers of a people with native American heritage. In 1919 the consciousness of Black Hawk reached New Orleans's spiritualistic churches through Leith Anderson, a woman of black and Indian ancestry who had come from Chicago.

In a WPA interview conducted during the Depression, Mother Dora, another spiritualistic leader, recalled Leith Anderson: "She wanted us to pray to Black Hawk because he was a great saint for spiritualism only . . . Ah think he came to her one time and said dat he was de first one to start spiritualism in dis country way before de white men come heah."

A Black Hawk cult flourishes in spiritualist churches today. Mother Leith Anderson—also called Leafy—is memorialized as well. The trancelike possessions are powerful testimony to the belief system—a benevolent Christian vision of spirits-as-seed-carriers of culture across space and time.

Voodoo rages on in the popular imagination, fed by the media. The tremors colonists once felt at the mention of voodoo are not such a far cry from the chills generated by voodoo scenes in horror movies like *Angel Heart,* set in contemporary New Orleans, or *The Serpent and the Rainbow,* which follows a young botanist into the world of zombies in modern-day Haiti.

In 1967, a crusty rock-and-roller named Mac Rebenneck adopted the stage name and persona of Dr. John. He sported bone and teeth necklaces, face paint, and turban with billowing colored feathers. Confronting this bizarre persona, Mac's mother, a good Catholic lady, fretted. "I didn't want him for his soul's sake to be doing this. But actually, I could see the creativeness of what he was doing."

In "Gris-Gris Gumbo Ya-Ya," Mac sang as Dr. John: "Got a satchel of gris-gris in my hand/ Got many clients that come from miles around."

Gris-gris dust surfaced again in an episode of the TV sitcom "Frank's Place" when Frank, the proprietor of a New Orleans restaurant, has a run-in with a practicing voodoo "witch" who leaves a gris-gris hex smack-dab on Frank's front porch.

Perhaps the most visible emblem of voodoo's hold on the popular imagination today is the number of visitors who flock to the tomb of Marie Laveau in St. Louis Cemetery No. 1 and to the Voodoo Museum in the French Quarter. Both are tributes to a time in Louisiana's history when mask and drum voice moved to an African beat. Their shadowy appeal is a reminder of the chthonic world of blood sacrifice and orisas still living within us all.

Carnival

by Millie Ball

*A staff writer for
New Orleans's*
Times-Picayune,
*Millie Ball has
won four
first-place feature
writing awards
from the
Associated Press
and two Alex
Waller Awards
from the Press
Club of New
Orleans.*

What could convince a prominent New Orleans businessman to wear a pageboy wig, gold crown, jeweled tunic, and white tights in public—and consider it the honor of a lifetime? Or cause people to ask with interest, "Who found the baby in the king cake?" Or prompt little old ladies to jostle strangers and shout that phrase New Orleanians learn at mama's knee—"Throw me something, Mister!"

Come to New Orleans during Carnival and find out.

Carnival is a mad game in which New Orleanians beg masked men on passing floats to toss them handfuls of plastic beads, go-cups, or aluminum doubloons (known generically as "throws") that eventually are pitched into the trash or mailed to family members who have married Yankees and moved away.

Don't be smug; if you visit, you'll catch the fervor. After a few moments of astonished gaping, you'll yell for throws, too, draping layers of beads around your neck, sipping from a plastic cup as you prance along the street, bebopping with the marching bands, and having a grand old time—assuming you like crowds.

Get one thing straight right away: There is a difference between Mardi Gras and Carnival—always with a capital *C* to differentiate it from carnivals that set up portable Ferris wheels and dart booths in vacant lots.

Carnival refers to an entire season that begins January 6, with an elegant debutante ball called Twelfth Night (as in "twelfth night after Christmas") and a separate, less aristocratic ball held on a streetcar by a group of Carnival devotees calling themselves Phunny Phorty Phellows.

Lasting for one to two months, Carnival explodes in its final days into a party that envelopes the entire city and suburbs, with balls in every hall and hotel room and on the final weekend, parades day and night, all of them organized and paid for by members of private clubs called "krewes." Since the parades are free (although the balls are strictly by invitation), New Orleanians refer to Carnival as "the greatest free show on earth."

During Carnival just about everybody overdoses on king cake, a sweet-dough coffee cake shaped like a wreath and topped with icing or sugar sprinkles in the Carnival colors of green, gold, and purple. Baked inside is the mysterious "baby," a fingernail-long pink plastic baby doll. Whoever bites into the baby is supposed to give the next king cake party or bring the next king cake to the office. Some New Orleanians prefer swallowing the baby to having to buy yet another king cake.

Mardi Gras (literally Fat Tuesday in French) is the final day of Carnival, the only day that it is legal to wear costumes, face paint, and masks in the streets. It's the final bash-of-a-celebration before Ash Wednesday, the beginning of Lent—that period of fasting for 40 days (and six Sundays that don't count) that leads up to Easter. Mardi Gras is an official city holiday, with just about everyone but policemen taking the day off.

It's also the day that a middle-age man in a pageboy wig reigns over the parade of Rex, the most important of the 50 or more parades and 100 or so Carnival balls (all with their own maids and queens accompanying their own draped and bewigged kings).

But there is only one Rex (the king of this Krewe is also known as Rex, latin for king) and he is always an outstanding citizen who has done some high-profile volunteer work and who is a member of the men's group sponsoring the parade. Unlike kings of some of the less social balls, who sometimes pay hundreds or even thousands of dollars to their organizations for the honor (and for their costumes), Rex pays nothing to be king, and his club owns his outfit.

The queen of Rex is a young debutante chosen by the group's leaders on the basis of her father's prominence. Rex and his queen are considered to be monarchs of the entire Carnival celebration. Their identities are kept secret until the day before Mardi Gras, when they are announced publicly.

The queen of Rex watches the parade from the city's most exclusive men's club (some would say most snobbish), the Boston Club (named after a card game, not the city) on Canal Street; though she wears a traditional white suit, she waves her arms for throws like everyone else. That night the king and queen of Carnival wear jeweled clothes as they promenade around the white-cloth-covered floor at a ball in the city's Municipal Auditorium. At 11:30 PM they leave the Rex ball and cross to the other side of the auditorium to join the ball of the Mistick Krewe of Comus, the oldest and most exclusive of all Carnival balls in New Orleans. (The identity of Comus is never revealed.)

The kings swap queens and all sit together on a throne, then leave the floor grandly, one at a time. This is called "the meeting of the courts," and is televised to a huge audience every year on WDSU-TV, Channel 6. And that is the end of Mardi Gras; at midnight, police cars cruise through the French Quarter, loudspeakers blaring "Mardi Gras is over."

The next morning, Ash Wednesday, the more than half of the New Orleans population who are Roman Catholic go to church to receive the sign of the cross on their foreheads in ashes. And Lent begins.

New Orleanians are of two minds about Carnival. Most think it's the grandest thing since the invention of beer; the rest leave town. So many locals seek exile skiing in Aspen, Colorado, that they call themselves the Krewe of Aspen.

There are complications to Mardi Gras. First there's the matter of the date, which changes yearly because it is based on the movable feast of Easter. Mardi Gras can occur from early February to early March, and, whenever it is, New Orleanians invariably say "Mardi Gras is early this year" or "Mardi Gras is late this year." Mardi Gras falls on the following dates in upcoming years: February 7, 1989; February 27, 1990; February 12, 1991; March 3, 1992; February 23, 1993; February 16, 1994.

How it all started, no one is absolutely sure. Some say the Carnival celebration is an offshoot of pagan holidays. Others point to the Middle Ages. The faithful abstained from meat, eggs, and milk during Lent and before the fasting began vast feasts were held. Rome held rowdy celebrations during the Renaissance; in fact, festivities were held in most Christian countries, including France. So when French-Canadian explorer Pierre Le Moyne, Sieur d'Iberville, landed on a plot of ground near the mouth of the Mississippi River on Mardi Gras, March 3, 1699, he named it Pointe du Mardi Gras.

There's not much in history books about early Louisiana Carnival celebrations until the 1800s, when private balls were held by the Creole descendants of French and Spanish settlers, the city's aristocracy in those days. And there were "quadroon" balls where wealthy white men mingled with beautiful "free women of color" who were one-quarter black.

There also were street processions of the raucous sort. Young men from the so-called good families (as well as the not-so-good) wore masks and costumes and sometimes dumped flour on passersby, and were more intent on getting drunk than anything else. Occasionally the parades were splendid, but more often they were coarse. Then, on Feb. 24, 1857, Mardi Gras changed forever.

At 9 PM, 60 or so men dressed like demons paraded in the streets with two floats in a torchlit cavalcade. The group called itself the Mistick Krewe of Comus, after the god of revelry. Arthur Burton LaCour wrote in his classic 1952 book *New Orleans Masquerade* that the men were Creoles from the French Quarter and Saxons (as LaCour referred to the nouveau riche Americans) from the other side of Canal Street, over the so-called "neutral ground" (a name still used in New Orleans to refer to the median of a wide street).

Comus, LaCour wrote, was started by 13 New Orleanians and six men from Mobile, Alabama, where Mardi Gras parades had begun a few years earlier. Wanting to observe the holiday more fully, they formed a secret men's society, went to Mobile for costumes, and sent 3,000 invitations to a ball held at New Orleans's Gaiety Theater. They had begun a tradition.

As time passed (with lapses for the Civil War) invitations to the Comus ball became so coveted that one year the krewe captain advertised a $2,000 reward for two missing invitations. Comus crowned Robert E. Lee's daughter, Mildred Lee, as its first queen in 1884.

Through the years, other groups of men organized Carnival krewes. Then, in 1872, 40 businessmen founded the Krewe of Rex and sponsored a daytime parade for the Mardi Gras visit of His Imperial Highness, the Grand Duke Alexis of Russia. They chose as Carnival colors green for faith, gold for power, and purple for justice. Today's standard Carnival song, "If Ever I Cease to Love," was from a play called *Bluebeard* that featured an actress who infatuated the grand duke, and bands of the day played it ceaselessly. The first Rex parade was thrown together quickly with borrowed costumes, and there was no ball. The first reception was not until the next year, when a queen was chosen on the spot at a public ball. Eventually invitations and formal dress became required.

As more and more carnival organizations were founded, young girls who made debuts at afternoon teas held by their grandmothers were invited to be queens and maids. Traditionally, debutantes wear subdued white dresses, giving the 18 or so socially prominent balls the nickname "white gown balls." Maids in less prominent balls tend to wear lavish costumes depicting some aspect of the ball's theme. As with the kings, debutantes of the social balls pay only for their dresses, while maids at less prestigious balls may also pay several hundred dollars for their right to reign.

Balls were strictly segregated; even Jews and Italians were banned from guest lists of the exclusive older balls (known as the "old-line krewes") until recently. (Even now, only Rex invites black guests.) So other segments of society started clubs of their own.

A black butler and dance instructor from Chicago started the Illinois Club in 1895, copying the format of the old-line balls. Though this club split into two krewes, the Original Illinois Club and the Young Men Illinois Club, the debutantes still perform the founder's dance, the Chicago Glide, in parallel black galas. The Illinois clubs don't sponsor parades, but the Zulu Social and Pleasure Club, organized in 1909 by working-class black men, does. The Zulu king (Louis Armstrong reigned in 1949) and his entourage toss glitter-covered coconuts to the crowds. In days gone by the Zulu parade would wander wherever the drivers chose, stopping at various bars along the way; these days, it's more organized. Doctors and bishops mingle with blue-collar members at a splashy, racially integrated party, and the parade follows a route published in city newspapers.

After the Depression and World War II, Carnival clubs started popping up everywhere. Some were for doctors, others for businessmen, some for residents of certain neighborhoods, for military men, or for gays. The gay balls are splendid extravaganzas, but invitations for "straights" are scarce. There are only a few organizations for women, none in the socially elite category; so a few years ago, former old-line debutantes started joining a women's Krewe, Iris, so they, too, could parade. Membership fees in krewes can range from $150 to $600, but joining parading krewes costs much more, because members must buy the trinkets they "throw."

Though new krewes proliferated after the Depression, their members never dreamed of competing for status with the older groups, revering their traditions. Then, in 1969, an upstart group of businessmen looking to entertain tourists the Sunday before Mardi Gras founded Bacchus, named after the god of wine. The sassy group stunned the city by setting new rules and strutting out with a show as stupendous as the Rex gala. The Bacchus floats were bigger than any seen before, and the king was Danny Kaye, not a homegrown humanitarian but a famous entertainer. The party was in the Rivergate Convention Center, not at Municipal Auditorium or a hotel ballroom. There was no queen, no court, and the party was called a Rendezvous, not a ball. All guests could dance, not just members and their wives, as was the custom in old-line balls, where nonmembers merely watched the proceedings. The floats rode right into the Rivergate, and you didn't have to be socially prominent to join —or even white.

The crowds have loved Bacchus from day one, and guessing what celebrities will follow the likes of Danny Kaye, Bob Hope, and Jackie Gleason has become almost as popular as wondering about the identity of Rex.

In 1974, another "krewe" of businessmen, Endymion, borrowed some of Bacchus's ideas and took over an abandoned slot in the Saturday night parade lineup. Nationally known celebrities are invited to be grand marshal and to entertain at a party for 10,000 called the Extravaganza, now held in the Louisiana Superdome. Endymion has super floats, a local king (drawn in a members' raffle at $25 a chance), and a court consisting of daughters of members. It can cost a queen's father $15,000 for expenses that include an elaborate dress and party. By the time members of Bacchus and Endymion buy throws and pay dues, they've dished out $2,000 to $3,000 each.

The last weekend before Mardi Gras is a whirlwind of parades and parties. Some krewes stage Carnival balls for convention groups willing to pay to see a simulated version of the real thing. Occasionally, lucky out-of-towners can buy extra tickets to the Bacchus or Endymion parties. Or they may be able to obtain invitations (always invitations, never tickets) to Rex, the most accessible of the old-line balls, if they happen to know a prominent New Orleanian with connections. The best parades tend to be near the end of Carnival, put on by wealthy krewes that have their own floats. A favored (and crowded!) spot to watch the floats and marching bands is downtown on Canal Street, where the parades end about 8 to 9 PM. Families of the old-line krewes usually watch from their uptown neighborhoods, many of the families gather at around 6 PM at Napoleon and St. Charles Avenues.

The big parades begin the Wednesday before Mardi Gras with the Knights of Babylon, the so-called doctors' krewe, whose path is lighted by flambeaux (torches) carried by young black men who dance as they collect change thrown by onlookers. Though some think it demeaning, the tradition flourishes.

Thursday night is Momus, an irreverent, old-line krewe that almost always spoofs politics or some other serious subject. Friday is the businessmen's krewe of Hermes parade. Saturday and Sunday there are parades all day long, in both the city and the suburbs, climaxing Saturday night with Endymion and Sunday with Bacchus. There's also a Carnival market in the French Market over the weekend.

Monday, Lundi Gras, used to be quiet, but in 1987 the city launched festivities both day and night. The old-line krewe of Proteus's parade is always a tasteful show.

Tuesday is Mardi Gras. Zulu and Rex are followed by parades of trucks decorated by anyone who wants to organize a group of friends. Walking clubs (they march instead of riding on floats), including the Jefferson City Buzzards and Pete Fountain's Half Fast Marching Club, zigzag all over town, stopping in bars and swapping kisses for paper flowers and beads.

The Mardi Gras Indians also roam the city, particularly near Canal Street and Claiborne Avenue. The Indians are neighborhood groups of black men in stupendous feather costumes. Hometowners and visitors alike enjoy wandering through the French Quarter, where those with the flashiest costumes tend to gather. Though the Quarter can be wild and drunken, it's worth seeing the mind-boggling costumes that frequently are the result of a year's work. If a woman is in a particularly stunning costume look twice—"he" may be a "she."

Those who last through the day end the season properly by attending the Comus Parade. Crowds are usually sparse and the theme esoteric; Comus waves a silver goblet instead of a scepter. Diehard Carnival fans watch from North Rampart Street, right before the parade disbands for the ball. The throws are meager by then, but it's oh, so pleasant to view Comus slowly, to take in details on the floats, to wave at the maskers instead of pleading for beads, and to smile good night and good-bye to Mardi Gras before heading home to eat the last crumbs of king cake.

For anyone serious about planning for Carnival, Arthur Hardy's *Annual Mardi Gras Guide* is a must. It costs $2.50 and can be ordered from Box 8058, New Orleans, LA 70182, tel. 504/282–2326.

The New Orleans daily *The Times-Picayune* publishes an annual Carnival guide a few weeks before Mardi Gras each year. Write the Special Sections Department, *Times-Picayune*, 3800 Howard Ave., New Orleans, LA 70140, tel. 504/826–3132.

Gambit, a weekly newspaper, also publishes parade guides in the weeks before Mardi Gras. Write *Gambit*, 921 Canal St., Ste. 740, New Orleans, LA 70112, tel. 504/525–5900.

If you won't be in town at Carnival but want to see some of the costumes, floats, or paraphernalia, there are several museums and showrooms where it's Mardi Gras all year long.

The **Louisiana State Museum's Old U.S. Mint** at the corner of Esplanade Avenue and Decatur Street, behind the French Quarter's French Market, has an extensive "Carnival in New Orleans" exhibit. There are costumes and memorabilia on display. *Tel. 504/568–6968. Admission: $3 adults; $1.50 children 12 and older, and senior citizens. Open Wed.– Sun. 10–5.*

Blaine Kern's Mardi Gras World is on the West Bank, across the Mississippi River Bridge at 233 Newton Street. Kern is the major float builder and designer in the city, and the exhibit focuses on floats, both finished and under construction. There is a large gift shop of Carnival souvenirs; guided tours must be booked in advance. *233 Newton St., tel. 504/362–8211. Tour cost $3.50 adults, $2 children; general admission without guide $2. Parties can be arranged. Open weekdays 9:30–4.*

Germaine Wells Mardi Gras Museum is on the second floor of Arnaud's Restaurant in the French Quarter. The late Mrs. Wells was a flamboyant woman who reigned as queen of more than 20 Carnival balls; her gowns and other Carnival costumes are on display. *813 Bienville St., tel. 504/523–5433. Admission free. Museum and restaurant open Sun.–Fri. 11:30–2:30 and 6–10.*

Musée Conti (Wax Museum) in the French Quarter has four Carnival displays and 10 mannequins in costume. *917 Conti St., tel. 504/525–2605. Admission: $4 adults, $3 teenagers, $2.50 children 6–12, children under 5 free. Open daily 10–5:30.*

Ripley's Believe It or Not, in the French Quarter, has one exhibit and a short film about Carnival. *501 Bourbon St., tel. 504/529–5131. Admission: $3.95 adults, $2.50 children, plus tax. Open daily 10 AM–midnight.*

The Cradle of Jazz
by Jason Berry

Music is the soul of New Orleans. Since the 1890s her melodies, rhythms, and musicians have enriched America's artistic heritage, and today, the city's musical texture is an interweaving of jazz, rhythm and blues, gospel, rock and roll, Latin beat, and then some.

The sound of New Orleans extends from the classic jazz of the early 1920s through the sterling sound of Louis Armstrong and his mates; from the mid-century dance-hall beat of Fats Domino, Professor Longhair, and a legion of rhythm-and-bluesmen to the polished modern improvisations of Wynton Marsalis and the young jazz lions of the 1980s.

As a distinctive sound, New Orleans's music is marked by a parade-time backbeat on drums, rocking, vocally suggestive horns, and a percussive piano style with liberal shadings of the blues.

The root of this sound is called the "second line"—the waves of marching dancers who engulf the brass bands with a dazzling body language of gyrating steps, following the musicians as they parade through the streets. Above all, it's music to make you clap your hands and move your feet.

The strength of the sound and the beauty of the tradition advance to a rare plateau at jazz funerals. One of the most poignant occurred on December 9, 1987, when saxophonist David Lastie, whose career spanned 30 years, was laid to rest.

Lastie was one of three brothers who learned music in a local church where their father played drums. A valued recording-session artist, David Lastie performed with a litany of rhythm-and-bluesmen, including Fats Domino, Huey "Piano" Smith, Jesse Hill, and Dr. John (on the 1967 *Gumbo* LP).

Lastie was equally at home with R&B and with traditional jazz standards like "When the Saints Go Marching In" and impressionist pieces like "Killer Joe," which he laced with cool, bluesy lines. His father, Frank Lastie, deacon of the Guiding Star spiritual church, played with Louis Armstrong in 1913 in the Colored Waifs Home, and was among the earliest ministers to introduce drums into local church services, in 1929.

Like his brothers—Melvin, a trumpeter who died in 1972, and Walter, a drummer who died in 1980—David carried jazz history in his genes. He played the music of the churches, of the clubs, of the streets. His funeral was an eloquent ritual—43 musicians, clad in black and white, played the slow dirge "Just a Closer Walk With Thee" as the hearse and limousines, backed by 300 friends of the departed, proceeded along Elysian Fields Avenue, slowing traffic to a crawl. At the cemetery, as the coffin was lowered into the earth, the musicians and mourners cut loose with "Oh, Didn't He Ramble?"—A fitting tribute to a musical hero.

The seeds of New Orleans jazz first took root in the 1890s. New Orleans was then legally segregated, but was a town where rare degrees of social intercourse prevailed. It was a society of many layers—Creole descendants of European settlers, Italians, Irish, and Germans, blacks, Indians, and Creoles of color (or *gens de couleur*).

Music held a common currency among these peoples. Outdoor festivals and indoor dances followed the calendar of Catholic feasts, the biggest of which was Mardi Gras, "Fat Tuesday," ushering in 40 days of Lent. The society orchestras and smaller ensembles that performed for parties and other events were playing syncopated rags; French quadrilles and polkas were popular, too.

A more potent influence, at least for the impetus of jazz, was the brass bands—groups that marched in uniforms, playing parade music with new rhythmic flavorings that reflected an African percussive tradition.

The musicianship of black Creoles was a primary factor in the emergence of jazz. They were a distinct caste, descendants of African mothers and fathers of French or Spanish ancestry; many first arrived from Haiti in the early 1800s, settling in the Treme neighborhood (behind what is now Louis Armstrong Park) and, in later years, the Seventh Ward, which lies downtown, well beyond the French Quarter. The lines of miscegenation were perpetuated by New Orleans aristocrats who kept mulatto mistresses and often supported second, "shadow" families.

Some Creoles amassed great wealth before the Civil War, and even owned slaves. They were generally better educated than the blacks who lived in uptown wards, upriver from the French Quarter. By the end of Reconstruction and with the tightening of racial laws, the sturdy familial lines and artisan skills of the downtown Creoles had produced a burgeoning tradition of families who taught music and performed professionally.

One such professor, James Brown Humphrey, played a variety of instruments and was a catalyst of jazz. In 1887 he began regular trips to outlying plantation communities to teach poor blacks, a number of whom moved to town to join brass bands. In 1987 two of his grandsons, Willie and Percy Humphrey, were regular performers in Preservation Hall.

A more legendary figure—universally deemed the first great jazzman—was Buddy Bolden, who played cornet (a smaller version of the trumpet) with strong, bluesy currents. Though his music was popular, Bolden suffered a mental breakdown in 1907 and never recorded.

In time, the musical division between blacks, who learned to play by ear—listening to songs, replicating what they heard— and Creoles, who read sheet music, began to blur. Meanwhile, a red-light district called Storyville gave piano professors like Jelly Roll Morton quite a venue until its closure in 1917.

Nineteen seventeen was a milestone year for another reason: In New York, a group of white New Orleans musicians led by Nick LaRocca, the Original Dixieland Jazz Band, recorded the first jazz disc. Jazz was an idiom rooted in the African improvisational genius; many white practitioners, whose style became known as Dixieland, began to flourish in New Orleans as well.

The first generation of New Orleans jazzmen produced three brilliant artists—Louis Armstrong, Jelly Roll Morton, and

Sidney Bechet—each of whom left the city to establish his reputation. Morton, a Creole with great talent as a composer-pianist, was a peripatetic figure who died in 1941, down on his luck. Bechet, also a Creole, was a virtuoso clarinetist who left behind a string of memorable recordings. He settled near Paris, where he became a celebrity, and died in 1959.

Armstrong's life was a rags-to-riches odyssey. His given birth date was July 4, 1900: He grew up in the Back-o'-Town ghetto, and after a stint in the Colored Waifs Home, found an early mentor in Papa Joe Oliver, the popular cornetist and bandleader also known as King Oliver. In 1918 Armstrong began traveling the Mississippi, playing on riverboats, refining his technique. In 1922, he left New Orleans to join Oliver's band in Chicago, and for the next half-century he traveled the globe, elevating jazz to an international art form.

The music stylizations and recordings of Armstrong, Morton, and Bechet had an enormous influence; yet to all but aficionados of jazz, the historical sensibility they shared is frequently overlooked. Each man worked hard on a biography; their books are solid works of literature, as well as classics of jazz history— Armstrong's *Satchmo: My Life in New Orleans*, Bechet's *Treat It Gentle*, and Morton's *Mister Jelly Roll* (written by Alan Lomax, but based on long interviews with Morton).

The sounds of jazz continued to flow in New Orleans through the 1930s and '40s. The tidal shift toward a new idiom came after World War II: rhythm and blues.

A blues sensibility ran deep in New Orleans, and the many lyrics about love lost, love found were fashioned into a style, enhanced by gospel techniques, the soaring choirs and drums of the churches, and saxophones and trumpets that blasted like preachers and moaned like bluesmen.

Fats Domino put R&B on the map. In 1949, "The Fat Man," with his rocking piano style and rolling, mellifluous voice, triggered a line of golden records that made teenagers put on their dancing shoes.

Domino had the advantage of a highly skilled producer, trumpeter-bandleader Dave Bartholomew, who molded Fats's sound for the Imperial label. His biggest hit, "Blueberry Hill," was a country boy's song that wedded Fats's appeal to an audience of blue-collar workers and rural folk.

The other influential early rhythm and bluesman was Henry Roeland Byrd, who took the stage name Professor Longhair in 1949, and who played in Domino's shadow most of his life. Fess, as he was fondly known among locals, was quite a ticket. A tap dancer in his youth, he made the rounds of Rampart Street honky-tonks in the Depression, studying the blues piano of Champion Jack Dupree and Sonny Boy Williamson.

Professor Longhair called his own style "a mixture of mambo, rumba, and calypso." He infused the dance steps of his youth into an intricate, percussive keyboard style and he sang with the deep heart of a bluesman. He simulated the street pace of Carnival in "Mardi Gras in New Orleans" and "Go to the Mardi Gras," which became local anthems. "Big Chief" was his homage to the Mardi Gras Indians, groups of blacks who create grand tribal Indian costumes and still parade in neighborhood tribes through New Orleans's back streets.

In a sense, Professor Longhair's death in 1980 marked the end of the postwar R&B era. His unique style never caught on as a national chart-buster, but he had enormous influence on younger musicians. Even before his death, younger jazzmen in the brass bands had begun performing his Carnival tunes.

Domino and Longhair divided New Orleans R&B into two stylistic camps—one a building block of rock and roll, the other a more improvisational, Afro-Caribbean beat. Between these styles ranged a generation of exceptional musicians.

Allen Toussaint harnessed the talents of a stable of singers in the 1960s. A skilled pianist with a seasoned lyrical touch, Toussaint composed songs for Irma Thomas ("Queen of the Blues"); Aaron Neville, a brawny balladeer with a falsetto reach that chills the spine; Ernie K-Doe, an extravagant stage performer and blues shouter who scored a hit with "Mother-in-Law"; and Benny Spellman, a hefty ex-football player for whom Toussaint penned the memorable "Fortune Teller."

The music of the 1950s fit a new urban groove. White teenagers were the big market; of the many New Orleans artists who reached the kids, Huey "Piano" Smith did it with a colorful entourage known as the Clowns. Drawing on nursery rhymes, Huey wrote uncomplicated, if offbeat lyrics—"I got the rockin' pneumonia and the boogie-woogie flu"—and the dancers loved it.

When the Beatles and Rolling Stones swept America in the 1960s, the New Orleans R&B scene fell into decline. In the early 1970s, the annual Jazz and Heritage Festival ignited a revival.

One of the most talented 1950s session artists, a white boy named Mac Rebenneck, played piano, guitar, and penned dozens of compositions before hitting pop stardom in 1968 as Dr. John. James Booker, who dubbed himself the Piano Prince, also had commanding talent; he could jump from classical chords into R&B bounces with sizzling heat and witty lyrics. Booker, Dr. John, and Art Neville were prime exponents of a piano idiom that roamed the bridge between the Longhair-Domino styles. Booker's death in 1983 was greatly felt in New Orleans's jazz community.

In 1977, Art joined his brothers to form the Neville Brothers band, today the city's preeminent pop group. Charles plays saxophone; Cyril sings and plays congas; Aaron, whose 1966 hit "Tell It Like It Is" is still a showstopper, sings and plays hand percussions. The Nevilles' four-part harmonies, set against Afro-Caribbean lines, gave R&B a warm new shading. At the same time, the Nevilles wrote a new chapter in popular music through their association with the Wild Tchoupitoulas, a Mardi Gras Indian tribe led by their uncle, George Landry.

There are approximately 25 black neighborhood groups that masquerade as Indians each Mardi Gras; the folk tradition dates to Reconstruction. As Big Chief Jolley, Landry founded the Wild Tchoupitoulas in the uptown neighborhood where he and his nephews lived. A 1976 LP, *The Wild Tchoupitoulas*, combined the instrumental prowess of the Nevilles and the Meters bands with Jolley's hearty vocals, based on the old *a capella* tribal chants, to become a classic. By the time Landry passed away in 1980, Mardi Gras Indian music was emblematic of the Neville sound.

I n the 1980s, New Orleans experienced a jazz renaissance led by a brilliant trumpeter named Wynton Marsalis, the product of yet another musical family. As high school students, Wynton and his brothers studied at the New Orleans Center for the Creative Arts, where Ellis Marsalis, their father, directed the jazz program. With brother Branford on saxophone, Wynton emerged as a national star by the time he was 20, and in 1984 won two Grammy awards.

A gifted composer-pianist in his own right, Ellis Marsalis molded three other young talents who have since achieved national recognition: trumpeter Terence Blanchard and saxophonist Donald Harrison, who perform together, and pianist Harry Connick, Jr., who in 1987 released his debut album at age 19. The Marsalis brothers, Blanchard, and Harrison all got their professional start in New York with Art Blakey's Jazz Messengers. Yet another Marsalis brother, Delfayo, produced the Blanchard-Harrison 1988 LP *Crystal Stair*.

The young lions of the 1980s are products of a teaching tradition and a society rooted in musical families. Their polished innovations draw from a large canvas of sounds. The Dirty Dozen and Rebirth bands have led the brass band resurgence, a fourth generation of young musicians improvising with blues, bebop, R&B, and jazz.

Nevertheless, as New Orleans nears the final decade of the century that gave birth to jazz, the strength of that heritage is problematic. Many musicians struggle, taking day jobs to pay the bills. The unsuccessful 1984 World's Fair had a devastating impact on the local economy, which, unlike Nashville, still has not developed an entertainment industry strong enough to support its own. Tourists flock to New Orleans in droves, spending more in music clubs than locals do, yet comparatively little of the local sound makes its way back up the river.

As a cultural commodity, jazz and pop are all too often exported only when local artists pick up and move, as the Marsalis family did—Wynton and Branford to New York, Ellis to a professorship in Virginia. Still, for all of the musicians who have left, many more have stayed. Despite the drawbacks, a cultural sensibility—more Latin and African than Anglo-American—has endowed New Orleans with a unique sense of musical community. That, coupled with the languorous pace and premium placed on food and good living, maintains New Orleans's magnetic appeal.

Some Like It Hot: New Orleans's Sultry Bill of Fare

by Lisa Le
Blanc-Berry

The "Urbane
Gourmet" food
critic for Gambit
newspaper, Lisa
LeBlanc-Berry
gives weekly
restaurant
reviews on New
Orleans's radio
station WWIW.
She is currently
the editor of
Where Magazine
in New Orleans.

Although a child of France, New Orleans has always been a melting pot of ethnic culinary styles. Africans, Spaniards, Frenchmen, Choctaw Indians, and Acadians all contributed to what is now known as New Orleans-style cooking.

Slaves, the foundation of the 18th-century colonial economy, brought with them from their native lands *gombo* (an African word for okra), *couscous* (a North African dish they transformed into a warm breakfast cereal made of cornmeal), and, most importantly, a vivid spicing technique.

New Orleans was ceded by France to Spain in 1762, but reclaimed in 1800 by Napoleon. Three years later, it was sold to Thomas Jefferson as part of the Louisiana Purchase. The Spanish legacy included a new style of cooking and a love of tomatoes and peppers, which were later utilized in jambalaya, a variation on Spanish paella.

The Choctaw Indians, who traded with the French, introduced them to sassafras, which is used to thicken certain non-okra-based gumbos, and to corn, which resulted in grits and *macque-choux*, an Acadian dish of corn, bell peppers, and onions.

The Acadians, exiles from Nova Scotia who arrived in New Orleans via the backwater regions of Louisiana, brought with them a peasant tradition of cookery. Impoverished at the outset, they used inexpensive meats, seasonal game, fish, and simple garden and farm products in their dishes. They, like the black slaves, fostered a gumbo tradition that remained in southwest Louisiana until the late 1880s, when the railroad broke down their isolation.

From this blending of cultures have come the innovations in Creole cooking that continue today, creating an array of regional talent.

Since New Orleans's recent leap into culinary acclaim, Chef Paul Prudhomme, the famous Cajun who opened K-Paul's Louisiana Kitchen in 1982, has assumed an ambassadorial role in the exportation of Acadian (Cajun) and Louisiana cooking. His most recognized dish, blackened redfish, has become so popular that a commercial fishing ban was levied on redfish in early 1988. The Cajun cooking craze, with staying power at the national level, has resulted in an explosion of the crawfish industry.

Another distinguished man of New Orleans cuisine is Austin Leslie, chef-owner of Chez Helene's, whose soul-food establishment spawned the hit TV series, "Frank's Place." The series aptly demonstrates New Orleanians' appreciation of good food and the star treatment bestowed upon local chefs.

While the Cajuns are taking an international spotlight, Creole cuisine is undergoing some important transformations—with a twist in nomenclature—into Nouvelle Creole. Establishments devoted to this style are currently the rage. Pasta is now more popular than rice in many Louisiana restaurants, and the growing presence of Vietnamese staff in some of the finest New Orleans kitchens has introduced diners to eastern herbs and spices.

A *roux*, a sauce that originated in the kitchens of France, is the basis of many Cajun and Creole dishes, but each type is distinctly different. A Cajun roux is made with flour and oil that is browned over a low fire, resulting in a deep, chocolate-colored sauce. Although Creole cooks are known occasionally to use the Cajun technique, they prefer to use butter or bacon fat—instead of oil—to thicken their stocks. Cajuns considered butter a luxury, as dairy products were scarce; hence, a roux without butter and a bisque without cream. The Creole roux is more akin to French roux, which mixes equal parts of butter and flour.

Hens were substituted for chickens in Cajun gumbos, since thrifty Cajuns wouldn't slaughter chickens until after laying time. The Creoles enjoyed more expensive ingredients for their gumbos, which resembled bouillabaisse.

The cuisine that Paul Prudhomme has popularized has little to do with what is considered typical Cajun cooking. Like a composer, he has taken the theme of his heritage and richly embellished it with innovative melodies of his own, all quite imaginative and superbly palatable. Cajuns would never have dreamed of creating either his blackened redfish or his oyster and brie soup. Etouffees and stuffed mirlitons (a vegetable pear), which Prudhomme also serves at K-Paul's, are closer to the heart of Cajun cookery. Generally, the food served at Prudhomme's restaurant, as well as at a handful of other Cajun establishments in the city, is far removed from what is consumed daily in the bayou parishes.

An Acadian's pantry is never without rice, filé, red pepper, Tabasco sauce, a hen, and the "Holy Trinity"—onion, bell pepper, and celery. Other necessities are wild game and fresh shellfish. It's said that a Cajun will cook and eat anything that won't eat him first.

A popular concept that helps to distinguish Cajun from Creole cuisine is the notion that the former is countrified and the latter is citified. However, despite the geographical implications, each is sophisticated and artful in its own right.

The French Market gave birth to many dining traditions that have remained in New Orleans. As a result of colonial trading, eating styles evolved around the marketplace. Brunch, a mainstay in New Orleans, was born here. Originally devised to accommodate the butchers and French Market merchants who breakfasted late in the day, it was introduced to the public by the chef-restaurateur Madame Begue in the mid-1800s. Tujague's Restaurant (823 Decatur St.) preserves her memory at the original site of her restaurant with a Madame Begue room, replete with photographs and memorabilia. Today, Brennan's Restaurant (417 Royal St.), the most popular brunch spot in town, carries on the brunch tradition and boasts of serving over 1,000 brunches each Saturday and Sunday.

Brunch is merely the beginning of what eating in New Orleans is about. Traditions abound here, and the best way to begin an exploration of them is with a cup of café au lait and a beignet. The famed Creole coffee, or café au lait, is sold everywhere, but the best version of this rich chickory blend laced with steaming hot milk or cream (a hearty version of the Parisian grande crème) can be savored at Café du Monde (open 24 hours a day), across from Jackson Square.

The accompaniment to this rich coffee is a Café du Monde beignet—a deep-fried sour-dough pastry doused with powdered sugar. (Try to avoid sneezing around beignets, especially when wearing dark colors.) This is a perfect way to finish off an evening or to start a morning of sightseeing. Café du Monde is also a nice place to people-watch.

The legacy of the New Orleans po-boy is rich. Available today at almost every lunch counter, restaurant, and grocery store, this oversized sandwich came into being during a late 1920s streetcar strike. The sandwich was originally made from a loaf of French bread sliced lengthwise and filled with a generous portion of potatoes, meat, or whatever the chef's whim of the day was; the cost was five cents. Today, po-boys are more expensive, but they're still as a rule as long as a person's forearm. The sandwiches today are stuffed with everything from roast beef to meatballs, Italian sausage, fried oysters, and soft-shell crabs. Mother's on Poydras Street, Parasol's in the Irish Channel Uptown, and R & O's Pizza Place in Bucktown make the best po-boys in the city.

Another great New Orleans sandwich is the Italian *muffuletta*, which is made with a dense, round bread dressed with olive salad and stuffed with layers of meats and cheeses. Central Grocery (923 Decatur St.) makes one of the best muffulettas in town. Napoleon House (500 Chartres St.) serves its own variation of the muffuletta, hot from the oven. Muffulettas are so large that most people halve and quarter them; one makes a meal for two adults.

Barbecue shrimp, Pascal Manale's original, succulent creation, is served in Manale's Italian-Creole restaurant on tree-lined Napoleon Avenue. This spicy dish isn't barbecued at all; instead, large shrimp are baked in butter and herbs and served still in their shells. Some restaurants, like Ruth's Chris Steak House, peel them; Manale's offers bibs. You can find barbecue shrimp everywhere from casual eateries to the best restaurants.

Oysters on the half shell are offered everywhere in town. The Acme Oyster Bar in the French Quarter has some of the best. Wherever they are consumed, the important thing to remember is that you shouldn't ever sit down to eat them. Tradition has it that cold oysters are eaten standing up, then washed down with a bottle of Dixie beer.

Oysters Rockefeller are served at many fine restaurants in the city, but none are as fine as those consumed at their place of birth, Antoine's (713 St. Louis St.)—founded in 1840 by Antoine Alciatore—the oldest dining establishment in New Orleans. Traditional oysters Rockefeller are served in a sauce of puréed greens tinged with Pernod. The dish is so rich that it was named for the richest man in the world at the time of its creation. Brennan's, unlike most restaurants, has an outstanding version that uses no spinach. Two other baked-oyster dishes that have become famous are Bienville and Lafayette; some better restaurants offer an appetizer of 2-2-2, which means two of each type on a platter.

Jambalaya, red beans and rice are sold almost everywhere, and some of the tastiest are found at lunch counters. One of the more savory jambalayas is served at Mr. B's in the French Quarter. Jambalaya, like gumbo, can be made with any variety of ingredients, from sausage to shellfish, and in some cases both. The common denominators are rice, tomatoes, onions, and plenty of pepper.

Steaming platters of red beans and rice, often with a huge link of spicy sausage, are a New Orleans mainstay. There are numerous places that do this dish justice, including Popeye's Famous Fried Chicken, a fast-food chain with 40 outlets in New Orleans, which sells a delicious liquidy, spicy version without meat. Most casual restaurants serve this dish on Mondays, a tradition that originated long ago when women served it after doing Monday's wash—the beans simmering all day while the women completed their chores.

Gumbo is considered a staple in most places, yet it is rare to find a great gumbo in New Orleans. It typically lacks a dark brown, slow-cooked roux, and it is often overladen with pepper, watered down or overly thick, and short on meat or fish. Seafood gumbo is served most frequently. Even gumbos made by the so-called specialists like the Gumbo Shop fall short when compared to what is lovingly prepared in Acadiana at such places as Don's Seafood Hut in Lafayette. Gumbo is an event. Most Cajuns make gumbos either with chicken, sausage, and oyster, or with duck and oyster. Unfortunately, very few restaurants in the city do justice to this dish.

Boiled seafood is quite popular, and the freshest seasonal shrimp, crabs, and crawfish can be had at numerous seafood restaurants around town. Orleanians eat boiled crawfish served cold, and in relatively small portions compared to Cajuns, who generally figure three pounds per person. Crawfish shacks like Richard's in Abbeville (a charming town of 12,000 near Lafayette) serve up enormous tubs of spicy crawfish, steaming hot and accompanied by boiled onions, potatoes, and corn. Patrons eat with their hands (yours will need a good scrubbing with hot water and lemon after this!). Nothing could be tastier than this small crustacean, which is far better served hot than cold.

Bananas Foster, the world-famous dessert, originated at Brennan's and is now a mainstay in most fine Creole kitchens, although none does it as well. Other flaming desserts associated with New Orleans are cherries Jubilee (great at Galatoire's), baked Alaska (the Blue Room in the Fairmont Hotel is tops), and crêpes Suzette (best at Arnaud's).

In the older restaurants, most locals have a favorite waiter. The conviviality enjoyed between patron and waiter is one of the nicest personal touches about New Orleans dining. It is best to play this to its full advantage, since many waiters in the finer restaurants are knowledgeable about the food, and they are often quite entertaining.

The thing to remember about dining in New Orleans is the pace: No one ever rushes through a meal here. In fact, dining out constitutes an event. Friends often talk about where they ate yesterday, as well as where they will eat tomorrow. The only other subject that interests Orleanians as much as food is politics—a topic almost as sizzling as their cuisine.

3 Essential Information

Important Numbers and Addresses

Tourist Information The **Greater New Orleans Tourist and Convention Commission** and the **Louisiana Tourist Development Commission** both operate a tourist information center at 529 St. Ann St., facing Jackson Square in the heart of the French Quarter (tel. 504/566–5011). Open daily 9–5.

Emergencies Dial 911 for assistance. Emergency rooms closest to the CBD and French Quarter are **Charity Hospital** (1532 Tulane Ave., tel. 504/568–2311) and the **Tulane University Medical Center** (220 Lasalle St., tel. 504/588–5711). In Uptown go to **Touro Infirmary**, 1401 Foucher St., tel. 504/897–8250).

Pharmacies In the CBD, **Walgreens** (900 Canal St., tel. 504/523–7201) remains open until 9 PM; Uptown, **Smith's Drug Store** (2025 St. Charles Ave., tel. 504/523–7601), next to the Pontchartrain Hotel, stays open until 8 PM, Mon.–Fri., and until 5 PM Sat.

Getting Around

By Streetcar The city's Regional Transit Authority (RTA) operates the historic St. Charles Avenue streetcar, established in 1835, that makes the 5-mile trek from the CBD to Carrollton along picturesque St. Charles Ave. The fare is 60 cents plus 5 cents for transfers.

The Riverfront streetcar covers a 1.9-mile route along the Mississippi River, connecting major sights from the end of the French Quarter (Esplanade Ave.) to the New Orleans Convention Center (Julia St.). Eight stops en route include the French Market, Jackson Brewery, Canal Place, the World Trade Center, the Riverwalk, and the Hilton Hotel. Two cars operate 24 hours a day passing each stop every 15 minutes. One of the cars is specially equipped for handicapped and elderly passengers. The fare is 60 cents a ride. One-day and three-day visitor passes are available at reasonable rates for unlimited rides on both the St. Charles Ave. and Riverfront streetcar lines. Call the RTA, tel. 504/569–2700.

By Bus The RTA also operates a public bus transportation system with interconnecting lines throughout the city. The buses are generally clean and on time. Bus fare is 60 cents plus 5 cents for transfers. Visiting senior citizens 65 or over who have a valid Medicare ID card may ride public transit for only 20 cents. For route information, call tel. 504/569–2700.

By Taxi Cabs are metered at $1.10 minimum plus $1 per mile. You can either hail cabs in some of the busier areas, or call one. **Checker Yellow Cabs**, 504/525–3311; **Liberty Bell Cabs**, 504/822–5974; **United Cabs**, 504/522–9771.

To the Airport **Airport Rhodes** (504/469–4555) has regular shuttle service from the CBD and French Quarter hotels to the airport. For pickup, call at least two hours in advance. The 40-minute trip costs $7 per person.

The least expensive way is by bus. The **Louisiana Transit** system (504/737–9611) also runs a bus from the CBD to the airport every 10 to 20 minutes. Catch it at Elks Pl. and Tulane Ave.

across from the city library. The last bus leaves at 6:20 P.M. The 45-minute ride costs $1.10 in exact change.

Taxis cost $18 for the first three people and $6 a person after that.

By car, take the I-10 Expressway west to the Airport Exit. Allow for an hour drive during afternoon rush hour.

Guided Tours

Orientation Tours Four local tour companies offer three- to four-hour city tours by bus that include the French Quarter, the Garden District, Uptown New Orleans, and the lakefront. Prices range from $15 to $25 per person, with some lower rates for children; call **American-Acadian** (tel. 504/467–1734), **Grayline** (tel.504/525–0138), **New Orleans Tours** (tel. 504/487–1991), or **Tours by Isabelle** (tel. 504/367–3963).

Both Grayline and New Orleans Tours offer a longer, seven-hour city tour by bus that includes a steamboat ride on the Mississippi River. **Escape with Travel** (tel. 504/242–5811) has a three-hour "City/Black Heritage" tour by bus or van. The tour covers the history of the city and highlights the many achievements by blacks since the 1770s.

Narrated steamboat cruises up and down the Mississippi River on authentic paddlewheelers are offered by the **New Orleans Steamboat Company** (tel. 504/586–8777 or 800/233–BOAT). Departures are 3 times daily from the wharf in front of Jackson Brewery in the French Quarter. **New Orleans Tours** has a river plantation and battlefield cruise twice daily departing from the Riverwalk.

Special-Interest Tours Plantation tours by bus from New Orleans usually include guided tours through two antebellum plantation homes along the Mississippi River, a drive through cypress swamps, and a stop for lunch in a Cajun-Creole restaurant outside the city. **Grayline** (tel. 504/525–0138) and **New Orleans Tours** (tel. 504/487–1991) have full-day tours, lunch not included. **Tours by Isabelle** (tel. 504/367–3963) includes lunch in its full-day plantation package that traces the history of the Cajun people. This company also has a city tour that includes a visit to one plantation. **American-Acadian** (tel. 504/467–1734) has a six-hour tour that includes the city's Garden District plus two plantations upriver, with the price of lunch at a restaurant included.

Nightlife tours feature escorted visits to popular jazz clubs and Bourbon Street nightclubs. Cocktails and admission are included in the price. Grayline offers an optional dinner in a traditional French Quarter restaurant with its "New Orleans After Dark" tour, while New Orleans Tours concludes its nightlife tour with café au lait and beignets at Café du Monde.

A fun way to see the river and Audubon Zoo is the "Zoo Cruise" by **New Orleans Steamboat Company** (tel. 504/586–8777 or 800/233–BOAT). The *Cotton Blossom*, a historic sternwheeler, departs the Riverwalk at the foot of Canal Street and travels 7 miles upriver to dock at Audubon Landing near the zoo. You can return via the *Cotton Blossom* or take a free shuttle to St. Charles Ave. and catch the streetcar back to Canal St. New Orleans Tours has a zoo express bus that transports guests from downtown hotels to the zoo and back.

Cajun Queen (tel. 504/524–0814), an authentic replica of an 1800s steamer, gives a narrated cruise of Bayou Country and the Algiers locks system; it departs daily from the Riverwalk. The same company also conducts a river plantation cruise that includes the site of the Battle of New Orleans.

Dinner on the river is a special treat, and several tour companies offer steamboat cruises that include dining and dancing under the stars to live jazz. Menus, bands, times, and prices vary. Contact the *Creole Queen* (tel. 504/529–4567), the *Cajun Queen*, or the *Natchez* (tel. 504/586–8777).

To visit churches, shrines, and cemeteries in the city, contact **Musicana Tours** (tel. 504/566–0999).

Two carriage companies operate mule-pulled carriages for half-hour, narrated drives through the narrow streets of the French Quarter: **Gay 90's Carriages, Inc.** (tel. 504/943–8820) and **Old Quarter Tours** (tel. 504/944–0446). Carriages depart from Decatur Street in front of Jackson Square. Carriages also can be rented for special occasions.

Walking Tours A wide selection of walking tours are available through the French Quarter and other neighborhoods of the city. Free general historical tours of the French Quarter are given daily by the **Jean Lafitte National Park** (tel. 504/689–2002), located in the Quarter. Park rangers conduct three of these 3-hour tours. They also have a "tour du jour" once a day which focuses on a particular cultural or historical aspect of the Quarter. **Friends of the Cabildo** (tel. 504/523–3939) also has a 3-hour walking tour of the Quarter. The admission cost includes two state museums.

For more specialized walking tours of the Quarter, try **Heritage Tours** (tel. 504/949–9805) for literary tours on William Faulkner and Tennessee Williams; **Royal Walks** (tel. 504/566–7592) for tours featuring architecture and literature, with an emphasis on Tennessee Williams; **Margaret Media, Inc.** (tel. 504/861–2921) for great women of New Orleans; the **New Orleans Historic Voodoo Museum** (tel. 504/523–7685) for voodoo and cemeteries; **Antiques** (tel. 504/283–8253) for antique shops on Royal Street; and **Local Art** (tel. 504/482–6623) for art galleries and studios. These tours are offered only by advance reservation and usually require a minimum of two persons.

Walking tours of the Garden District are included in some city bus tours; try the **Preservation Resource Center** (tel.504/581–7032) or **Specialty Tours** (tel. 504/861–2921).

The **Superdome** (tel. 504/587–3810) offers guided tours from 9 to 4 daily. For sports fans, touring this unique facility can highlight a visit to New Orleans.

In addition to two Mardi Gras museums in the French Quarter, don't forget **Blaine Kern's Mardi Gras World** (tel. 504/362–8211) across the river in Algiers; visitors can tour the large warehouses where the famous Mardi Gras floats are made.

Your Sound Promenade (tel. 504/282–1932) has a self-guided French Quarter tour on two 90-minute cassettes, which you can keep for a great souvenir.

For visitors who wish to browse through the French Quarter at their own leisure, there are maps for self-guided walking tours available through the **New Orleans Tourist and Convention**

Commission (tel. 504/566–5011) at the Tourist Information Center, 529 St. Ann St., on Jackson Square.

Multilingual Tours To accommodate the many international visitors, most tour companies have access to interpreters and foreign-language guides. Some companies cater to specific nationalities. **Pacheco Tours** (tel. 504/482–7127) and **Family Tours** (tel. 504/468–1688) have Spanish-language tours, **Derwent Tours** (tel. 504/943–6182) has German and French tours, and **Yamaguchi Travel Service** (tel. 504/454–6644) offers Japanese-language tours.

Other Tours Personalized, multi-tour services are offered by a number of tour companies that arrange everything from airport transportation to dining to nightlife. **Specialty Tours** (tel. 504/861–2921) specializes in unique aspects of the city, from voodoo to women's history and local literary characters. **Tours by Isabelle** (tel. 504/367–3963) and **Tours by Andrea** (tel. 504/524–8521 or 800/535–2732) are both geared toward small-scale tours with personalized service. **Escape with Travel** (tel. 504/242–5811) conducts private tours.

Limousine services also make arrangements for personal interests and private guides; rentals vary. Best known are **London Livery, Ltd.** (tel. 504/944–1984), **Carey-Bonomolo Limousines** (tel. 504/523–5466), **A Touch of Class Limousine Service** (tel. 504/522–7565), **Celebrity Limousine** (tel. 504/888–LIMO), and **New Orleans Limousine Service** (tel. 504/529–5226).

For a view of the city from the air, **Southern Seaplane, Inc.** (tel. 504/394–5633) will fly you over the city and its surrounding areas.

Saja's Video Tours (tel. 504/522–7252) can record your visit on videotape, which can serve as a great souvenir.

4 Exploring New Orleans

Orientation
by Mary Gehman

"Do you know what it means to miss New Orleans?" The old jazz song, so popular in this city, aptly suggests that there is much to experience while one is here and much to miss when one is away. Despite its sprawling size, to its residents New Orleans is intimate and small-town, made up of dozens of neighborhoods where families have lived within the same blocks for generations. Red beans and rice are served throughout the city on Mondays, people visit the tombs of their departed on All Saints Day, and from the smartest office to the most down-home local bar, folks are ready to celebrate anything at the drop of a hat. As they say in New Orleans, *laissez les bon temps rouler* (let the good times roll)!

To experience this fun-filled city, you can begin with the usual tourist attractions, but you must go beyond them to linger in a corner grocery store, sip a cold drink in a local joint, or chat with a stoop-sitter. Orleanians love their city—most of them wouldn't live anywhere else. They treasure custom and tradition, take in stride the heat and humidity of a semitropical climate, and look at life with a laid-back attitude that makes New Orleans seem a close cousin to her Caribbean neighbors.

The city radiates out from an eight-mile stretch between the Mississippi River and Lake Pontchartrain, covering roughly 365 square miles of flat, swamp-drained land. The heart of the city, Downtown, includes the famous old French area called the *Vieux Carré* (Old Square) or the French Quarter, the Central Business District or the CBD, and the riverfront. Across the river from Downtown is an extension of New Orleans known as the West Bank, which includes the areas of Algiers and Gretna.

The city of New Orleans is composed of four sections that spread out from Downtown: Uptown to the southwest, Mid-City to the north, and Faubourg Marigny and Gentilly to the east. Large suburban areas such as Metairie and Kenner to the west and New Orleans East to the east have developed in the past 30 years and today make up what is called Greater New Orleans.

Receiving directions in a city that bases its compass on the curve of the river can be hopelessly confusing. Canal Street, a long avenue that runs from the river to the lake, divides the city roughly into uptown and downtown sections. Streets to the north of Canal are named North and run downtown, while those to the south of Canal are named South and run uptown. Only the French Quarter is laid out in a grid pattern. Ask an Orleanian for directions and you are likely to hear about so many blocks downriver or upriver on the lake or river side. The best advice is to keep a map handy at all times.

New Orleans's housing patterns are very mixed. It is not uncommon to find mansions on one block and run-down tenements on the next, or nearby. Visitors should be alert to conditions around them, taking precautions not to wander alone on deserted streets or in questionable areas. A high crime rate, as in other cities, is a problem in New Orleans. If in doubt about the safety of sites to visit, ask hotel personnel for advice, tour areas in groups when possible, and take a cab at night. (Areas requiring special precautions are noted in the tours that follow.)

The tours described here introduce various areas of New Orleans and suggest things to see and do in each. The Downtown and Algiers sections are best explored on foot because sites are near each other and should be experienced at a slow pace. For the other areas, biking or driving is recommended due to the long distances covered. For further ideas, check Off the Beaten Track, New Orleans for Free, and What to See and Do with Children before starting out on a given tour. Finding the unexpected is what makes New Orleans fun; the tours that follow are designed with that sense of adventure in mind.

The heart of New Orleans is the French Quarter or Vieux Carré, a six-by-twelve-block rectangle along the Mississippi River where the city originally was settled by the French in 1718. Here the Creoles (children born in the colony to French and Spanish settlers) built their stately town houses, cathedral, marketplace, opera houses, and theaters. Here, served by African slaves, they developed one of the most sophisticated styles of living in North America.

Much of this Old World influence began to fade when in 1803 the Louisiana Purchase was signed and the Americans, predominantly Anglo-Saxon, moved into power. Eventually, the Civil War in the 1860s put an end to the Golden Age of antebellum New Orleans, and the French Quarter went through years of decline and neglect. Only in the past 50 years have the buildings been restored and the French Quarter regained its place as a rare and fascinating center of the city.

Unlike historic downtown areas of many other American cities, the French Quarter is a residential district, sharing streets with shops, restaurants, and offices. It is alive with the sights, sounds, and odors of a major port city and entertainment hub. Yet, behind the wrought iron gates of its buildings are tranquil, intimate courtyards hidden from view. This intertwining of the public and private fronts in the Quarter give it a charm rarely matched in other U.S. cities. The Vieux Carré Commission, formed in 1936 to preserve the historic integrity of the Quarter, controls all renovation and rebuilding with strict codes. Notice that with the exception of Bourbon Street, there are no neon signs or garish flashing lights, and that buildings throughout the Quarter conform to the architectural style of the late 1700s to mid-1800s.

To see and do everything available in the French Quarter can take days. The area is best savored on several different occasions, allowing for leisure time to browse in shops, tour museums, snack at cafes, and listen to a street musician or watch a portrait artist at work.

The Inner French Quarter includes Jackson Square, the riverfront, and several immediate blocks containing the most frequented and photographed sites. For adventurers with more time and stamina for walking, we recommend the Outer French Quarter, which encompasses some exciting fringe places not as well known but still well worth the effort. Tours of both areas are given here; you may wish to combine aspects of both tours into one, depending on your interests and the amount of time you have.

The numbers in the margins correspond with the numbered points of interest on the French Quarter map.

Inner French Quarter

❶ Tours conventionally begin in **Jackson Square.** It is the heart of the French Quarter, much as almost every French town has a square around which are built the church, seat of government, and major shops. Until the 1850s, the square was called the Place d'Armes, a military marching ground. It was also the site of public executions carried out in various styles, including burning at the stake, beheading, breaking on the wheel, and hanging.

Today Jackson Square is a beautifully landscaped park. A statue of Andrew Jackson, victorious leader of the Battle of New Orleans in the War of 1812, graces the center of the square. The words carved in the base on the cathedral side of the statue—"The Union must and shall be preserved"—are a lasting reminder of the Federal troops who occupied New Orleans during the Civil War and who inscribed those words.

The park is landscaped in a sun pattern, with walkways set like rays streaming out from the center, a popular garden design in the royal court of King Louis XIV, the Sun King. Beware of feeding the pigeons in the park; signs warn of fines imposed on bird-feeders. This law is necessary to keep the number of pigeons in the area to a minimum. Park gates are open from 8 AM to 6 PM except for special events. In the daytime, dozens of artists hang their paintings on the park fence and set up outdoor studios where they work on canvases or offer to draw portraits of passersby. These artists are easy to engage in conversation and are knowledgeable about many aspects of the Quarter and New Orleans.

Surrounding the park is a flagstone pedestrian mall, which is closed to traffic. All sorts of top-rate street performers entertain here: musicians, break dancers, tap dancers, jugglers, acrobats, mimes, and clowns. Performers are licensed by the city and depend on donations from their audiences to make a living.

❷ **St. Louis Cathedral,** named for the French king who led two crusades, is the oldest active cathedral in the United States. The current building, which replaced two former structures destroyed by fire, dates back to 1794, although it was remodeled and enlarged in 1851. In 1964 the cathedral was elevated to the status of minor basilica, one of only 15 such churches in the United States. Pope John Paul II held a prayer service for clergy here during his New Orleans visit in 1987; to honor the occasion, the pedestrian mall in front of the cathedral was renamed Place Jean Paul Deux. The cathedral is open to the public. Worshipers are always welcome; tours of the building are given daily, 9–5, free of charge.

In the rectory behind the cathedral are the church archives, which chronicle baptisms, marriages, and deaths from as early as 1731. St. Anthony's Garden, which extends behind the rectory to Royal Street, is dominated by the statue of the Sacred Heart of Jesus at its center. From Royal Street can be seen a monument to 30 members of a French ship who died in a yellow fever epidemic in 1857. In the right-hand alley beside the gar-

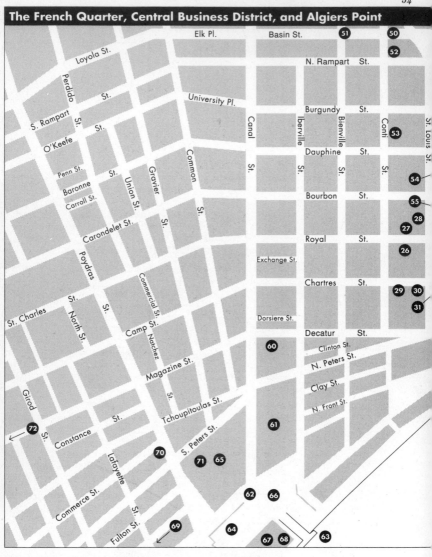

The French Quarter, Central Business District, and Algiers Point

Louisiana Children's
Museum, **72**

Louisiana Information
Center, **7**

Madame John's
Legacy, **19**

Mardi Gras Museum, **38**

Maspero's
Exchange, **30**

Miltenberger
Houses, **18**

Moon Walk, **11**

Musée Conti, **53**

Napoleon House, **31**

New Orleans
Convention Center, **69**

New Orleans Historic
Voodoo Museum, **46**

New Orleans Jazz
Collection, **39**

New Orleans Pharmacy
Museum, **32**

New Orleans School
of Cooking, **10**

Old Farmer's
Market, **35**

Old Mint, **37**

Old New Orleans Court
Building, **26**

Old Ursuline
Convent, **15**

Opelousas Street,
Old Algiers, **74**

Our Lady of
Guadalupe Church, **52**

Overview of Square
and River, **8**

Pat O'Brien's, **58**

Piazza d'Italia, **70**

Pontalba Apartments, **5**

Presbytere, **3**

Preservation Hall, **59**

Quadroon Ballroom, **22**

Ripley's Believe It or
Not Museum, **55**

Riverfront
Aquarium, **62**

Rivergate Exhibition
Center, **65**

Riverwalk, **68**

St. Louis Cathedral, **2**

St. Louis
Cemetery #1, **50**

Spanish Plaza, **67**

Spring Fiesta Historic
Townhouse, **47**

Storyville (former
site), **51**

World Trade Center, **66**

den, at 624 Pirates Alley, William Faulkner lived and wrote in the 1920s. Sherwood Anderson, who resided in the nearby Pontalba Apartments, persuaded Faulkner to go back to his home town in Mississippi and write about the people and places he knew best.

③ ④ The Presbytere and the Cabildo. Return to the front of the cathedral. The Spanish colonial-style buildings that flank the cathedral were the seat of government for New Orleans during the colonial period; today they are part of the Louisiana State Museum Complex, housing some permanent and some changing exhibits. The Presbytere originally was designed to house the priests of the cathedral; instead, it served as a courthouse under the Spanish and later under the Americans. The *Pioneer*, the first submarine used by the Confederate Navy in the Civil War, is the curious metal object on display in front of the Presbytere. To the left of the cathedral is the Cabildo, named for the Spanish council—or cabildo—that met there. In 1988 the Cabildo suffered terrific damage from a four-alarm fire. Most of the historical pieces inside the building were saved, but the top floor and roof were destroyed. Efforts are underway to restore this treasured meeting place. The transfer of Louisiana to the United States was made in 1803 in the front room on the second floor overlooking the square. After 1803, the Cabildo served as the city hall and later the supreme court. Exhibits today include Napoleon Bonaparte's death mask. A gift shop occupies the lower right corner. The Cabildo is the older of the two buildings, dating to 1799; the Presbytere was under construction from 1795 to 1847. *Jackson Square, tel. 504/568–6968. Admission: $3, $1.50 senior citizens. Open Wed.–Sun. 10–5.*

⑤ The **Pontalba Apartments,** two sets of buildings, one on each side of Jackson Square, were built in the late 1840s by the Baroness Micaela Pontalba. The daughter of a wealthy Spaniard, Don Almonester y Rojas, she inherited the prime real estate around the square and had these apartment buildings constructed to leave a permanent European imprint on the heart of the old city. She also helped to fund the landscaping of the square and the erection of Jackson's statue in its center. The strong-willed baroness married her cousin Baron Celestin de Pontalba in France. She caused a scandal on both sides of the Atlantic when she had a near fatal fight with her father-in-law, left her husband, and returned to Louisiana in the 1840s to build the apartments on the square. She later returned to Paris and is buried there.

The Pontalba Apartments are publicly owned, the side to the right of the cathedral by the state and the other side, by the **⑥** city. In the state side is the **1850s House,** a model of one of the apartments as it looked in 1850 for the first residents. Notice the lovely ironwork on the balconies of the apartments. The baroness introduced cast (or molded) iron with these buildings, and it eventually replaced much of the old handwrought ironwork in the French Quarter. The initials for her families, A and P—Almonester and Pontalba—are worked into the design. *523 St. Ann St., tel. 504/568–6968. Admission: $3 adults, $1.50 senior citizens. Open Wed.–Sun. 10–5.*

⑦ The **Louisiana Office of Tourism** is a few doors away and a good place to pick up brochures and information about the Quarter,

the city, and Louisiana in general. *529 St. Ann St., tel. 504/568
-5661. Open daily 9–5.*

As you walk up St. Ann Street away from the cathedral you'll
notice the carriage stand in front of Jackson Square on Decatur
Street, where mule-drawn carriages await passengers from
early morning till midnight. These carriages, integral to the
Quarter, take half-hour tours around the narrow streets while
drivers recite a mixture of folklore and fact about the old city.
The mules replaced horses several years ago because mules
were found to be more tolerant of high temperatures in summer
and could go longer without water.

⑧ Overview of Square and River. Cross Decatur Street (beware of
the heavy traffic here) and walk up a flight of steps leading to
an overview of the square on one side and of the Mississippi River on the other. This is a great spot for photographing both
attractions.

⑨ Across the square, to your left on Decatur Street, will be **Jackson Brewery,** also called Jax Brewery, a former brewery now
remodeled to house a three-section shopping and entertainment complex. Outside are multilevel terraces facing the river
and inside is a collection of shops, galleries, restaurants, and
lounges. Live music often sounds from various areas. **The Hard
Rock Cafe** in the third, and newest, section of Jax is a favorite
attraction for young people. *Jackson Sq. and the River, tel.
504/529–1211. Open Sun.–Thurs. 10–9, Fri.–Sat. 10–10.*

⑩ For those interested in Creole and Cajun cooking, the **New Orleans School of Cooking** in the first section of the brewery
features television cooking personality and local chef Joe Cahn.
Reservations for classes and demonstrations are a must. *Tel.
504/525–2665. Admission prices vary. Open Mon.–Sat. 10–1.*

⑪ Moon Walk. In front of the overview, beyond the railroad
tracks, is a promenade along the levee called Moon Walk. This
landscaped arcade is named for Moon Landrieu, who was may-
or of the city in the 1970s when the walk was built. Here is a
breathtaking view of the mighty Mississippi as it curves around
New Orleans, giving the city the name of the Crescent City.
When facing the river, you see to the right the Greater New Orleans Bridge, a twin span connecting New Orleans to the West
Bank, and a ferryboat that crosses the river every 20 minutes
as an alternative to the bridge. The river flows to the left down-
stream for another 100 miles until it meets with the Gulf of
Mexico. Directly across the river is the ferry landing and a
ship-repair dry dock. A bit farther to the left is a ramshackle
multilayer building that is actually a good restaurant and popular night spot, Algiers Landing. The river is always active with
steamboats carrying tour groups, tugboats pushing enormous
barges, and oceangoing ships plying its waters. Sometimes a
dredge boat is visible, dredging the river's bottom of silt to
keep the channel open for large ships. If you are lucky, the
steamboat will be readying to leave its dock upriver to the
right, and the burst of steam from the engines, followed by the
playing of the calliope, will give you the age-old sound of life on
the river.

⑫ After a stroll along the levee, go back to the overview and walk
down to your right to a canopied landmark, **Café du Monde.** For
generations locals and visitors have come here for around-the-

clock café au lait (equal parts of strong chickory-laced coffee
and hot milk) and beignets (pronounced ben-yays), square
French doughnuts dipped in powdered sugar. If you step
around to the large window behind the cafe, you can watch the
beignets being rolled, cut, and flipped into vats of deep fat for
frying. This is especially fun for children.

⑬ Café du Monde marks the beginning of the **French Market,** a
complex of renovated buildings that extends several blocks
along Decatur and N. Peters streets. Originally an Indian trading post, later a bustling open-air market under the French and
Spanish, the French Market has always figured strongly in the
life of the city. The buildings, some of them now glass-enclosed,
house shops, offices, and eating places. You'll enjoy exploring
them not only from the street, but also from the flagstone areas
alongside and behind the buildings. On weekends there are
usually street performers and musicians enlivening the outdoor
areas of the market.

⑭ Check with the **Folklife and Visitor Center** of the Jean Lafitte
National Historical Park for free exhibits on the life and cus-
toms of various ethnic groups in Louisiana, as well as for free
daily history tours of the French Quarter and outlying areas.
This office also supervises and provides information on the
Jean Lafitte National Park, located across the river from New
Orleans, and the Chalmette Battlefield, where the Battle of
New Orleans was fought in the War of 1812. *916–918 N. Peters
St., in the French Market, tel. 504/589–2636. Open daily 9–5.*

Time Out If you are ready for a little relaxation, the **Mediterranean Café,**
at the intersection of N. Peters and Decatur streets, and the
Gazebo, a short walk back behind the Mediterranean Café, offer live jazz and cool drinks outdoors in graceful settings.
Across Decatur Street is the Central Grocery (923 Decatur
St.), known for its imported foods and its muffuletta sandwiches (a round loaf of Italian bread filled with ham and other
cold cuts, cheese, and an olive salad), which have long been a
local favorite.

When you leave the vibrant French Market, walk down Decatur Street to Ursulines Street, named for the nearby convent
and grounds of the Ursuline nuns. The Ursulines were the first
of many orders of religious women who came to New Orleans
and founded schools, orphanages, and asylums, and ministered
⑮ to the needs of the poor. The **Old Ursuline Convent** stands to the
right at the next corner, Chartres Street. Built in 1734, the
convent is believed to be the oldest French colonial building in
the Mississippi valley. St. Mary's Italian Church, adjoining the
convent, was added in 1846. The original tract of convent land
covered several French Quarter blocks, and the sisters were attended by slaves who occupied a small narrow building still
visible from the side facing Ursulines Street. Now an archive
for the archdiocese, the convent was used by the Ursulines for
90 years. The Ursuline Academy, the convent's girls' school
founded in 1727, is now located uptown on State Street, where
the newer convent and chapel were built. The academy is the
oldest girls' school in the country.

⑯ Across Chartres Street from the convent is the **Beauregard-
Keyes House.** This stately 19th-century mansion was the tem-
porary home for Confederate General P.G.T. Beauregard. The

house and grounds had severely deteriorated in the 1930s when well-known novelist Frances Parkinson Keyes moved in and helped restore it to its former glory. Her studio at the back of the large courtyard remains intact. Keyes wrote 40 novels in this studio, all in longhand, among them the local favorite, *Dinner at Antoine's*. If you do not have time to tour the house, be sure to take a peek through the gates at the beautiful walled garden at the corner of Chartres and Ursulines Streets. Landscaped in the same sun pattern as Jackson Square, the garden is in bloom throughout the year. Both garden and courtyard have been a popular romantic setting for several movies filmed in New Orleans. *1113 Chartres St., tel. 504/523-7257. Admission: $3 adults, $2 senior citizens, $1 children. Open Mon.-Sat. 10-3.*

Continuing down Ursulines Street, you'll notice a cafe on the right, **Croissant d'Or/Patisserie** (617 Ursulines St.), where French pastries are baked on the premises. This used to be an Italian ice-cream parlor, Brocato's, and the interior is still adorned with ornate Italian decorations. At the next corner turn right on Royal Street and walk a few doors down to **Gallier House** on the right. Gallier House is a restored 1857 town house, originally built by local architect James Gallier as his personal residence. Besides tours of the house and grounds, there are also short films on architectural crafts, changing exhibits on 19th-century life in the city, and a gift shop. Take a moment to look through the carriageway; it is the only one in the city with a carriage parked in it. You can almost hear the horses in the stable shaking their harnesses in anticipation of a trip. *1118 Royal St., tel. 504/523-6722. Admission: $3. Open Mon.-Sat. 10-4:30.*

Turn and stroll down Royal Street, back past Ursulines Street, and note why this is called the street of balconies. Royal Street boasts some of the most celebrated and beautiful balconies in the country. During the Civil War, while New Orleans was occupied by Federal troops, women in the Quarter used the protection of their balconies to hurl household objects at passing troops and shout out insults. The situation between the ladies and the unwelcomed soldiers became so tense that General Benjamin Butler issued the Woman Order in 1862, threatening to arrest offenders and treat them as women of the street "plying their avocation"—a challenge that was met by some local women and that shocked and outraged men of the North and South alike.

Two blocks down Royal Street, at the corner of Dumaine Street, is a complex of three town houses built in 1838 by the widow Marie Miltenberger, the **Miltenberger Houses** (900–906 Royal St.). Besides their beautiful iron balconies, the houses also are known for being the birthplace of Alice Heine, the first American princess of Monaco at the turn of the century, preceding Grace Kelly by many years. Princess Alice divorced the prince, however, before any children were born.

At this corner, turn left on Dumaine Street and walk a few doors up to **Madame John's Legacy** (632 Dumaine St.) across the street on the right. Notice the West Indian architecture, with the first floor built high off the ground and a porch (called "gallery" in New Orleans) running around the front and side of the house. The original building dates back to 1726, but the building you see here is an exact replica that was built in the late 1700s, when the 1726 structure was destroyed by fire. The house has undergone some renovation through the years and has had a colorful past. The first owner, Jean Pascal, a French sea captain, was killed by Natchez Indians. Today, the historic building is owned and operated by the State Museum Complex and is currently closed to the public. The name "Madame John's Legacy" was adapted in the late 1800s from a short story by New Orleans writer George W. Cable. The popular tale was about Madame John, a "free woman of color" (a localism for free blacks), who, like many women of her race, became the mistress of a Frenchman. Having never married, her master, John (Jean), bequeathed his house and estate to her on his deathbed.

20 Turn back to Royal Street and walk a few doors down to one of the Quarter's most unusual shops, **Hové Parfumeur.** This perfume shop was founded in 1931 by Mrs. Alvin Hovey-King, whose granddaughter now runs the business. Hové perfumes, colognes, and soaps are known internationally, mainly through mail order. Today, fragrances created from the recipes of Mrs. Hovey-King are still much in demand. New Orleans once had many such shops, but only this one remains. *824 Royal St., tel. 504/525-7827. Open Mon.–Sat. 9–5.*

A few doors down from the parfumeur, stop and examine the building to the left, an art gallery, and the one across the street and a door down. Both houses are of a modern, 1930s style, in sharp contrast to the balconied buildings on either side of them. The contrast gives you a feeling for the buildings of the Quarter that were lost before 1936 when the Vieux Carré Commission was formed to restrict the rapid destruction of the old Quarter.

21 Around the corner, left on St. Ann Street, is the **Elizebeth Werlein House** (630 St. Ann St.), the residence of Elizebeth Werlein, who was instrumental in saving many of these old abandoned buildings in the 1930s and 1940s. She died in 1946, but her preservationist efforts continue to this day.

Go back to Royal Street and pass the park behind the cathedral. Pause at Orleans Street, which begins there, and look down Orleans on the right. The former **Quadroon Ballroom** (717 Orleans **22** St.) is the white wooden balcony on the second floor where, it is believed, free women of color met their French suitors (as Madame John of the house on Dumaine Street is said to have done). The quadroons (people whose ethnic makeup is one-quarter Negro) who met here were young, unmarried women. The girls' mothers traditionally accompanied them to the balls to make sure that any man who took a serious interest in their daughters had the means to support both a mistress and the several children who would be born to the relationship. If the Frenchman married a woman of his own race and had a legitimate second family, he often continued to support his first family. If you read the plaque on the building at 717 Orleans Street, you'll learn that the ballroom later became part of a convent and school for the Sisters of the Holy Family, a religious order founded in New Orleans in 1842 by the daughter of a quadroon. The nuns moved in 1964 to a suburb in eastern New Orleans, and the building is now the elegant Bourbon Orleans Hotel.

Royal Street at Orleans Street is closed to traffic for several blocks from 11 AM to 5:30 PM to allow pedestrian access to the lovely shops, art galleries, antique stores, and restaurants on both sides of the street. At the corner of the next block, at St.

(23) Peter Street, on the left is **Labranche House** (700 Royal St.), which has some of the finest examples of ironwork in New Orleans on its balconies. Notice the intricate design of oak leaves and acorns. The building and ironwork date back to the 1830s. This corner is one of the most photographed spots in the city, and it is easy to see why. The **A&P Supermarket** across the street is the only such store in the French Quarter. Small and antiquated by today's standards, it nevertheless does a good business with locals.

(24) Continue down Royal Street and on the right is the **Court of Two Sisters Restaurant** (613 Royal St.), which is housed in a building that dates to 1832 and has one of the most beautiful courtyards in the Quarter. It is named for two sisters, long since gone, who ran a dry goods shop there. You might want to step down the carriageway and take a look at the courtyard (or court) with permission of the maître d'.

Among the shops on the next block is a local research treasure,
(25) the **Historic New Orleans Collection.** This private archive, with thousands of historic photos, documents, and books, is one of the finest research centers in the South. Housed in the 19th-century town house of General Kemper Williams and the 1792 Merrieult House, the collection offers changing exhibits on local history and tours of the houses, grounds, and archives. *533 Royal St., tel. 504/523–4662. Open Tues.–Sat. 10–5. Tours $2; gallery exhibit and use of research library free.*

The imposing Victorian building that takes up the whole next
(26) block between St. Louis and Conti streets is the **Old New Orleans Court Building** (known today as the Wildlife and Fisheries Building), erected in 1908 to replace a former court facility. Empty in recent years, the building has been proposed as the site for a casino if and when such business is legalized in Louisiana. Several old and famous New Orleans restau-
(27) rants are in this area, including **Brennan's Restaurant** (417 Royal St.), across the street from the court building,
(28) and **Antoine's Restaurant** (713 St. Louis St.), just around the corner on the right. Both establishments are located in historic houses and known for their traditional Creole cuisine.

Walk around the court building to Chartres Street and take a
(29) left. On the right-hand side in the middle of that block is **K-Paul's Louisiana Kitchen** (416 Chartres St.), named for the Cajun chef Paul Prudhomme and his wife Kay. In recent years Prudhomme has been creating and serving the Cajun specialties here that have become the rage in other parts of the country. At the corner on the right is another well-known local
(30) eatery, **Maspero's Exchange** (440 Chartres St.), which once was a slave auction house, and for many years thereafter the Exchange Coffee House, where the city's notable Creoles gathered. An interesting feature of the building is that it seems from the outside to have only two floors, whereas inside there is a middle floor, called an entresol, in the section above the window arch at the top of what appears to be the first floor. This narrow middle floor was used for storage. Only a few buildings in the Quarter have an entresol.

(31) On the corner across from Maspero's is another landmark, the **Napoleon House** (500 Chartres St.). A longtime favorite haunt for local writers and artists, the house was built in 1814 and reportedly offered to Napoleon when he was exiled on St. Helena in 1821, but Napoleon died before arrangements for his rescue could be completed. The Napoleon House is a good place to soak up local color and atmosphere.

(32) Just up Chartres Street is the **New Orleans Pharmacy Museum.** It bills itself as "the finest historical pharmacy museum in the U.S." This building was the apothecary shop and residence of America's first licensed pharmacist, Louis J. Dufilho, in the 1820s. His botanical and herbal gardens are still cultivated in the courtyard. Touring the museum is to step back into 19th-century medicine. Even the window display, with its enormous leech jar and other antiquated paraphernalia, is fascinating. *514 Chartres St., tel. 504/524–9077. Admission: $1. Open Tues.–Sun. 11–5.*

La Marquise, across the street at 625 Chartres Street, is a fine French pastry shop. A half block to the right, on Chartres Street, is Wilkinson Row, an alley lined with shops that is closed to traffic during the day to provide a mall effect. On the **(33)** next corner at the square and on the left is **Le Petit Théâtre** with its entrance around the building on St. Peter Street. Founded in 1916, this is the oldest community theater in continuous operation in the United States. The building was erected in 1797 and underwent considerable reconstruction in 1960. The patio is itself a Quarter landmark. Seven plays are produced here each season, plus several children's plays. *616 St. Peter St., tel. 504/522–9958. Admission is by ticket during the theater season, Sept.–June.*

(34) Next to the theater is **Le Petit Salon** (620 St. Peter St.), a typical Creole home, that has housed a women's salon or literary group since 1924. Founded by local author and historian Grace King, the salon originally entertained the casts and staff of productions at Le Petit Théâtre. Notice that there is a different design in the railing of each of the three balconies, and that the building leans a bit to one side, evidence of age and of the soft soil on which the city of New Orleans rests.

A few doors down, at 632 St. Peter Street, is the house where Tennessee Williams wrote *A Streetcar Named Desire*. The streetcar, which used to run on Desire Street, is now on display outside the Old Mint on Barracks Street at the edge of the French Quarter.

If you duck into the little half-block Cabildo Alley off St. Peter Street and across from the salon, you will pass several shops and end up on the side of the cathedral at Pirates Alley. A turn right and up Pirates Alley brings you back into Jackson Square and the spot at which you began.

Time Out For the taste of French New Orleans, try the croissants and French breads baked in a brick oven at **La Madeleine** on Jackson Square, corner of Chartres and St. Ann streets. A cup of café au lait adds the crowning touch. *547 St. Ann St., tel. 504/568–9950. Open Mon.–Thurs. 7 AM–8 PM, Fri.–Sun. 7 AM–9 PM. No credit cards.*

Outer French Quarter

To enjoy the Outer French Quarter tour will require more walking than the Inner French Quarter tour. The effort will be worth it, as you will get to explore the fringe elements of the Quarter and dabble in voodoo. Numbers in the margin correspond with the numbered points of interest on the French Quarter, Central Business District, and Algiers Point map.

35 Begin at the end of the French Market at a covered fruit and vegetable area called the **Old Farmer's Market.** You will see farmers hauling their produce into the city from outlying areas and salespeople hawking garlands of onions, boxes of mirlitons, and other Louisiana produce. Toward the end of this building is
36 the **Community Flea Market,** a child of the 1960s, where dozens of merchants rent tables to sell a variety of goods. The sharp-eyed shopper can find bargains here, especially among the collectibles and local memorabilia, jewelry, ceramics, old magazines, and record albums. *Admission: free. Open Fri.–Sun. 10–6.*

37 Walk across Barracks Street, at the end of the market, into the entryway of the **Old Mint,** an imposing building between Decatur, Barracks, and Esplanade streets. Built in 1835, it was here that the Confederacy minted its money during the Civil War; later Confederate soldiers were imprisoned in the thick-walled mint while Union troops occupied New Orleans. After the war, legal tender again was printed in this building until 1909. Thereafter the Mint served a number of needs, among them as an office for the U.S. Coast Guard.

38 39 In the late 1970s the state undertook a complete restoration of the mint, turning it into the landmark **Louisiana State Museum.** Housed there are the **Mardi Gras Museum** and the **New Orleans Jazz Collection.** The Mardi Gras exhibit includes extravagant costumes, gowns, and Carnival floats. A visit here is not the same thing as a trip to New Orleans during Mardi Gras, but the museum conveys the feeling that stirs the city on Fat Tuesday (Mardi Gras Day). The Jazz Collection is filled with memorabilia of this native music form; a highlight is Louis Armstrong's first trumpet. Also housed in the Old Mint is the **Louisiana Historical Center,** which includes French and Spanish Louisiana archives, open free to researchers. *Tel. 504/394– 7334. Admission to either museum: $3, $1.50 senior citizens. Open Wed.–Sat. 10–3.*

40 An item of interest outside the Mint, at the Barracks Street entrance, is the **Desire Streetcar,** canonized in Tennessee Williams's play *A Streetcar Named Desire.* At one time streetcars ran through many New Orleans streets, including Desire Street. The one remaining sample of the Mint's old walls gives you an idea of the building's deterioration before its restoration.

Walk back to the Mint, turn right on Decatur Street, and go one block up to Esplanade Avenue, the once-grand promenade for Creoles of the French Quarter. You can imagine the sound of horses' hooves and the sight of bonneted women in long dresses carrying their dainty parasols, or of gentlemen in top hats toting walking canes.

41 Make a left on Esplanade Avenue to reach the **Lamothe Guest**

House (621 Esplanade Ave.), a typical example of the 19th-century mansions that once lined both sides of this tree-covered avenue.

Continue along Esplanade Avenue and at Royal Street (the next corner) turn left toward the French Quarter, walk one block to Barracks Street, and make a right. The **first studio of John James Audubon** (706 Barracks St.), a naturalist painter, was a few doors around the corner of the next block. In 1821, Audubon rented a small room here for several months before going to rural Louisiana to work on his bird drawings. His association with New Orleans is memorialized in the name of Audubon Park and the internationally acclaimed Audubon Zoo.

One block up Royal at the corner of Governor Nicholls Street is a **haunted house** (1140 Royal St.). Within this splendid mansion, in the 1830s, Delphine Lalaurie, wealthy mistress of the house, reportedly tortured her slaves in a most heinous manner; when a fire broke out in the attic in 1834, firefighters found slaves shackled to the walls and in horrible physical condition. An outraged community is said to have run Madame Lalaurie from the house and demolished what was left of it after the fire. Although much of this story was later proved to be in doubt, rumors persist to this day that the house is haunted by the groans and screams of the unfortunate slaves.

Turn left on Governor Nicholls Street, away from the haunted house, to the **Latrobe House** (721 Governor Nicholls St.), which dates back to 1814. Built by the young New Orleans architect Henry Latrobe, this house, with its modest porticos, started a passion for Greek Revival architecture in Louisiana, evidenced later in many plantation houses upriver, as well as in a significant number of buildings in New Orleans.

Continuing down Governor Nicholls Street, you come to Bourbon Street. The raucous nightclub-filled area that makes Bourbon Street synonymous with New Orleans doesn't begin for another few blocks. At upper Bourbon you get a sense of the quiet, residential street it was until the 1940s, when lower Bourbon developed its current reputation as "the playground of the South." This area of upper Bourbon has its own reputation as the center of the gay community. In the surrounding blocks are bars and clubs of gay men, many of whom perform as female impersonators in the clubs farther down on Bourbon Street. This community also stages the outrageous male beauty queen contests at Mardi Gras.

On the next corner, at St. Philip Street, is an ancient, weathered building, **Lafitte's Blacksmith Shop** (941 Bourbon St.). The striking anvil no longer sounds here, only the clinking of glasses—this has long been a favorite local bar for patrons from all walks of life. Legend has it that the pirate Jean Lafitte and his cronies operated a blacksmith shop here as a front for their vast, illicit trade in contraband, though no historic records have been found to support this legend. The building, dating to 1772, is interesting because it is one of the few surviving examples of soft bricks reinforced with timbers, a construction form used by early settlers.

This area of Bourbon Street was once known as the home of voodoo queens and doctors. There are no more public voodoo rituals in the city, but some followers still believe in aspects of the religion brought to New Orleans by their ancestors from

46 Haiti and Sainte Domingue. The **New Orleans Historic Voodoo Museum,** to the right on Dumaine Street, is the only such museum in the world and has a large collection of artifacts and information on voodoo. The gift shop sells gris-gris potions and voodoo dolls; readings, lectures, and voodoo tours are also available through the museum. *724 Dumaine St., tel. 504/523–7685. Admission: $3 adults, $2 senior citizens, $1 children. Open daily 10–dusk.*

The famous voodoo queen Marie Laveau lived nearby, but before visiting her stomping grounds, return to Bourbon Street **47** and walk one block to the **Spring Fiesta historic townhouse.** This lovely 19th-century home has been restored to its former splendor by the same people who sponsor the annual Spring Fiesta, a celebration of the Quarter's beautiful homes and genteel lifestyle of days gone by. *826 St. Ann St., tel. 504/581–1367. Admission: $3 adults, children under 12 free. Open weekdays 1–4.*

Make a left on St. Ann Street and continue another two blocks; in the 1000 block, on the edge of the Quarter, was the home of Marie Laveau, the greatly feared and respected voodoo queen of antebellum New Orleans. Little is known of her historically, although dozens of stories, folktales, and rumors persist today. With her power to cast spells and heal physical ailments as well as heartaches, she became quite influential, counting among her clients some of the wealthiest people in the city. It is not certain which of the small houses on the left side of this block was hers, or even if the original house has survived. Important, though, was the proximity of her house to the park across the next cross street, where the slaves and "free persons of color" congregated in her day in Congo Square, spoke in their native African tongues, danced to their own music, and joined Marie Laveau in solemn voodoo rituals.

As you reach the next block, N. Rampart Street, the large park **48** that runs for several blocks in front of you is **Louis Armstrong Park,** named for native son and world-famous musician Louis Armstrong, whose statue is located near the brightly lit entrance. To the left of the park is a stone-inlaid circle of ground **49** with a fountain at its center, **Congo Square,** now renamed **Beauregard Square,** but still referred to by locals by its original name. In the distant background is the **Theater for the Performing Arts,** and to the left, behind Congo Square, is a large gray building, the **Municipal Auditorium.** Plans are afoot to transform Armstrong Park into an entertainment complex like Tivoli Gardens in Copenhagen. It is ironic that Louis Armstrong was not welcome to play the better clubs of his home city during his illustrious musical career. *Be very careful about exploring the park. Unless a special activity is going on there, the park is not well guarded, and it is not advisable to linger.*

The name N. Rampart Street indicates that a wall once stood here, at the back of the French Quarter; it was built to protect early settlers against Indian attacks. Walking down N. Rampart Street to the left you will pass **Covenant House,** a complex of buildings recently constructed to house teenage runaways. Another block down turn right on St. Louis Street, which intersects at the next corner with Basin Street, for which the "Basin Street Blues" were named.

50 Ahead on Basin Street is **St. Louis Cemetery,** the oldest cemetery in the city and typical of the unique, aboveground burial practices of the French and Spanish. Due to the high water level, it was difficult to bury bodies underground without having the coffin float to the surface after the first hard rain. Modern-day burial methods permit underground interment, but many people prefer these ornate family tombs and vaults, which have figured in several movies, among them *Easy Rider*.

Buried here are such notables as Etienne Boré, father of the sugar industry; Homer Plessy of the *Plessy* v. *Ferguson* 1892 U.S. Supreme Court decision establishing the separate-but-equal Jim Crow laws for blacks and whites in the South; and most notably, Marie Laveau, voodoo queen. Her tomb is marked with *X*s freshly chalked by those who still believe in her supernatural powers.

A second Marie Laveau, believed to be her daughter, is buried in **St. Louis Cemetery #2,** four blocks beyond this cemetery, on Claiborne Avenue. A third St. Louis Cemetery is located at the end of Esplanade Avenue, a good drive from here. Although these cemeteries are open to the public daily from about 10 AM to 5 PM, it is not advisable to enter them unescorted. Group tours, arranged through local tour agencies, are a much safer way to explore these areas.

51 Continue down Basin Street one block to Conti Street. In the next blocks of Basin Street to the right is a government housing project, the **Iberville project,** which stands on the former site of **Storyville.** A legitimatized red-light district that lasted from 1897 to 1917, Storyville spawned splendid Victorian homes that served as brothels, and brought uptown and downtown jazz players together for the first time to create what became known as New Orleans jazz. This area has been the subject of many novels, songs, and films; the Louis Malle film *Pretty Baby*, starring a teenage Brooke Shields, was inspired by a Storyville photographer. Always controversial, the district was shut down in 1917 and the buildings razed almost overnight; the housing project was built in the 1930s. Only a historical marker on the "neutral ground" (median) of Basin Street remains to mark alderman Sidney Story's notorious experiment attempting to legalize prostitution and vice.

52 Going from vice to virtue, take a left on Conti Street and follow it to N. Rampart Street where **Our Lady of Guadalope Chapel** (411 N. Rampart St.) dominates the corner on the left. Known for its large St. Jude shrine, this church was built in 1826 at the edge of the Quarter and found much use as a burying chapel during the waves of yellow fever that hit the city in the 1800s. From time to time the church holds a midnight jazz mass on Saturday. Check the rectory for a schedule.

53 Follow Conti Street for another two blocks to the **Musée Conti Wax Museum.** Over 100 wax figures of past and present Louisiana celebrities are arranged in tableaus with written and audio explanations; the gift shop stocks a variety of local memorabilia. *917 Conti St., tel. 504/525-2605. Admission: $4 adults, $3.50 senior citizens, $3 children, under 6 free. Open weekdays 10–5:30, weekends 10–9.*

Make a left on Conti Street to Dauphine Street, left again on Dauphine Street to St. Louis Street, where you will find the **54** **Hermann-Grima House** in the middle of the block. This is one of the largest and best preserved examples of American architecture in the Quarter. It has the only restored private stable and the only working 1830s Creole kitchen in the Quarter. Cooking demonstrations on the open hearth are held here from October to May by reservation only. You'll want to check the gift shop that contains many local crafts and books. *820 St. Louis St., tel. 504/525–5661. Admission: $3 adults, $2.50 senior citizens, $2 children 8 years and older. Open Mon.–Sat. 10–4. Last tour at 3:30.*

55 An experience of a different nature awaits you at the next corner on Bourbon Street, **Ripley's Believe it or not Museum**. Among many of the unusual items displayed here is an exhibit of the New Orleans Mardi Gras Indians, explaining their dances and intricate handmade costumes. This is an aspect of local lore not treated in any other museum in the city, and is in itself worth the cost of admission. *501 Bourbon St., tel. 504/529–5131. Admission: $3.95 adults, $2.50 children. Open daily 10–midnight.*

56 Take a left outside Ripley's and continue along **Bourbon Street**, the busy, world-famous entertainment strip. There is probably a **Lucky Dog vendor** nearby, with a vending cart shaped like a hot dog—John Kennedy Toole immortalized these in his Pulitzer Prize–winning novel about New Orleans, *A Confederacy of Dunces*. **Chris Owens Club** (502 Bourbon St.) is the last of a tradition of one-woman shows on the strip. For several decades Owens has been a favorite local cabaret dancer and performer.

57 At the next corner, Toulouse Street, is an engraved marker pointing out the former location of the **French Opera House**, which burned down in 1919 and was never rebuilt. Probably no other building in the South saw more celebrities and musical hits in its day; the elegant elliptical auditorium, with its four tiers of seats, accommodated 1800 guests. While on rowdy Bourbon Street, keep in mind that until the end of World War II, this was a quiet residential area, with small shops and an occasional cabaret or theater.

58 At the corner of the next block (St. Peter St.), music blares from several clubs. To your right is the party animal's landmark, **Pat O'Brien's Bar** (718 St. Peter St.). Many visitors don't consider their stay in New Orleans complete without a Pat O'Brien's Hurricane, a sweet, highly intoxicating mixed drink served in a tall lantern-shaped glass (which you may keep). You can toast to your future in a beautiful courtyard to the sounds of a rousing piano tune.

59 Our tour concludes on a slightly less boisterous musical note at **Preservation Hall**. Although a neighbor to Pat O'Brien's, this music club offers strictly old-time New Orleans jazz, and it is one of the best places in town to catch native singers and musicians. The $2 admission allows you to stay for as many sets as you wish. One note: No food or drink is served on the premises, and none can be brought in. Also, the room is not heated or air-conditioned; this is serious, no-frills music, but the best that can be found in the city where jazz was born. *726 St. Peter St., tel. 504/522–2238. Admission: $2. Open daily 8 PM–12:30AM.*

Time Out **Johnny White's Bar,** across St. Peter Street from Preservation Hall, is as New Orleans as one can get. It has a colorful history and a loyal local clientele; a cold Dixie beer here could be your invitation to some lively conversation and local atmosphere. *733 St. Peter St., tel. 504/523–6153. AE, MC, V.*

Foot of Canal Street

One of the fastest-growing and most exciting areas of New Orleans is where Canal Street meets the river. Referred to by locals as the foot of Canal Street, it is within walking distance of the French Quarter (about 10 minutes) and most downtown hotels. The riverfront has been dramatically developed in recent years, and the former riverfront site of the 1984 World's Fair has been incorporated into the commercial area known as the Central Business District. The RTA (Regional Transit Authority) has just added a new streetcar that rolls through the bustling riverfront area. You may want to catch it to some of the sites covered in the following tour (*see* Getting Around). Numbers in the margins correspond with the numbered points of interest on the French Quarter, Central Business District, and Algiers Point map.

Begin a few blocks from the river on Canal Street at Decatur Street, where 200 years ago the river met the land; look down the four blocks to the left that lead to the Mississippi River and note how much alluvial soil has been deposited by the river over the years—land that today is some of the most valuable in the city.

A word about the wide median strip in Canal Street, called neutral ground by locals: In the early 1800s, after the Louisiana Purchase, the French Creoles residing in the French Quarter were strictly segregated from the Americans who settled on the upriver side of Canal Street. The two communities had separate governments and police systems, and the middle of Canal Street became the "neutral ground" where they skirmished from time to time. Today these animosities are amusing history, but the term neutral ground has survived as the name for all medians throughout the city.

60 On the corner of Decatur and Canal streets is an enormous building, the old **Custom House**, which occupies the whole block. Built in 1849, it replaced what had been Fort St. Louis, which guarded the old French city. The building has identical entrances on all four sides, because at the time it was completed no decision had been made as to which side would be the main entrance. The Custom House has been home to many, including General Butler, commanding officer of the Union troops during occupation of New Orleans during the Civil War; today it houses government offices.

61 Down Canal Street to the left is **Canal Place,** a fashionable shopping complex with stores such as Saks Fifth Avenue, Brooks Brothers, and Ralph Lauren Polo. The Westin Canal Place Hotel is on the top floor of the complex; its dining rooms and lobby have a fantastic view of the river.

62 Below Canal Place is the **Aquarium of the Americas and Riverfront Park,** expected to be completed in late 1989 or early 1990. It will be the largest aquatic facility in the South and will include a landscaped park along the river.

63 Directly ahead on Canal Street is the terminal for the **Canal Street Ferry,** offering a free ride across the river to a part of New Orleans called Algiers. Pedestrians climb the stairs and board the ferry from above, while bicycles and cars board from below on the left of the terminal. The trip takes about 20 minutes; ferries run from 6:30 AM to around 9:30 PM. Be sure to check with the attendants if you are crossing late in the evening —it is no fun to be stranded on the wrong side. Keep in mind, too, that there are no rest-room facilities in the terminals or on the ferry itself, and no food or drink concessions. Special arrangements for the disabled must be made with an attendant. The ferry ride is an experience in itself, offering great views of the river and the New Orleans skyline, and the heady feeling of being on one of the largest and most powerful rivers in the world.

If you ride the ferry, you can explore the historic district of Old Algiers and tour the warehouses in **Blaine Kern's Mardi Gras World,** where the parade floats are made. This could be a morning or afternoon excursion by itself (*see* Algiers Point Side Trip).

Return to the Canal Street side of the river. The small island in the middle of Canal Street near the ferry terminal is **Liberty Place,** with its tall **obelisk** monument to white supremacy. Shrouded now by tall bushes, this obelisk is a curious piece of local history; if you brave the traffic to study it up close you can see many of the words engraved on its base have been obscured by a cementlike substance, and that graffiti is spray-painted on its sides. Little is known today of the purpose of the monument, which honored the 16 men who died nearby in the Battle of Liberty Place during the 1891 armed rebellion of the White League against the Reconstructionist government of New Orleans. In an attempt to quell the controversy about the monument that surfaces from time to time and as an alternative to removing the obelisk altogether, a bronze plaque was installed in 1974 in front of the obelisk explaining that although the monument constitutes an event in local history, the sentiments it expresses are contrary to those of present-day New Orleans.

Directly across the street from the monument is the **Rivergate Exhibition Center,** a convention center with fluid lines evoking the movement of water. Built in the late 1960s, it was once the main convention facility for the city, but has long since been replaced by larger buildings like the Superdome and the New Orleans Convention Center. The Rivergate continues, however, to host seminars and smaller exhibits.

Across the landscaped median is the **World Trade Center** (2 Canal St.), home to dozens of foreign consulates and many international trade offices. There is an observation deck near the top of this 33-floor building. *Admission: $2 adults, $1 children. Open daily 9–5.*

For adult visitors to the Trade Center there is a revolving bar on the top floor called **Top of the Mart.** A live dance band makes this a most romantic spot. *Open weekdays mid-morning–midnight, weekends mid-morning–1AM.*

The World Trade Center is surrounded by statues and plazas from three countries. Joan of Arc straddles her horse in a gold-plate statue in **Place de France.** Winston Churchill is memorialized in a bronze statue in **British Park Place,** to the right. A bronze equestrian statue of Bernardo de Galvez, Spanish governor of Louisiana in the 1780s, guards the entrance of **Spanish Plaza.** These statues represent the countries that contributed to the settlement and success of New Orleans—France, Spain, and England.

(67) Behind the World Trade Center toward the river is a large plateau with beautiful inlaid tiles and a magnificent 50-foot fountain. This **Spanish Plaza** was a gift from Spain in the mid-1970s; a platform near the fountain often hosts local bands.

(68) To the right, down several steps, is the entrance into **Riverwalk,** an old warehouse district that has been transformed into a half-mile marketplace holding more than 200 shops, cafes, and restaurants. There are three tiers of restaurants, entertainments, and local and national shops, all connected by a promenade that stretches along the river's edge. Plaques along the walkway relate bits of the Mississippi River's history and folklore. Test your memory of history and geography on this educational minitour.

If you exit from the third level of the Riverwalk, you can see how the marketplace complex conveniently ties the Hilton Hotel and Spanish Plaza at its lower end to the New Orleans Convention Center at its upper end. This stretch of land held the 1984 Louisiana World Exposition (World's Fair).

(69) The **New Orleans Convention Center** (900 Convention Center Blvd.) is another outgrowth of the World's Fair. One of the largest convention facilities in the country, it was completed in 1985 and already is undergoing expansion to accommodate the overwhelming bookings that extend to the year 2000.

A less fortunate leftover from the World's Fair is the **gondola,** a cableway stretching across the Mississippi from the tall, red, cranelike structure beside the Convention Center. During the fair it was a novelty ride with glass-enclosed cable cars. Plans to incorporate it into the commuter transport system never materialized. The gondola, which is privately owned by local businessmen, may yet return!

(70) Take Convention Center Boulevard back to Poydras Street and walk left on Poydras for three short blocks to **Piazza d'Italia.** *(The areas around the Convention Center and the Piazza tend to be deserted at times and can be unsafe; use caution when displaying cameras and travel bags.)* This modern, award-winning plaza has been featured in several movies, most prominently in the opening scene of *The Big Easy.*

(71) To the left of the piazza is the **American-Italian Museum.** Here Italian New Orleans customs are explained. Family records of local Italian immigrants are included in the research library. *537 S. Peters St., tel. 504/891–1904. Admission free. Open Wed. –Fri. 10–4.*

(72) This concludes the tour of the foot of Canal Street. The **Louisiana Children's Museum** is a few blocks behind the piazza, but to walk there is not recommended, as this is an unsafe area. The museum, with its hands-on activities and miniature hospital, grocery store, and so forth, is a special treat for children; plan to make a separate expedition there. *428 Julia St., tel. 504/523–1357. Admission: $2.50. Open Tues.–Sun. 9:30–4:30.*

Time Out The **Economy Restaurant,** a block behind Piazza d'Italia, is a no-frills local bar frequented by workers from the neighborhood warehouses by day and by poets and artists by night. It is one of the few places serving Abita beer, brewed with care by two local entrepreneurs in Abita Springs, an enclave across the lake known for its pure spring water. Abita beer is no competition for the old standby Dixie beer, but it is developing a loyal following. *325 Girod St., tel. 504/524–7405. No credit cards.*

Algiers Point Side Trip Directly across the Mississippi River from the French Quarter and Canal Street is the neighborhood of Algiers. Extending out into the curve of the river is the area known as **Algiers Point.** This 25-block area is accessible by a ferry ride across the river that departs from Canal Street (*see* Foot of Canal Street).

Settled at the turn of the century, this extension of New Orleans is a world apart from the city. Its quiet, tree-lined streets, quaint shops, and renovated Victorian houses are aspects of a community that has managed to remain somewhat isolated. In the early days of New Orleans, Algiers was a holding area for the African slaves from the many ships that made their way into the port. The slaves were ferried across the river to the French Quarter where they were to be placed on the auction block. It is speculated that Algiers is named for the North African slave port. Numbers in the margin correspond with the numbered points of interest on the French Quarter, Central Business District, and Algiers Point map.

The best way to appreciate the beauty of the houses and their varied architecture in Algiers Point is on foot. As you disembark the ferry, walk down to the right where Delaronde Street curves around to the left and follow it several blocks past the

73 finest homes in **Algiers Point's historic renovation district.** On the left is a large sand-colored building owned by Louisiana Power & Light Co.; notice how the initials LP&L are worked into a decorative pattern within the blocks used to make the building.

There is a one-man Algiers welcoming and information committee, Russell Templet, in the Hair and Style Shop across from the LP&L building. Feel free to drop in at Templet's shop to say hello.

Follow Delaronde Street for three more blocks to Verret Street. Note the various sizes and styles of houses from ornate mansions to modest shotgun houses (all the doors open one behind another in a straight line, so you could fire a gun from the front step to a backyard wall without hitting a wall in between), a popular working-class architecture in New Orleans. Since these homes were all built around the early 1900s, they reflect the Victorian influence in vogue at that time. In the last 30 years, a movement has been undertaken to restore many of these old homes to their original elegance.

Turn right at Verret Street; around the next corner is the **Lemieux Art Gallery** (508 Pelican St.). In the next block down Verret Street, in a scene reminiscent of provincial French towns, is a triangular park surrounded by small houses and shops with a large Catholic church, **The Holy Name of Mary Church,** dominating the left side.

74 Follow Verret another two blocks to **Opelousas Street,** heart of Old Algiers. This wide tree-canopied avenue looks much like those of Uptown New Orleans. The playground to the right has six great magnolia trees. Across Opelousas Street are shops and churches like those found in any small-town center.

The operational **firehouse** on the next corner looks straight out of the 1930s. A few doors down from it is the **Abalon Theater,** a local landmark and the only cinema in the area, which is fighting to stay in business. The **Olde Town Antique Shop** near the corner of Teche Street lends to the nostalgic atmosphere of this tranquil area.

Opelousas Street ends after the next block, and predictably curves left to follow the river on Brooklyn Avenue. Straight ahead is a cluster of newly renovated cottages purchased and moved here to use as offices for the Compass Barge Company. Surprisingly, these offices create a harmonious, almost rural setting.

75 To the left, three blocks down Brooklyn Avenue, is the real attraction on this side of the river, **Blaine Kern's Mardi Gras World,** the largest float-building firm in the world. A tour here takes you through the warehouses, or dens, where the spectacular floats for over 40 Mardi Gras parades are constructed. Visitors can watch the artists and builders at work, view a film about Mardi Gras, and buy Carnival memorabilia in the gift shop. A photo of yourself with one of the giant figures used on the floats makes a terrific souvenir. Blaine Kern has for many years been the best-known artist and creator of Mardi Gras floats; he often personally conducts tours through this one-of-a-kind facility. The three long blocks of Brooklyn Avenue before Mardi Gras World are through a warehouse area that is often deserted; be sure to take proper precautions. A cab can be called from pay phones on Opelousas Street. *233 Newton St., tel. 504/362–8211. Admission: $3.50 adults, $2.50 children. Open weekdays 10–4.*

The **gondola,** a cable car over the river, which is housed in the red, cranelike structure across the street from Mardi Gras World, has not operated since the World's Fair in 1984, but plans are to use it for commuters and Mardi Gras World visitors in the future.

To conclude the Algiers Point tour and return to the ferry, follow Powder Street, right from the end of Opelousas Street, back along the river. **Algiers Iron Works and Dry Dock Company** is on the left, as evidenced by the huge steel equipment used to repair river-going vessels. Where Powder Street curves into Pelican Street, take the footpath to the left leading up onto the **76** **levee** and follow this for two blocks back to the ferry landing. This is a great spot for picture-taking, with a view of the river and the New Orleans skyline.

Algiers Landing, a deceptively ramshackle multilevel building visible from the bend of the river, is a fine restaurant and offers romantic dining, especially at sunset.

St. Charles Avenue Streetcar Tour

The best way to explore the Central Business District, the Garden District, and Uptown New Orleans is a ride on the historic **New Orleans Streetcar,** the hallmark of the city. In the early 1900s streetcars were the most prominent mode of public transit and ran on many streets, but today there is only the 6½ miles of track mainly along St. Charles Avenue; the streetcars are well maintained by the Regional Transit Authority, which also operates the city buses. *Cost: 60 cents one way (exact change).*

Streetcar runs 24 hours daily, about every 10 min. 7 AM–8 PM, every half hour 8 PM–midnight, every hour midnight–7 AM.

People living and working along its route depend heavily on the streetcar; plan your trip to avoid rush hours—7–9 AM and 3–6 PM— or you may have to stand much of the way and will not be able to enjoy the scenery or sites.

A number of sightseeing points in the area are not visible from the streetcar route and require walking several blocks. These side trips can be condensed into three main points of diversion, each taking from one to two hours. You may want to skip one or two of them this time and plan a return trip later. The streetcar route also has been shortened here to end at Riverbend, where St. Charles Avenue becomes Carrollton Avenue. If you have more time and want to take the streetcar to its end at Claiborne Avenue, stay on for about another 10 minutes and enjoy the ride through what was once the separate town of Carrollton.

Whether you exit the streetcar at Riverbend or Claiborne Avenue, you can return to Canal Street and the French Quarter either by streetcar or bus. Remember to exit the streetcar from the front; the signs may say to exit in the rear, but no one does there —only the tourist! Streetcar enthusiasts may want to pick up a copy of *The Streetcar Guide*, published by Transitour in 1980 and available in most local bookstores.

Numbers in the margins correspond with the numbered points of interest on the St. Charles Avenue Streetcar map.

❶ To begin the tour, board the streetcar in the **first block of St. Charles Avenue,** off Canal Street (in the French Quarter, Royal Street changes its name to St. Charles Avenue upon crossing Canal Street). The stop is at Common Street, marked by a small yellow sign. If you miss one streetcar, duck into the **Pearl Restaurant's** oyster bar, two doors down on St. Charles, and have some fresh, salty, raw oysters while awaiting the next streetcar.

The first four blocks up St. Charles are not remarkable; they include office buildings and banks typical of any central business district. At the third stop, Poydras Street, the skyscrapers on either side are among the most impressive in the city—the 27-story **Pan American Life Insurance building** on the left and the 50-story **One Shell Square** on the right. Exit at Poydras Street for the Civic Center and Superdome side trip.

Superdome and Civic Center Side Trip A good walk—about eight blocks—down Poydras to the right off St. Charles Avenue brings you to the Louisiana Superdome and the nearby Civic Center. Along the way you will pass several impressive office buildings, the newest and most innovative being the **Louisiana Land and Exploration Building** (901 Poydras St.) and the **Energy Centre** (1100 Poydras St.), with its towering fountain sculpture in front. Don't be intimidated by the policeman poised near the fountain; he is made of bronze and is one of several lifelike bronzes scattered around the city.

Across Loyola Avenue, on the left, is a complex of interconnected buildings that includes the **Hyatt Regency Hotel,** the **Texaco Building,** and **Poydras Plaza** (facing Loyola Ave.). The **❷** **New Orleans Centre,** farther down on the left, is the city's newest and poshest shopping mall, positioned opportunely

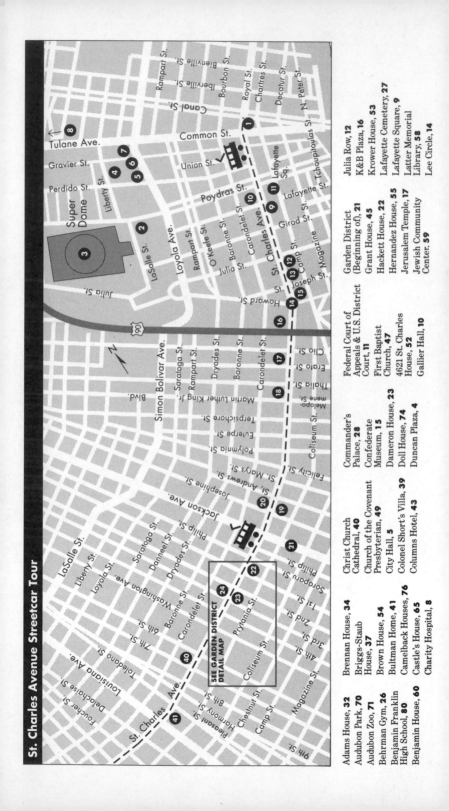

St. Charles Avenue Streetcar Tour

Adams House, **32**
Audubon Park, **70**
Audubon Zoo, **71**
Behrman Gym, **26**
Benjamin Franklin
High School, **80**
Benjamin House, **60**

Brennan House, **34**
Briggs-Staub
House, **37**
Brown House, **54**
Bultman Home, **41**
Camelback Houses, **76**
Castle's House, **65**
Charity Hospital, **8**

Christ Church
Cathedral, **40**
Church of the Covenant
Presbyterian, **49**
City Hall, **5**
Colonel Short's Villa, **39**
Columns Hotel, **43**

Commander's
Palace, **28**
Confederate
Museum, **15**
Dameron House, **23**
Doll House, **74**
Duncan Plaza, **4**

Federal Court of
Appeals & U.S. District
Court, **11**
First Baptist
Church, **47**
4621 St. Charles
House, **52**
Gallier Hall, **10**

Garden District
(Beginning of), **21**
Grant House, **45**
Hackett House, **22**
Hernandez House, **55**
Jerusalem Temple, **17**
Jewish Community
Center, **59**

Julia Row, **12**
K&B Plaza, **16**
Krower House, **53**
Lafayette Cemetery, **27**
Lafayette Square, **9**
Latter Memorial
Library, **58**
Lee Circle, **14**

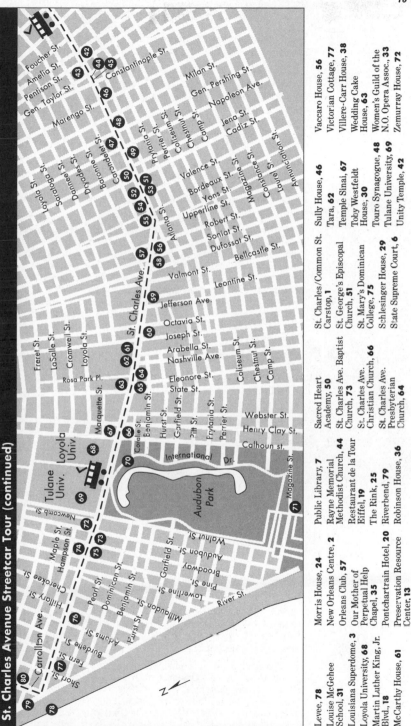

75

St. Charles Avenue Streetcar Tour (continued)

St. Charles/Common St.
Carstop, 1
St. George's Episcopal
Church, 51
St. Mary's Dominican
College, 75
Schlesinger House, 29
State Supreme Court, 6

Sacred Heart
Academy, 50
St. Charles Ave. Baptist
Church, 73
St. Charles Ave.
Christian Church, 66
St. Charles Ave.
Presbyterian
Church, 64

Public Library, 7
Rayne Memorial
Methodist Church, 44
Restaurant de la Tour
Eiffel, 19
The Rink, 25
Riverbend, 79
Robinson House, 36

Morris House, 24
New Orleans Centre, 2
Orleans Club, 57
Our Mother of
Perpetual Help
Chapel, 35
Pontchartrain Hotel, 20
Preservation Resource
Center, 13

Vaccaro House, 56
Victorian Cottage, 77
Villere-Carr House, 38
Wedding Cake
House, 63
Women's Guild of the
N.O. Opera Assoc., 33
Zemurray House, 72

Sully House, 46
Tara, 62
Temple Sinai, 67
Toby Westfeldt
House, 30
Touro Synagogue, 48
Tulane University, 69
Unity Temple, 42

Levee, 78
Louise McGehee
School, 31
Louisiana Superdome, 3
Loyola University, 68
Martin Luther King, Jr.
Blvd., 18
McCarthy House, 61

between the Superdome and the Hyatt Regency. The center
③ services the many conventions and events held in the **Louisiana
Superdome,** famed site of many Sugar Bowls and Super Bowls
and home to the New Orleans Saints football team. The dome
seats up to 100,000 people and can be partitioned into smaller
areas for special events. The parking garage accommodates
5,000 cars and 250 buses. With a 166,000-square-foot playing
field and a roof that covers almost eight acres at a height of 27
stories, this is one of the largest buildings of its kind in the
world, built in 1975 for more than $180 million.

In addition to sports events, the Superdome has a full schedule
of conventions, Mardi Gras balls, and events such as the circus
and ice-skating shows. The National Republican Convention
was held here in 1988. *One Sugar Bowl Dr., tel. 504/587–3810.
Tour admission: $4 adults, $3 children over 5. Open daily 9–4,
except during some Superdome events.*

Across from the Superdome on Poydras is a large abstract
sculpture called **The Krewe of Poydras,** designed to evoke the
frivolity and zany spirit of Mardi Gras. It can and has had many
other interpretations. Walk back one block to Loyola Avenue
and take a left at the Juvenile Court Building at the corner. Be-
④ yond the courthouse on the left is a wide open area, **Duncan
Plaza,** newly landscaped with grassy knolls and a large, open,
African-style pavilion in the center. Around the plaza are the
⑤ ⑥ buildings that make up the **Civic Center: City Hall** on the left,
the **State Office Building** straight ahead, and the **State Supreme
Court** to its right.

⑦ ⑧ To the right, across Gravier Street, is the **public library,** and a
block behind it towers **Charity Hospital.** The massive public
hospital system includes two nearby medical schools—
Louisiana State University and Tulane University.

The streets around the Superdome and Civic Center are usually busy during business hours, but at nights and on weekends
this area generally is deserted and should not be explored alone
after dark.

To see more of the Central Business District, return to the
streetcar by way of Gravier Street, at the lower end of Duncan
Plaza.

The next three stops along St. Charles Avenue pass through
what used to be the city of Lafayette and the seat of the American government during New Orleans's antebellum years.
⑨ ⑩ **Lafayette Square** is on the left at the first stop (Lafayette St.),
and **Gallier Hall,** the former city hall, is on the right. (The
French Creoles controlled the French Quarter and had their
own city government on Jackson Square.) The statue in Lafayette Square on the white granite pedestal and facing St.
Charles Avenue is of John McDonogh, benefactor of public edu-
cation in New Orleans and the man for whom many public
schools are named. The bronze statue in the center of the
square is of Henry Clay, the U.S. Senator who was a frequent
visitor to the city in the mid-1800s.

Gallier Hall is considered the finest example of Greek Revival
architecture in New Orleans, with Grecian Ionic touches and a
portico of white marble. Built in 1850, it was designed by local
architect James Gallier, whose name it bears. This was the seat
of Reconstructionist rule after the Civil War, and the building
saw many political demonstrations in its days as city hall. In the

1950s a new city hall was built in the civic center, six blocks to
the right on Loyola Avenue. Gallier Hall has since been used for
city offices and as a reception facility.

⑪ On the far side of Lafayette Square is the **Federal Court of Appeals,** and barely visible to its left the **U.S. District Court,** site of
the two lengthy federal trials of Louisiana Governor Edwin
Edwards in 1986 and 1987. The Cajun governor, nicknamed the
Silver Fox, was acquitted of racketeering in both trials but lost
his bid for another term as governor to Buddy Roemer in 1987.

⑫ Just past the next stop is Julia Street; the block on the left, **Julia Row,** has 13 row houses lining the entire right side of the
block. These homes were occupied by prominent Americans in
the 1840s, but the whole area deteriorated badly during the
20th century. Ambitious and extensive renovations in the early
1980s have brought the original row houses back to some of
their former finery.

⑬ Located in Julia Row is the **Preservation Resource Center,** with
materials and displays on local historic architecture. The center also offers architectural tours through various
neighborhoods in the city; check for details. *604 Julia St., tel.
504/581-7032. Admission free. Open weekdays 8:30-5.*

The most notable establishment in the next block of St. Charles
is the **Hummingbird Grill** (804 St. Charles Ave.), an aging
greasy-spoon fictionalized by New Orleans novelists and
dear to many Orleanians of all social strata. Com-
⑭ ing up at the intersection of Howard Avenue is **Lee Circle,** a
neatly trimmed mound with a pyramidlike base that supports a
60-foot white marble column topped with a bronze statue of
Confederate leader General Robert E. Lee. He stands facing
due north as he has since 1884, but he appears today to be looking at the YWCA across the circle; a local joke has it that the
tall letters taunt the general that "The Yanks Will Come
Again."

To the left of the circle, barely visible from the streetcar, is an
⑮ ivy-covered stone building, the **Confederate Museum.** Built in
1891, the museum contains artifacts and records from the Civil
War. The Civil War buff will find the museum's extensive collection worth a visit. *929 Camp St., tel. 504/523-4522.
Admission: $2 adults, $1 senior citizens, 50 cents children under 12. Open Mon-Sat. 10-4.*

⑯ To the right, as the streetcar turns at Lee Circle, is the **K&B
Plaza** (1055 St. Charles Ave.), a tall office building with a wonderful collection of outdoor sculptures. The eye-catching
abstract piece facing Lee Circle is titled "The Mississippi," by
Isamu Noguchi. Other sculptures include ones by Henry Moore
and George Segal. The plaza, erected in 1973, won an award
from the American Institute of Architects. A collection of
works by local and international artists is displayed throughout
the building (*see* New Orleans for Free).

On the next corner, where the I-10 expressway enters St.
⑰ Charles Avenue, is the **Jerusalem Temple** (1137 St. Charles
Ave.), home to the city's large Shriner community. Built in
1916, the temple features intricate mosaic tile scenes on its fa-
⑱ cade. Two stops after Lee Circle is the intersection of **Martin
Luther King, Jr. Blvd.** on the right, which is called Melpomene
Street on the left. The stretch was renamed in the early 1970s
to honor the civil rights leader; his bust is displayed on

Claiborne Avenue near the intersection of Martin Luther King, Jr. Blvd. King helped to found the Southern Christian Leadership Conference (SCLC) in New Orleans in the **New Zion Baptist Church** (2319 Third St.) in this area.

19 After three more stops comes a wildly different building on the left, the **Restaurant de la Tour Eiffel** (2040 St. Charles Ave.). Adding a modern French touch to New Orleans, this structure was salvaged from the original restaurant inside the Eiffel Tower in Paris. Each piece was shipped here where it was carefully reassembled in 1986, to become one of the more novel restaurants in the city. On the right approaching the next stop **20** is the **Pontchartrain Hotel** (2031 St. Charles Ave.), a venerable, old-style grand hotel, locally owned and renowned.

21 The wide intersection at the next stop is Jackson Avenue, traditionally considered the beginning of the **Garden District**. Stately mansions on either side of the avenue attest to the taste and wealth of the American settlers who swarmed to New Orleans after the Louisiana Purchase in 1803. St. Charles Avenue cuts through the edge of the fashionable Garden District; most of the district is located in the next five blocks on the left. To get a closer look at these homes, exit the streetcar three stops up at Washington Avenue and take the Garden District side trip.

22 On the left before the next stop, First Street, is the **Hackett House** (2336 St. Charles Ave.), dating back to the 1850s. The Greek Revival style (a simple, columned design) of the Hackett House is typical of the early days of the Garden District. An-**23 24** other house of note is the **Dameron House** (2524 St. Charles Ave.), on the left at the Third Street stop, and the **Morris House** (2525 St. Charles Ave.) across on the right. Washington Avenue, intersecting at the next stop, is in the heart of the Garden District. Exit here for the Garden District side trip.

Garden District The Garden District lives up to its name in its beautifully land-
Side Trip scaped gardens surrounding elegant antebellum homes. None of these private homes are open to the public on a regular basis, but their occupants do not mind visitors enjoying the sights from behind the wrought iron fences that surround these magnificent estates.

Adams House, **32**
Behrman Gym, **26**
Brennan House, **34**
Briggs-Staub House, **37**
Colonel Short's Villa, **39**
Commander's Palace, **28**
Lafayette Cemetery, **27**
McGehee School, **31**
Our Mother Chapel, **35**
The Rink, **25**
Robinson House, **36**
Schlesinger House, **29**
Westfeldt House, **30**
Villere-Carr House, **38**
Guild Opera Assn., **33**

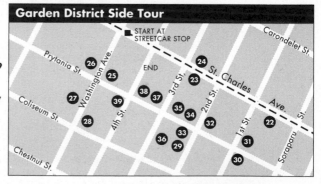

Garden District Side Tour

Group tours of this area are available (*see* Guided Tours). The helpful book *The Great Days of the Garden District*, by Ray

Samuel, can be bought at the first stop on the Garden District tour, The Rink.

Begin one block from the streetcar at the intersection of Washington Avenue and Prytania Street. On the left corner is **The Rink** (2727 Prytania St.), a skating rink in the 1880s but converted in recent years into a shopping center. **Maple Street Bookstore** in the Rink has the book mentioned above and many other locally published books about New Orleans.

Across Washington Avenue is the **Behrman Gym** (1500 Washington Ave.), which also dates back to the turn of the century, when it was the Southern Athletic Club. Today it is again a private sports facility.

Continuing down Washington Avenue toward Coliseum Street, notice that the next block on the right is taken up by the white-walled **Lafayette Cemetery** (1600 Block Washington Ave.). This area used to be Lafayette City in the early 1800s; the Americans settled in this area when the French Creoles would not welcome them into the older part of the city.

From the gates of the cemetery you can see the lavish aboveground vaults and tombs of the families who built the surrounding mansions. Although the gates are generally open during working hours, it is not advisable to wander among the tombs—this isolated, unguarded area can be dangerous.

One of the grandest Victorian homes in the area is **Commander's Palace** (1403 Washington Ave.), across from the cemetery, now a restaurant. Owned by the Brennan family, this is considered one of the finest Creole restaurants in the city.

Turn left at the corner, onto Coliseum Street, and walk three blocks to Second Street. This stroll will give you a general overview of the area.

What cannot be appreciated from the outside of these mansions are the sumptuous, carefully preserved interiors: ceilings as high as 22 feet, crystal chandeliers, hand-painted murals, Italianate marble mantels and fireplaces, pine floors, spiraling staircases, mahogany window and door frames, handmade windowpanes, and beautiful carved moldings. The histories of only a few of the more unusual houses in the district are known; those few houses in this four-block area are highlighted below.

Turn left on Second Street and walk to the **Schlesinger House** (1427 Second St.). This home is a classic example of the Greek Revival style popular in the 1850s when this mansion was built. The lovely ironwork on the front gallery was added in the 1930s.

Continue down Second Street and turn right onto Prytania Street, and walk one block down to the **Toby-Westfeldt House** (2340 Prytania St.). This unpretentious raised cottage dates back to the 1830s and sits amid a large, plantationlike garden, surrounded by the original white picket fence. Thomas Toby, a Philadelphia businessman, moved to New Orleans and had this house built well above the ground to protect it from flooding. The simple Greek Revival architecture lacks the embellishments that later became popular on homes of that style. This home is thought to be the oldest in the Garden District.

Across Prytania Street, on the opposite corner, is **Louise S. McGehee School for Girls** (2343 Prytania St.), built in 1872, 40 years later than the Toby House. Originally a private residence, it has been home to a private girls' school since 1929. The building is in a style called Renaissance Revival, and it combines several features: fluted Corinthian columns, classic window design, and a sweeping spiral staircase inside.

③² Walk back up Prytania Street and stop at the **Adams House** (2423 Prytania St.) and admire the unusual curved gallery on its left. Here again the Greek Revival style is evident in the columns and the windows; this house is believed to have been built around 1860.

③³ In the next block, the **Women's Guild of the New Orleans Opera Association House** (2504 Prytania St.) is one of the few houses in the area open to the public, but only for groups of 20 or more with advance reservations. This Greek Revival house, built in 1858, has a distinctive octagonal turret, which was added in the late 19th century. The last private owner, Nettie Seebold, willed the estate to the Women's Guild of the New Orleans Opera upon her death in 1955. *Tel. 504/529–2278. Tours for groups of 20 or more only. Open weekdays 1–4.*

③⁴ Across Prytania Street is the **Brennan House** (2507 Prytania St.), built in 1852, also in Greek Revival style. Notice the Ionic and Corinthian columns that support the broad galleries; inside is a magnificent gold ballroom decorated by a Viennese artist for the original owners.

③⁵ A few doors down is **Our Mother of Perpetual Help Chapel** (2521 Prytania St.), built as a private residence in 1856. Its marble entrance hall is distinctive; also notice the detail in the extravagant cast ironwork on the galleries. The house is now a chapel maintained by the Redemptorist Fathers.

③⁶ Cross Prytania at Third Street and walk up Third Street to the **Robinson House** (1415 Third St.) on the left. Built in the late 1850s, this home is one of the largest and most elegant in the district, styled after an Italian villa with rounded galleries supported by Doric and Corinthian columns. This is believed to be the first house in New Orleans with indoor plumbing.

③⁷ Return to Prytania Street and cross to the other side to the **Briggs-Staub House** (2605 Prytania St.), one of the few Gothic Revival houses in the city. It was built around 1849 and contrasts sharply with its neighbors. Farther down this block,
③⁸ on the same side of the street, is the **Villere-Carr House** (2621 Prytania St.), interesting for its Greek Revival features that include a squared Greek-key doorway and squared window frames. This eclectic mansion was built around 1870.

③⁹ Cross Prytania at the corner of Fourth Street to more closely observe the cast-iron cornstalk fence around **Colonel Short's Villa** (1448 Fourth St.). In addition to the prevalent Greek Revival style and the unusually abundant ironwork of the gallery, the house is known for its iron fence, with its pattern of morning glories intertwining cornstalks. Legend has it that Colonel Short purchased the fence for his wife, who was homesick for Iowa. Another cornstalk fence very much like this one appears in the French Quarter at 915 Royal Street. It is not known if both fences were cast by the same Philadelphia company.

Concluding the Garden District side trip, walk down Fourth Street to St. Charles Avenue to board the streetcar and continue up the avenue. There are many more mansions along the route of the same style and magnitude as those of the Garden District, though most gardens along St. Charles Avenue are not as large.

⓵ Continuing on the streetcar, past the next stop on the right is a beautiful Gothic Revival Episcopalian Church, **Christ Church Cathedral** (2919 St. Charles Ave.), completed in 1887. Note its arched windows and steeply pitched gables, architectural features that were precursors to the Victorian era.

⓶ Look to the left at the intersection of Louisiana Avenue for a huge white mansion, the **Bultman Funeral Home** (3338 St. Charles Ave.), built in 1852. This is considered by many Orleanians to be the most prestigious funeral home in the city.

Several hospitals are located in the few blocks directly past Louisiana Avenue. **St. Charles General Hospital** is on the avenue to the left, and two blocks behind it (but not visible from the streetcar) is **Touro Hospital** and a related medical complex.

⓷ At the next stop on the left is a circular church building called **Unity Temple** (3722 St. Charles Ave.). Designed by a student of Frank Lloyd Wright, it was built in 1960. The harmonious and simplistic design reflects Wright's influence on that period.

⓸ Coming up on the right in the next block is the **Columns Hotel** (3811 St. Charles Ave.), which was built in 1884 as a family home but in recent years has been renovated and operated as a hotel. The interior was used to film the Louis Malle movie *Pretty Baby*, starring a young Brooke Shields. The hotel sports a veranda for sipping cocktails alfresco on the avenue.

⓹ In the next block, on the left is **Rayne Memorial Methodist Church** (3900 St. Charles Ave.), built in 1875 and notable for its Gothic-style gables and arched windows. A few houses down **⓺** from the church on the same side is **Grant House** (3932 St. Charles Ave.), a good example of the Queen Anne style, with a highly decorative porch and balcony balustrades; this house dates back to 1887. Popular architect Thomas Sully built the Grant House and the house in the middle of the next block, **⓻** **Sully House** (4010 St. Charles Ave.), his family home. The gables, towers, and gingerbread look of the Sully House were prized in that era and appear on many other homes in the vicinity.

The next blocks near Napoleon Avenue begin to reflect the large university student population in Uptown New Orleans. The restaurant and night spot **4141 St. Charles,** on the right after the next stop, and **Fat Harry's Bar** (4330 St. Charles Ave.), two blocks up on the left, are popular with the students.

⓼ Between the two bars is the **First Baptist Church** (4301 St. Charles Ave.), built in 1954, though its congregation dates **⓽** back to the early 1800s. On the left is **Touro Synagogue** (4238 St. Charles Ave.), built in 1908 and named for one of the city's great philanthropists, Judah Touro.

The large avenue intersecting at the next stop is **Napoleon Avenue,** the starting point for the many Mardi Gras parades that wind their way down St. Charles Avenue to Canal Street. **Copeland's Restaurant** on the corner to the left is named for its owner, Popeye's Fried Chicken magnate Al Copeland, a New Orleans native whose spicy Cajun cooking has become popular

on a national level. Dominating the opposite corner is the
(49) **Church of the Covenant Presbyterian** (4422 St. Charles Ave.).
The church, built in the early 1900s, reflects a Colonial Revival
style, favoring English houses of two centuries before.

(50) On the right in the next block is the even more spectacular **Sacred Heart Academy** (4521 St. Charles Ave.), one of the most
beautiful sites on the avenue. Built in 1899 by the Sisters of the
Sacred Heart, it has housed their private girls' school since.
Unique aspects of this building include wide, wraparound balconies (or galleries) and colonnades that face a large garden.

(51) **St. George's Episcopal Church** (4600 St. Charles Ave.) is another fine building from 1900; it reflects a Romanesque style with
its softly curved arches. The oldest house on St. Charles Avenue is the **4621 St. Charles House** on the right in this same block.
(52) Its history is not certain, but it is believed to date back to the
1850s. Renovations have since added details that are obviously
not part of the original building.

(53) The **Krower House** (4630 St. Charles Ave.), on the left, is unique
for its partially underground basement, a rare feature in New
Orleans. The basement was probably used to house servants
rather than quartering them in a wing of the house or in separate quarters, as was popular. Coming up on the right is the
largest mansion on St. Charles Avenue and obviously among
(54) the most expensive, the **Brown House** (4717 St. Charles Ave.).
Completed in 1902, it took five years to build at a cost of a quarter of a million dollars. The structure is a choice example of
Romanesque Revival with its solid, monumental look, Syrian
(55) arches, and steep gables. The **Hernandez House** (4803 St.
Charles Ave.), in the next block to the right, illustrates the
Second Empire style, characterized by the mansard roof, relatively rare in New Orleans. This house, originally located back
a half block, had become sadly neglected until the early 1980s
when it was moved to face the avenue and was miraculously restored to the showcase home it is today.

Several houses in the next block are turn-of-the-century buildings, though they artfully re-create an antebellum style. The
(56) **Vaccaro House** (5010 St. Charles Ave.), after the streetcar stop
on the left, dates to the 1910s. The Tudor style, with its steep
gables, Gothic arches, and half timbering was popular when banana magnate Joseph Vaccaro built the home for his family.

(57) In the next block on the right is the **Orleans Club** (5005 St.
Charles Ave.). It was built as a residence in 1868 but in 1925
became the home of one of the city's oldest women's organizations, the Orleans Club, which remains active today. On the left
(58) in the next block is the **Milton H. Latter Memorial Library** (5120
St. Charles Ave.). Occupying a complete city block, this mansion was built in 1907 and donated to the city in 1948; silent-film
star Marguerite Clark married the former owner and lived
there in the 1940s. Today it serves as the most elegant public
library in New Orleans. Its spacious Beaux Arts architecture
and lovely lawns make it a prized site on the avenue (*see* Off the
Beaten Track).

(59) **De la Salle Boys' High School** is ahead on the left. At the streetcar stop is the **Jewish Community Center** (5342 St. Charles
Ave.), one of the most modern buildings in the area, built in
1963 where the Jewish Home for Children once stood. **Benja-**

60 **min House** (5331 St. Charles Ave.), on the right at the next stop, is a stunning building from around 1916, made of limestone, an expensive and unusual building material for New Orleans.

61 In the next block is **McCarthy House** (5603 St. Charles Ave.), a typical Greek Revival home, with ornate columns and flat-
62 topped doors and windows. Watch for **Tara** (5705 St. Charles Ave.), coming up on the same side of the avenue in the next block. Tara, the plantation home used in the film *Gone with the Wind*, was a set, but this house in New Orleans is an exact replica built from the actual plans of the movie set.

63 Look carefully or you will miss the Georgian Colonial Revival style **Wedding Cake House** (5809 St. Charles Ave.), in the next block on the right. Outshining Tara with its portico and decorative balconies, the house's key beauty is the beveled lead glass on its front door, one of the most beautiful entryways in the city.

64 65 As you enter the university district, dominating the next block on the left is the Gothic **St. Charles Avenue Presbyterian Church.** On the same side in the next block is **Castle's House** (6000 St. Charles Ave.), another Georgian Colonial Revival similar to the Wedding Cake House. The **St. Charles Avenue**
66 67 **Christian Church** (6200 St. Charles Ave.), two blocks farther on the left, is 1923 Colonial Revival. On the right is **Temple Sinai** (6227 St. Charles Ave.), the first Reform Congregation in New Orleans. This building dates back to 1928; the annex on the corner was built in 1970.

68 **Loyola University** (6363 St. Charles Ave.), on the right, takes up the next block. The modernistic Gothic-style building on the corner is the new communications building, the **Louis J. Roussel Building.** Lining the horseshoe curve farther down is **Marquette Hall,** directly ahead, with **Thomas Hall** to the right and **Church of the Holy Name of Jesus** on the left. The Jesuits built this complex in 1914 for their university, which today extends for two blocks behind the masterfully constructed Gothic and Tudor edifice. (Loyola University also owns the local CBS-TV station and WWL radio.)

69 Directly beside Loyola is **Tulane University** (6823 St. Charles Ave.), which was founded in 1884. The central building facing St. Charles Avenue is **Gibson Hall,** built in 1894, with the additions of **Tilton Hall** on the left (in 1901) and **Dinwiddie Hall** on the right (in 1936). The Romanesque style, with its massive stone look and arched windows and doors, is repeated in the campus buildings behind these. Modern campus buildings extend another three blocks to the rear. Tulane is sometimes called the "Harvard of the South" and is known for its medical school, law school, and fine library. The **Sophie H. Newcomb College for Women** shares part of the Tulane campus, but has a separate dean and faculty.

70 The streetcar makes three stops in this stretch, but there is so much to see that you must watch carefully. On the left, across the avenue from the two universities, is **Audubon Park,** formerly the plantation of Etienne Boré, the father of the granulated-sugar industry in Louisiana. The World's Industrial and Cotton Centennial Exposition was held here in 1884–85 and brought New Orleans its first international publicity since the Civil

War. (New Orleans hosted another World Exposition a century later in 1984, but on a site nearer the business district.)

Audubon Park is one of the largest and most highly acclaimed metropolitan parks in the United States. Its 340 acres include a world-class zoo, a golf course, swimming pool, miniature train, riding stables, tennis court, and a river view. There are miles of winding lagoons and trails for biking, hiking, and jogging. The park is closed to all vehicles but bicycles. The park was developed as an outgrowth of the 1884 Exposition and was named for the famous naturalist and painter, John James Audubon, who spent many years working in and around New Orleans. The zoo is also named for him, and his statue stands in the park. Exit here for the Audubon Park and Zoo side trip.

Audubon Park and Zoo Side Trip The 340 acres of parkland that lie beyond the entrance to Audubon Park on St. Charles Avenue were once part of a plantation belonging to Etienne de Boré. None of the original buildings are standing; in fact, none of the buildings that housed the 1884–85 World's Industrial and Cotton Centennial Exposition, held on these acres, have survived. The park, however, began its development with the exposition a century ago. In 1914 the Audubon Park Commission was formed, and governs the area to this day.

Internationally known landscape architect Frederick Law Olmsted designed the current layout of the park, which includes a zoo, golf course, wading pool, swimming pool, riding stables, picnic and play areas, tennis courts, and winding paths for biking, hiking, and jogging.

The **Audubon Zoo** did not receive much attention until the late 1970s, when a major fund-raising effort brought about a new and greatly enlarged zoo, using the natural-habitat concept of displaying and breeding animals. Since the 1980s the zoo has taken its place as one of the most outstanding in the country.

As you exit the streetcar, at Walnut Street, and pass through the dramatic columned entrance to Audubon Park, the Audubon Zoo lies directly ahead, about 12 city blocks in the distance. You can walk there by taking the macadam path to the right across the park (approximately a 25-minute walk), or you can walk to your left along a lagoon for a more picturesque stroll and then return to the St. Charles Avenue entrance to catch the free shuttle van to the zoo, which operates every 15 minutes daily 9:30–5.

Walkers can also continue along the route to the left, across the park to the zoo; although scenic, this is a considerably longer walk. The aforementioned, shorter route to the right takes you through the golf course and down Oak Alley, a stretch of aged moss-hung oak trees that form a canopy over the path, one of the most enchanting settings in New Orleans. Emerging from Oak Alley you will cross Magazine Street, a busy thoroughfare; from there signs will direct you to the zoo entrance, another two blocks ahead. *6500 Magazine St., tel. 504/861–2537. Admission: $5.50 adults, $2.75 children 2–12. Mon.–Fri. 9:30–5, weekends 9:30–6.*

Once inside the zoo you may wish to wander for several hours. Of special interest are the seasonal exhibits, the Louisiana Swamp, the flamingo pond, the sea lions, and the white tiger.

Directions are clearly marked; there are concession stands and a neat gift shop.

To return to the streetcar on St. Charles Avenue, board the free shuttle van outside the zoo. To go directly back downtown, the Magazine Street bus passes the zoo entrance regularly and goes to Canal Street. You can also take a boat to Canal Street, as explained below.

Audubon Park includes a long stretch of land behind the zoo, on the levee overlooking the Mississippi River. If time permits, you may want to take the road to the left as you exit the zoo, cross the railroad tracks, and stroll along **Riverview Drive.** The river lookout includes **Audubon Landing,** where the **Cotton Blossom** cruise boat docks. *Tel. 504/586–8777. Cost (one way): $5.25 adults, $3.25 children 3–11. Cruises leave daily 2:15 PM and 5 PM for the 7-mi river ride to the French Quarter and Canal St. Refreshments are sold on board.*

71 The heavy stone archway on the right just after Tulane University is the entrance to **Audubon Place,** referred to locally as Millionaire's Row. A security guard checks people entering the two-block-long private drive that boasts some of the most ele-
72 gant mansions in the city. **Zemurray House** (No. 2 Audubon Place), the columned white mansion facing the archway, is the stately home of the president of Tulane University. It was built in 1907 by Sam Zemurray, president of the United Fruit Company. If you glance quickly to the left of the avenue here, you will catch the splendid beveled lead-glass door and transom of the **Parkview Guest House.**

73 On that same side at the next stop is **St. Charles Avenue Baptist Church** (7100 St. Charles Ave.). It was constructed in 1926, but the establishment of the congregation dates back to the late 1800s. The intersection at the next stop is Broadway, with a row of fraternity houses a few blocks down on the right. Notice
74 the miniature house in the corner yard on the right. The **Doll House** (7209 St. Charles Ave.), designed in the same Tudor style as the main house beside it for the daughter of a former owner, it is the smallest house in New Orleans to have its own postal address.

75 To the left you can see a collection of buildings, the Italianate, main one being the former center of **St. Mary's Dominican College for Women** (7214 St. Charles Ave.). This building was the main house of the Dominican Sisters who operated the Dominican School for Girls from around 1864. The college opened in 1910, but was forced to close a few years ago and has since been bought by Loyola University to house its law school. The Dominican Sisters still maintain several buildings on the campus.

St. Charles Avenue continues for two more stops until it turns just short of the levee. Some of the houses in this stretch, originally part of the small town of Carrollton, are more modest structures. Especially interesting are two houses on the left,
76 called the **Camelback Houses** (7628-30 and 7632-34 St. Charles Ave.) and built in the late 1800s. A house in those days was taxed by the width and height of its facade; working-class homes were usually narrow and long. Sometimes a second floor was added to the back half of the house, giving it the architectural designation of "camelback." The camelback and the gingerbread-type decoration on porches were very popular fea-

tures in the 1800s; another house in much the same style (but minus a camelback) is the **Victorian Cottage** (7922 St. Charles Ave.), on the left another three blocks up. This style is also known as a "shotgun" house (*see* the Algiers Point Side Trip).

As the streetcar makes the bend in the following block, St. Charles turns into Carrollton Avenue. To the left in the distance is the grassy knoll of the **levee,** a man-made earthen wall built for flood protection and to keep the Mississippi River flowing in its original course. Around the turn is an area filled with shops and restaurants, called **Riverbend.** The tour ends at the next stop, so prepare to leave the streetcar, unless you wish to stay aboard another 10 minutes to ride to the end of the line.

As you exit, the large, white columned building on the right is **Benjamin Franklin High School** (719 S. Carrollton Ave.). This college-prep public high school, thought to be one of the best in the country, is in the process of moving to a new facility on the University of New Orleans lakefront campus. The future of this stately building, which once housed the city hall for the town of Carrollton and later the Jefferson Parish Court House, is uncertain.

Time Out One of the city's first and favorite fast-food establishments is the **Camellia Grill,** a columned building a block back toward St. Charles Avenue. The service here is renowned and the food highly recommended. *626 S. Carrollton Ave., tel. 504/866–9573. No credit cards.*

Bayou St. John–Lakefront Car Route

The following car route, will occupy at least half a day. Numbers in the margins correspond with numbered points of interest on the Bayou St. John–Lakefront Car Route map.

Begin on **Canal Street,** the main avenue of downtown New Orleans that connects the Mississippi River with Lake Pontchartrain. Take a right at S. Jefferson Davis Parkway, approximately three miles from where Canal Street begins at the river. Follow Jefferson Davis four blocks and over the railroad tracks. Directly ahead on the left begins an inlet of water called **Bayou St. John,** which leads into Lake Pontchartrain about five miles out. This is the only remaining bayou in New Orleans.

Take a left immediately after the railroad tracks and just before the end of the bayou; turn right after a half block to follow the bayou to Moss Street. Pass the traffic light at the Orleans Avenue Bridge and continue for one more long block to the Dumaine Street Bridge; take a right, cross over the bridge, and turn left at the end onto Moss Street. Bayou St. John will now be on your left.

The first stop is the **Pitot House** (1440 Moss St.). This is one of the few surviving houses that lined the bayou in the late 1700s. It was bought by James Pitot in 1810 and used as a country home for his family; Pitot built one of the first cotton presses in New Orleans and served as the city's mayor from 1804 to 1805, and later as parish court judge. The Pitot House was restored and moved to its current location in the 1960s to mark the 1708 site of the first French settlement in the New Orleans area. The house is noteworthy for its stucco-covered brick-between-post construction. The galleries across the front and right side are typical of the West Indies style brought to Louisiana by early planters. Inside, the house is furnished with American antiques of the early 1800s. *1440 Moss St., tel. 504/482–0312. Admission: $3 adults, $1 children under 12. Open Wed–Sat. 10–3.*

Leaving Pitot House, follow Moss Street for another few blocks as it curves with the bayou until it intersects with Esplanade Avenue. Turn left and cross the Esplanade Avenue Bridge; **City Park** lies directly ahead. Go halfway around the **statue of General P.G.T. Beauregard,** Civil War hero mounted on his horse, and enter City Park, once the sugar plantation of Louis

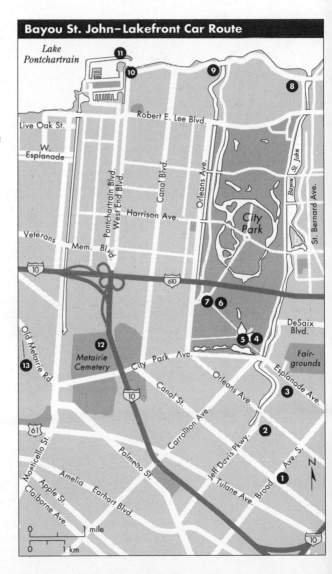

Allard in the late 1700s. The 1,500 acres make City Park one of the largest in the country and include an art museum, winding lagoons, a golf course, tennis courts, a children's entertainment park, a botanical garden, two sports stadiums, and lots of picturesque picnic and hiking areas. The man-made lagoons are home to a variety of wild geese, ducks, and swans; among the ancient moss-draped oaks is a proliferation of local flowers and fauna.

5 As you enter the park the **New Orleans Museum of Art** comes into view directly ahead on Lelong Avenue. This nationally recognized museum has a large permanent collection that specializes in pre-Columbian, African, and local art, with representation from the European and American masters as well. The museum has gained considerable attention in recent years via international traveling exhibitions including "The Treasures of Tutankhaman" and "Peru's Golden Treasures." *City Park, tel. 504/488–2631. Admission: $3 adults, $1.50 senior citizens and children 3–17; free Thurs. Open Tues.–Sun. 10–5.*

After touring the museum, drive around the half circle behind the museum to the right and over the bridge. Directly after the **6** bridge turn left onto Victory Avenue; the **Botanical Garden** is on the right, with a lovely conservatory, a parterre garden, and rose, herb, and vegetable gardens decorated with sculptures by local artist Enrique Alferez. *City Park, tel. 504/483–9385. Admission: $1.50. Open weekends 10–5, according to season.*

7 Past the gardens is **Storyland,** a whimsical and entertaining theme park for children featuring fairy-tale characters. Right next door is the exquisitely refurbished **Last Carousel,** replete with authentic wooden horses, giraffes, zebras, and other exotic creatures. The spectacular carousel and grounds cost $1.5 million to renovate (each horse was shipped to Connecticut for expert restoration). *City Park, tel. 504/483–9381. Admission: $1.50 Storyland, 50 cents carousel. Open Tues–Sun 10–5, according to season.*

As you drive away from Storyland, on the left are tennis courts. Make a left at the end of the courts, and left again onto Dreyfous Avenue. The peristyle on the right, with its tall columns and cement lions overlooking the lagoon, is a favorite spot for picnics and parties. Farther along this avenue is the **Casino,** a concession stand with rest-room facilities and a large playground for small children. In the lagoon beyond paddleboats ply the water; they can be rented for $6.50 an hour at the Casino. Bicycles are also available from the same rental office for $5 an hour.

Cross the narrow bridge, keeping to the left; the two large gnarled oaks on the left in the curve are known as the **Dueling Oaks** from the frequent duels held under them in the late 1700s to early 1800s. Follow the road to the right, past the museum, and back to the front of the park where you entered. Notice the Art Deco lines of the benches along the avenue as you leave; these same lines are prevalent in the cement work throughout City Park, a remnant of the 1930s refurbishment during the Works Progress Administration. There are many illustrations of this style in the fountains, bridges, ironwork, and statues of the park.

Take a left halfway around the Beauregard statue onto Wisner Boulevard, along Bayou St. John (now to your right). To the left is the City Park golf course, and farther out, Pan-American Stadium, where soccer games are played on weekends. Continue on Wisner Boulevard for another 3½ miles to the lakefront. City Park will be on the left most of the way. At Harrison Avenue look to the right for **Park Island,** with its beautiful modern homes and gardens facing the bayou. Farther up on the left is the driving range for the City Park golf club, then John F. Kennedy High School, and the U.S. Department of Agriculture Southern Regional Research Laboratory. Cross Robert E. Lee Boulevard, go straight a few blocks until the road bears to the right and around to the right again. The lake—not yet visible from behind the levee—is on the right. Keep right on **Lakeshore Drive** along **Lake Pontchartrain,** for about 2 miles.

The sight of the lake is impressive; it measures 24 miles across and stretches as far as the eye can see. **The University of New Orleans Lakefront Arena,** a new sports and entertainment facility, and **Lakefront Airport** (for small aircraft) are to the right, but not visible from here. To the left, farther out, is the marina, and beyond that the suburb of Metairie.

The seawall (the cement steps bordering the lake) is a 5½-mile levee and seawall protection system, built in the 1940s by the U.S. Army Corps of Engineers. Occupied by Army and Navy installations during and after World War II, the land was turned into private residential districts in the 1950s; the large modern homes in the subdivisions behind the levee were built around that time. Lakefront real estate is among the most expensive in the city.

Along Lakeshore Drive you can see many park and picnic areas that are generally filled on warm weekends and holidays. This is also a popular spot for fishing and boating. Swimming is not advisable; the lake is heavily polluted. There are many parking bays along Lakeshore Drive; you may want to stop here for a walk around the lake. Open to the public from 8 AM to 10 PM daily, the lakefront recreational area is relatively safe because of frequent police patrol.

Along Lakeshore Drive you will notice several shelters with rest-room facilities and telephones. Soon after passing Marconi Drive, on the left are the **Mardi Gras Fountains.** These circular, 60-foot fountains rise and fall in varying heights with changing Mardi Gras colors—gold, purple, and green. (Don't be surprised if the fountains are out of order; their upkeep is expensive and they have been dry for months at a time between repairs.) Worth the walk from the parking area to the fountains is a series of ceramic tiles bearing the names, symbols, and colors of the different Mardi Gras krewes (clubs). The fountains and plaques were installed in 1962.

Coming to the end of Lakeshore Drive (about three miles from where you began) is a **lighthouse** on land that juts out into the harbor, where sailboats move through the **Orleans Marina.**

To get a better view of the yacht harbor and marina, follow Lakeshore Drive as it turns left into West End Boulevard, past **Bart's,** a popular restaurant and night spot, and on for another third of a mile to Lake Marina Avenue, the first street to the right. This avenue winds around a row of boat houses and becomes Breakwater Drive. Take the very first right and make a long, horseshoe curve around **West End Park,** which is actually a very wide median. Enter the Orleans Marina parking lot to the right, almost at the end of the horseshoe curve. When you walk down the pier of the marina, the **Southern Yacht Club** will be to the right. This is one of the most refreshing scenes in New Orleans, far from downtown, with soft breezes blowing, gulls calling, and the rhythmic patter of sailboat cables slapping the masts.

As you leave the marina and turn left back onto Breakwater Drive, a collection of restaurants and night spots surrounds the parking lot to the right. These seafood restaurants cater not only to the marina, but to New Orleanians from all areas of the city.

To return downtown, continue on Breakwater Drive to West End Boulevard, take a right, and at the first traffic light turn right again, then circle to the left onto Pontchartrain Boulevard. A large civil defense air-raid shelter is on the left, partially underground. The boulevard eventually becomes Pontchartrain Expressway, part of I-10.

About a mile down the expressway, prepare to take the first exit at the "Metairie Road–City Park" sign. Metairie Road **(12)** runs along the expressway; on the right is **Metairie Cemetery,** which you can drive through to observe a variety of lavish aboveground tombs and vaults. To reach the cemetery, continue to Metairie Road at the traffic light, turn left under the overpass, and left again to drive along the other side of the expressway. A sign will direct you where to turn to enter the cemetery. If you are interested in a particular tomb or aspect of the cemetery, personnel in the office, in the back to the right, will be glad to assist.

Leaving Metairie Cemetery, return on the feeder road beside the expressway, turning right at the traffic light onto Metairie Road. On the left is the **New Orleans Country Club.** Turn left **(13)** at the sign for **Longvue House and Gardens** on Bamboo Road; this city estate, fashioned after the great country houses of England, is surrounded by eight acres of beautiful gardens embellished with fountains. The Greek Revival mansion is decorated with its original furnishings of English and American antiques, and priceless tapestries, modern art, porcelain and pottery. The gardens have various themes and the formal Spanish court is modeled after a 14th-century Spanish garden. Longvue was once the private residence of Edith and Edgar Stern, two great New Orleans philanthropists. Since their deaths the house and gardens have been open to the public for guided tours. Carefully preserved, this estate provides an educational experience in horticulture, art, and history. *7 Bamboo Road, tel. 504/488–5488. Admission: $5 adults, $3 children. Open Tues.–Fri. 10– 4:30, weekends 1–5. Last house tour begins 45 min. before closing.*

After the tour of Longvue, return to Metairie Road, turn right, and go under the expressway overpass. At the next traffic light turn right onto Canal Street, which will take you downtown and to the French Quarter.

Historical Buildings and Sites

New Orleans's major sites and attractions have already been described in the preceding tours. If you have more time for exploring, here are some other interesting stops.

Chalmette National Cemetery is the final resting place for hundreds of Louisiana soldiers from various wars since 1864. Visitors are free to drive through and view the war monument. *Rte. 42, 6 mi from downtown New Orleans, tel. 504/589–4428. Admission: free. Open daily 8–5.*

Chalmette National Historic Park includes the site of the Battle of New Orleans, fought in 1815 by the United States under Andrew Jackson against the British under Gen. Sir Edward Packenham. The **Beauregard Plantation House,** constructed in 1840, serves as a visitor's center, with historical exhibits, a diorama, and films about the battle. *Rte. 42, 6 mi from downtown New Orleans, tel. 504/589–4428. Admission is free. Open daily 8–5.*

Both the Chalmette National Cemetery and the Chalmette National Historic Park are operated by the Jean Lafitte National Park of the National Park Service. Park headquarters are in the Chalmette National Cemetery.

Margaret statue (at the intersection of Camp and Prytania Sts.) depicts Margaret Gaffney Haughery, who during the mid-1800s gave bread and milk from her dairy and bakery to feed the destitute of the city. Erected in 1884, hers was the first statue of a woman erected in the United States. The large Margaret Park surrounding the statue was reduced to a small triangle when an expressway exit ramp was cut through the area.

Martin Luther King, Jr. statue (on the median of Claiborne Ave., at the intersection of Martin Luther King, Jr. Blvd.) stands at the boulevard named for the famous civil rights leader who often visited New Orleans. The bust of King rests on a pillar engraved with excerpts of his "I have a dream" speech; it is also the site of an annual rally and wreath-laying ceremony on the Martin Luther King, Jr. national holiday.

Molly Marine statue (Canal St. and Elks Pl. Park) is the only statue to honor women in the U.S. military. It was sculpted by Enrique Alferez and was installed in 1943.

Rivertown, USA (located at the end of Williams Blvd.) is the historical district of Kenner, a town that has become part of the greater New Orleans area because of its proximity to the New Orleans (Moisant) International Airport. Turn-of-the-century buildings have been refurbished, commercial residences and business properties have been renovated, public areas landscaped, and an area of quaint shops, antique stores, art galleries, museums, and a community theater has been developed. There's a beautiful overview of the Mississippi River at Lasalle's Landing.

Steamboat Houses (at the end of Egania St. off St. Claude Ave.) are two identical houses built in 1904 and 1909 by the husband and wife river captains the Doullouts. One house was for them, the other for their son. The houses look like steamboats, with authentic wooden decorations, and are situated to allow a view of boats passing on the river. They are privately owned and closed to the public, and can be seen only from a car or tour bus. The neighborhood around them is not considered safe, and precaution should be taken.

What follows is a list of historical sites that have already been described. For further information see the specific tours in this chapter, noted below in parentheses.

Desire Streetcar (Outer French Quarter)
French Market (Inner French Quarter)
Gallier Hall (St. Charles Avenue Streetcar Tour)
Jackson Square (Inner French Quarter)
Julia Row (St. Charles Avenue Streetcar Tour)
Lafitte's Blacksmith Shop (Outer French Quarter)
Latrobe House (Outer French Quarter)
Le Petit Théâtre (Inner French Quarter)
Liberty Place Monument (Foot of Canal Street)
Madame John's Legacy (Inner French Quarter)
Miltenberger Houses (Inner French Quarter)
Napoleon House (Inner French Quarter)
New Zion Baptist Church (St. Charles Avenue Streetcar Tour)
Old Ursuline Convent (Inner French Quarter)
Piazza d'Italia (Foot of Canal Street)
Pontalba Apartments (Inner French Quarter)
Preservation Hall (Outer French Quarter)
Quadroon Ballroom (Inner French Quarter)
St. Charles Streetcar (St. Charles Avenue Streetcar Tour)
St. Louis Cathedral (Inner French Quarter)
St. Louis Cemetery (Outer French Quarter)
Spanish Plaza (Foot of Canal Street)
Spring Fiesta Historic Townhouse (Outer French Quarter)

Museums, Galleries, and Collections

New Orleans is a city rich in tradition. A number of historic houses have been restored with their original furnishings and are open to the public; there are also many museums and collections that cater to browsing visitors and professional researchers. (A number of the city's major museums, galleries, and collections have already been described in the preceding tours.)

Amistad Research Center is an important archive of primary source materials on the history of America's ethnic minorities, race relations, and the civil rights movement. It is the only such archive in the Deep South and the largest collection of primary documents on Afro-Americans in the United States. *Housed at Tulane University, Tilton Hall, tel. 504/865–5535. Admission free. Open Mon.–Sat. 8:30–5:30.*
Contemporary Arts Center features works by local artists and traveling special exhibits. The center also hosts concerts, films, theatrical and dance performances, and art-related workshops and seminars. *900 Camp St., tel. 504/523–1216. Admission varies with event. Open Tues.–Sun. noon–5.*
Ducros Museum is one of the earliest Creole cottages in St. Bernard Parish, south of New Orleans. Built around 1800, it contains parish artifacts and a library. *Rte. 39, near the Violet*

Canal, tel. 504/277-6317. Admission free. Open weekdays 10–noon and 1–5.

Elms House is a St. Charles Avenue mansion open for tours and receptions. The house, built around 1869, features marble fireplaces, stained-glass windows, and original tapestries. *3029 St. Charles Ave., tel. 504/895-5493. Admission: $2. Open by appointment only for group tours of at least 25.*

Fortier Gallery is an art gallery featuring the work of regional artists. The historic French Quarter house, built in 1803, was used in the TV series *Longstreet* as the home of detective James Longstreet. The house is open for tours by appointment only. *835 Chartres St., tel. 504/523-6791. Admission to gallery free; house tour: $2.50. Open Oct.–June, Tues.–Sat. 11–5.*

The Germaine Wells Mardi Gras Museum, a private family collection owned by Germaine Wells and her parents, exhibits mannequins dressed in the many gowns and costumes worn by Wells and her family, as kings and queens of various Mardi Gras krewes from about 1910 to 1960. Located on the second floor of *Arnaud's Restaurant, 813 Bienville St. (enter through restaurant), tel. 504/523-5433. Admission free. Open Sun.–Fri. 11:30–10:30, Sat. 3–10:30.*

Kenner Historical Museum is part of the Rivertown development in a New Orleans suburb near the International Airport. The museum includes a collection of Presidential papers, photos and local artifacts, and a Black History Room. *1922 Third St., Kenner, tel. 504/469-7459. Admission: $1 adults, 50 cents children. Open daily 9–5.*

The Louisiana National Guard Museum is an outdoor display of aircraft and tanks used by Louisiana's Air National Guard and Army National Guard. *Jackson Barracks, St. Claude Ave. at the Orleans Parish line, tel. 504/278-6472. Admission free. Open weekdays 9–5.*

The Louisiana Nature and Science Center is an 86-acre wilderness park dedicated to preserving what little is left of the natural environs that once surrounded the city. The center's main building contains exhibitions on south Louisiana flora and wildlife, a media center, lecture hall, and gift shop. The center offers guided nature walks through woodland trails, bird-watching classes, canoe trips through swamplands, craft workshops, and field trips. A planetarium offers shows at 2, 3, and 4 PM weekends. *11000 Lake Forest Blvd., in New Orleans East, tel. 504/246-9381. Admission: $3 adults, $2 senior citizens, $1 children over 4, $7 per family. Separate admission to planetarium shows. Open Tues.–Fri. 9–5, weekends noon–5.*

The Louisiana Railroad Museum depicts railroad history through a display of photos, model trains, films, and slide shows. It also features 4-4-0 10"-gauge steam locomotives. Children will love the hands-on displays. *519 Williams Blvd., Kenner, tel. 504/468-7223. Admission: $1 adults, 50 cents children under 12. Open Wed.–Sun. 10–6.*

The Louisiana Wildlife and Fisheries Museum is part of the Rivertown complex in the suburb of Kenner. The exhibit displays 700 species of animals, some in their natural habitat, and has a large public aquarium. *303 Williams Blvd., tel. 504/468-7232. Admission: $1 adults, 50 cents children under 12. Open Tues.–Sat. 9–5, Sun 1–5.*

The Middle American Research Institute has exhibits of pre-

Columbian and Central and South American culture. Established in 1924, the institute has an extensive collection of pre-Columbian Mayan artifacts and the largest collection of Guatemalan textiles in the nation, as well as a large library on Central America. *Tulane University, 4th fl., Dinwiddie Hall, tel. 504/ 865–5110. Admission free. Open weekdays 8:30–5.*

Sun Oak House is a beautifully restored Creole cottage in the Faubourg Marigny section outside the French Quarter. The cottage is furnished with fine French, Creole, and Acadian antiques and has landscaped subtropical gardens. *2020 Burgundy St., tel. 504/945–0322. Admission: $5, by appointment only.*

The Ursuline Museum is a collection of memorabilia and documents tracing the history of the Ursuline nuns from France to New Orleans in 1727. *2635 State St., tel. 504/866–1472. Admission free, by appointment only.*

American-Italian Museum and Library (Foot of Canal Street)
Beauregard-Keyes House (Inner French Quarter)
Blaine Kern's Mardi Gras World (Algiers Point Side Trip)
Confederate Museum (St. Charles Avenue Streetcar Tour)
Folklife and Visitor Center (Inner French Quarter)
Gallier House (Inner French Quarter)
Hermann-Grima House (Outer French Quarter)
Historic New Orleans Collection (Inner French Quarter)
K&B Plaza of Sculpture (St. Charles Avenue Streetcar Tour)
Longvue House and Gardens (Bayou St. John Car Route)
Louisiana Children's Museum (Foot of Canal Street)
Louisiana State Museum Complex: Cabildo (Inner French Quarter); Presbytere (Inner French Quarter); 1850s House (Inner French Quarter); Old Mint (Outer French Quarter)
Mardi Gras Museum (Outer French Quarter)
Musée Conti Wax Museum (Outer French Quarter)
New Orleans Historic Voodoo Museum (Outer French Quarter)
New Orleans Jazz Collection (Outer French Quarter)
New Orleans Museum of Art (Bayou St. John Car Route)
New Orleans Pharmacy Museum (Inner French Quarter)
Pitot House (Bayou St. John Car Route)
Preservation Resource Center (St. Charles Avenue Streetcar Tour)
Ripley's Believe It or Not Museum (Outer French Quarter)
Women's Guild of the New Orleans Opera Association House (St. Charles Avenue Streetcar Tour)

Parks, Zoos, and Gardens

New Orleans is fortunate to have a warm climate and lots of green, open spaces for outdoor activities. There are two large public parks within the city, a nationally acclaimed zoo, and a national park, plus several state parks surrounding the city. Some of these have already been discussed in the tours in the Exploring Chapter.

Jean Lafitte National Historical Park is one of the newer parks in the national park system and celebrates the diversity of the Delta region. The park has three major units: the **French Quarter, Chalmette,** and **Barataria.** The French Quarter unit, headquartered at the Old French Market, introduces visitors to New Orleans and the cultural traditions of the region through a Folklife and Visitor Center and a variety of free guided tours of the area. The Chalmette unit preserves the battlefield where in 1815 the American forces turned back the British advance on New Orleans. The Barataria unit preserves an area of rich and beautiful coastal wetlands. The park is also a study center, researching the history of the region and documenting the culture of the many ethnic groups that have contributed to the special flavor of the Delta. *National Park Service, U.S. Dept. of the Interior, Superintendent's Office, 423 Canal St., tel. 504/589–3882. Admission to all functions of the park is free.*

Louisiana State Parks is a system of 40 state parks and state commemorative areas throughout Louisiana. Those within quick driving distance from New Orleans are the **St. Bernard State Park** in Violet, 18 miles southeast of New Orleans; **Bayou Segnette State Park** in Westwego, across the Huey P. Long Bridge; and **Fontainebleau State Park** southeast of Mandeville across Lake Pontchartrain on U.S. 190. All three parks feature camping and picnic areas as well as nature trails, fishing, and general sightseeing. Some also offer cabins and meeting facilities. *Dept. of Culture, Recreation and Tourism, Baton Rouge, tel. 504/925–3830. Brochures on various parks available at visitor's center in New Orleans.*

What follows are parks, zoos, and gardens that have already been described. For further information see specific tours in this chapter, noted below in parentheses.

Armstrong Park (Outer French Quarter)
Audubon Park (St. Charles Avenue Streetcar Tour)
Audubon Zoo (St. Charles Avenue Streetcar Tour)
City Park (Bayou St. John Car Route)
Longvue House and Gardens (Bayou St. John Car Route)
New Orleans Lakefront (Bayou St. John Car Route)
Riverwalk (Foot of Canal Street)

New Orleans for Free

Billed as the "greatest free show on earth," Mardi Gras must head any list of freebies in New Orleans. But while Mardi Gras comes only once a year, there are many year-round activities and seasonal events that charge no admission and are easily accessible to visitor and resident alike. With its mild, sunny climate and its location between a river and a lake, New Orleans is a city of outdoor attractions, appealing to both adults and children.

Mardi Gras The day before Lent, in February or early March, is New Orleans's world-famous Mardi Gras. During the week and weekend before Fat Tuesday (Mardi Gras day), certain streets are filled with long, winding parades of magnificent floats, marching bands, and entertainers. Schedules for parades are printed in the daily newspaper. Revelers riding two- and three-story floats toss plastic bead necklaces, silver-dollar-size coins called doubloons, and a variety of plastic toys and cups. Those lining the parade route push, shove, and holler "Throw me something, Mister!" as they try to catch a small memento.

If you miss the real thing, there are several museums in the city that give you a sample of what Mardi Gras is like. Both the **Mardi Gras Museum** (*see* Outer French Quarter Tour in Exploring) and **Blaine Kern's Mardi Gras World** (*see* Algiers Point Side Trip in Exploring) charge admission, but the **Germaine Wells Mardi Gras Museum** (*see* Museums in Exploring) is free. **Accent Annex Enterprises** (1120 S. Jefferson Davis Pkwy., tel. 504/821-8999) sells items used by Mardi Gras revelers and is a good place to catch the spirit of the season.

Walking Tours of the French Quarter The Quarter is part of the Jean Lafitte National Park, and park rangers conduct free tours of the Quarter daily at 10:30, 11:30, 1, and 3. No reservations are required; just check in at the Visitor Center (916 S. Peters St.) in the French Market. Tours last about 90 minutes. The park service also offers free tours of other parts of the city.

French Quarter Street Performers The entire French Quarter is a living museum filled with sights, sounds, and scents to delight and entertain. During the day, performers of all varieties can be found on the streets around Jackson Square. Clowns, jugglers, mimes, tap dancers, break dancers, and all sorts of musicians perform solo or in groups; some perform well into the night, depending upon the reception of the crowds. An open instrument case or upside-down hat is usually provided to receive tips from appreciative passersby.

There are free outdoor concerts throughout the year in Jackson Square. Check the daily newspaper for listings. And since many jazz clubs along Bourbon Street leave their doors open when weather permits, it is often possible to linger near a club door and catch excellent performers.

Art Shows Browsers are welcome to the daily art exhibits around Jackson Square and along the street in back of St. Louis Cathedral. Portrait artists will sketch your likeness for $15 to $25. These artists are also usually talkative, friendly people who can answer your questions about the French Quarter and the city. Near the square are numerous art and poster galleries whose doors are always open to visitors. Other galleries, accessible by bus or taxi, are clustered along Julia Street in the Central Business District and farther uptown on Magazine Street.

K&B Plaza, Virlane Foundation The Virlane Foundation is a private organization dedicated to developing public interest in the arts, with an emphasis on contemporary sculpture. The idea of the sculpture plaza, which surrounds the corporate headquarters, was conceived in August 1973 when K&B's organization (K&B stands for Katz and Besthoff, the name of a locally owned drugstore chain) purchased the building. The collection is considered to be the most important assemblage of sculpture in New Orleans. To fully enjoy this stunning collection, you will want to explore the building's lobby where, among other works, you can see the amazing life-like sculpture created by hyper-realist Duane Hanson. The foundation's diverse art collection contains the works of such notables as Renoir, Boccioni, and Calder, to name a few. *Lee Circle, 1055 St. Charles Ave., tel. 504/586-1234. Plaza open 24 hrs. daily; lobby open Mon.-Fri. 8-5.*

Walk Along the River The mighty Mississippi River is at its mightiest in the curving stretch that gives New Orleans its second name, the Crescent

City. River-watching is a favorite local pastime. If you are lucky, the calliope will sound as steamboats ready their engines to leave the dock. **Moon Walk** (*see* Inner Quarter Tour) is a well-landscaped promenade facing the river in front of Jackson Square. There are benches where you can sit and enjoy the activity of ships, tugboats, and cruise paddlewheelers on the river.

Another good place to watch the river is along **Riverwalk** (*see* Foot of Canal Street Tour). Seats are provided along the promenade at the river, and a series of markers tell the history and lore of the river.

The French Market   A good place for browsing in the French Quarter is the French Market (*see* Inner Quarter Tour and Outer Quarter Tour). The restoration of this centuries-old marketplace includes specialty shops, restaurants, open-air cafes, a farmer's market of fresh local vegetables, and a flea market open on weekends. The market stays open late at night, the farmer's market is open 24 hours, and day or night the area is bustling with activity.

Stroll Along Lake   The Mississippi is not New Orleans's only water attraction;
Pontchartrain   the very large Lake Pontchartrain (*see* Bayou St. John Tour) has miles of seawall where you can relax along the cool lakefront, and lots of walking and picnic areas. Fishing, swimming, and boating on the lake are favorite local sports enjoyed.

Lark in the Park   Two major city parks offer a variety of free outdoor activities for people of all ages. **City Park** (*see* Bayou St. John Tour) and **Audubon Park** (*see* Streetcar Tour) are both accessible by public transportation and have beautiful old oak trees draped with Spanish moss, delicate gazebos, lagoons, and lots of space for hiking, jogging, and picnicking.

New Orleans   This nationally recognized art museum is free to the public
Museum of Art   Thursdays (*see* Bayou St. John Tour). After browsing through the exhibits, try to spend some time in the surrounding City Park.

What to See and Do with Children

Don't be reluctant to bring the children to New Orleans. Daytime activities are plentiful, and for those evenings when parents want to be out on the town, most of the city's major hotels offer baby-sitting services. The pleasures of New Orleans generally appeal to adults and children alike; however, there are a number of things to see and do that are especially recommended for children.

French Quarter Rentals. Baby strollers and bicycles with child carriers can be rented here, and are a good way to see the Quarter and surrounding areas with small children. Check the Sports and Fitness section for bike trails. *931 St. Louis St., tel. 504/524–8231. Rentals $10 first day, $5 per day thereafter per vehicle. Open daily 9–5.*
Past Finders is a workbook of things for children to do in the French Quarter. Each page asks the child to look for some special point of interest, describe it, draw it, or answer questions about it. Children who complete the approximately 30 activi-

ties are given instructions on how to contact the authors and receive a certificate stating that they are certified "past finders." Available at the Cabildo Book Shop or from the authors at *La Latania Press, Box 50464, 70150, tel. 504/288–5430 or 504/888–3798.*

Pontalba Historical Puppetorium. This puppet shop has 12 settings depicting various aspects of New Orleans history. Performances are given only for groups of 20 or more, with advance notice. *514 St. Peter St., on Jackson Sq., tel. 504/ 522–0344. Admission: $2 adults, $1 children. Open daily 10–6.*

The following children's activities have been discussed in the Exploring chapter:

Audubon Park (St. Charles Avenue Streetcar Tour)
Audubon Zoo (St. Charles Avenue Streetcar Tour)
Blaine Kern's Mardi Gras World (Algiers Point Side Trip)
Café du Monde (Inner French Quarter)
Canal Street Ferry (Foot of Canal Street)
City Park (Bayou St. John Car Route)
Germaine Wells Mardi Gras Museum (*see* Museums, Galleries, and Collections)
Louisiana Children's Museum (Foot of Canal Street Side Trip)
Louisiana Nature and Science Center (*see* Museums, Galleries, and Collections)
Mardi Gras Museum (Outer French Quarter)
Moon Walk (Inner French Quarter)
Musée Conti Wax Museum (Outer French Quarter)
New Orleans Historic Streetcar (St. Charles Avenue Streetcar Tour)
Ripley's Believe it or not Museum (Outer French Quarter)
Riverfront Aquarium (Foot of Canal Street)
Steamboat Ride (*see* Guided Tours)
Storyland (Bayou St. John Car Route)

Off the Beaten Track

Avenue Plaza Hotel Lounge. Recently opened, this lounge is a hideaway at the moment, but we anticipate that discovery of the lounge by the masses will soon change this. Enjoy an intimate conversation in this quiet, dark, romantic room, which is made comfortable with elegant European appointments. *2111 St. Charles Ave., tel. 504/566–1212. Open daily 11 AM–11 PM. AE, DC, MC, V.*

The Café Kafic. This funky, out-of-the-way artists' cafe, with its hip crowd reading *Rolling Stone* magazine or playing chess while listening to local musicians in search of a following, could have been transported from New York's Greenwich Village. The walls of this spacious restaurant act as gallery space for not-so-well-known local artists; the abstract sculptures planted around the place make great conversation pieces. The cafe serves cappuccino, wine, beer, soft drinks, light fare, and unusual desserts such as kosher cheesecake (is that because it's made without crawfish?). Things don't usually get underway here until late Friday and Saturday nights. *1818 Magazine St., tel. 504/525–0247. Open Mon.–Fri. 9 AM–7 PM, Fri. and Sat. 9 AM–1 AM. V, MC.*

Christmas Eve Bonfires. Giant bonfires are lighted on the Mississippi levees in St. James Parish every Christmas Eve. The bonfires, legend says, originally were lit by the early settlers to help Papa Noel (the Cajun Santa Claus) find his way to their new homes. The natives begin gathering wood for these huge pyres on Thanksgiving. *New Orleans Paddlewheels* (tel. 504/529–4567) and *New Orleans Steamboat* (tel. 504/586–8777) run boats up the muddy Mississippi for this blazing festival.

Hansen's Sno-Bliz Sweet Shop. New Orleans's hot, humid summers led to the creation of a local specialty, the snowball, a refreshing, cooling treat. Today the snowball is known by several different names, but the place to go for the best is Hansen's. There's almost always a long line, but it's worth the wait. *4801 Tchoupitoulas St., tel. 504/891–9788. Closed Oct.–Mar.*

The Milton H. Latter Memorial Library. Gracing its own beautifully landscaped block, this mansion was once the home of silent-screen star Marguerite Clark. It was later purchased by the Latter family and given to the city as a library in memory of their son, who was killed in World War II. Here you can sit a spell and leaf through a copy of Walker Percy's *The Moviegoer* or Anne Rice's *The Vampire Lestat* (two popular novels set in New Orleans), or just relax in a white wicker chair on the library's glass-enclosed porch; this is one of the only mansions on St. Charles Avenue that are open to the public. As you look across glorious St. Charles Avenue you may find yourself remembering Tara and those days gone with the wind. (To return to Tara, you may want to make the walk down St. Charles Avenue to Arabella Street where you can admire the outstanding replica of Margaret Mitchell's fictitious Southern icon, set far from the turmoil of Scarlett O'Hara's home (*see* St. Charles Avenue Streetcar Tour). *5120 St. Charles Ave., tel. 504/899–6021. Open Mon. 10–8, Tues.–Thurs. 10–6, Fri. and Sat. 10–5.*

St. Alphonsus Church and St. Mary's Assumption Church. Not as well known as St. Louis Cathedral, these two Baroque churches in the 2000 block of Constance Street date back to the mid-1800s. Located in the Irish Channel section of New Orleans, St. Alphonsus originally served the English-speaking Irish immigrants, while St. Mary's Assumption served the German-speaking immigrants of the neighborhood. Today St. Alphonsus is closed due to deterioration (notice also that the Baroque bell towers were never completed), but St. Mary's Assumption across the street continues to function as a local parish church. The church, built in the Baroque architecture that was popular among Germans of that day, is well restored and contains some of the largest stained-glass windows in the city. The exterior brickwork is noteworthy and the elaborate works you can see inside the church were crafted in Germany. This church is the final resting place of Father Seelos, currently under consideration for canonization for his services to his parishoners. For a tour of the glorious church contact the rectory. Just be sure to exercise caution when traveling through this less touristed neighborhood; we recommend you go with a group. *St. Mary's Assumption Church, 2030 Constance St., tel. 504/522–6748. Open to the public daily 8:30–4:30.*

Whitney's Seafood. For those who want to indulge in real New Orleans boiled seafood—crabs, crawfish, shrimp—this is the place to go. Crawfish and shrimp are brought to the table in plastic bags (ordered by the pound); Styrofoam containers are provided for the shells. It's messy (please, don't dress up) and delicious. Crabs (sometimes still hot) are served on trays; order a half-dozen or a dozen of these. Wash this succulent seafood down with pitchers of beer (no mixed drinks here). Whitney's menu is limited to the above, but who cares? *4314 Dowman Rd., tel. 504/241–2893. Closed Tues.*

The Witchcraft Shop. This may be one of the strangest stops you make in the city that put voodoo on the U.S. map. The store, the only witchcraft shop in Louisiana, operated by certified witches, offers a large selection of candles, herbs, oils, books, and statues—something for whatever, or whoever, ails you. The owners are members of the religious order of witchcraft and serve as spiritual advisers to their many local customers (New Orleans is not only a romantic town, but a superstitious one as well). This is the place to go to learn much about a little-known religion. *521 St. Philip St., French Quarter, tel. 504/586–0449. Open Mon.–Sat. noon–8 PM. Closed Sun.*

Your Daily Bread. The streetcar stops a block away from this bakery/deli located in the Uptown area of the city. The bread here is absolute heaven; they also pack breakfast baskets and picnic lunches to enjoy in Audubon Park, just four blocks away. *7457 St. Charles Ave., tel. 504/861–GOOD. Open daily 7 AM– 9 PM.*

5 Shopping

Orientation
by Mary Gehman and Nancy Ries

The fun of shopping in New Orleans is in the many regional items available throughout the city, in the smallest shops or the biggest department stores. You can take home some of the flavor of the city: its pralines (pecan candies), seafood (packaged to go), Louisiana rice and red beans, coffee (pure or with chickory), Creole and Cajun spices (cayenne pepper, chili, and garlic), and packaged mixes of local dishes such as jambalaya, gumbo, beignets, and a sweet, red local cocktail called the Hurricane. A variety of cookbooks also share the secrets of preparing distinctive New Orleans dishes.

The color and vibrancy of the city are captured in many art forms. Beautiful posters celebrating Mardi Gras, the Jazz and Heritage Festival, and the Crescent City Classic all are issued each year and quickly become collector's items.

Ceramic or feather masks are popular articles that serve both as masks for Mardi Gras and as attractive wall hangings during the rest of the year. Mardi Gras costumes, beads, and doubloons make wonderful gifts, too.

Posters, photographs, and paintings on canvas and slate capture the more notable scenes in New Orleans. Jewelry, antiques, ceramics, carved wooden toys, kites, jazz umbrellas, and wreaths of dried flowers are often handmade and make lovely gifts and souvenirs.

The sounds of New Orleans are available on tapes and albums in music stores throughout the city. There is a wide spectrum, including old Dixieland jazz, contemporary jazz, swinging Cajun and zydeco, and the hot, sweet wail of rhythm and blues.

All major bookstores carry an impressive selection of books about the city; local history and photography books are especially popular. Good bets are cookbooks, guides to special-interest sightseeing, and books that specialize in local ethnic history. There are a number of small, independently operated bookshops where perseverance can yield some real finds in local literature and lore. Stock in these shops often combines old photographs, posters, and postcards.

There are many clothing shops that offer fabric designs popular in the semitropical heat: Panama hats, lacy lingerie, and the ubiquitous T-shirt and sports clothes. Designer clothes have become more available in recent years with the opening of national stores such as Macy's, Saks Fifth Avenue, and Brooks Brothers. Top fashions and high quality can also be found in the two original New Orleans department stores, D.H. Holmes and Maison Blanche.

The main shopping areas in the city are the French Quarter, with its narrow streets lined with specialty, gift, and antique shops and art galleries; the Central Business District, including Canal Street, which features department stores and clothing and jewelry shops; Magazine Street, known for its antique shops and galleries; and Uptown, with its neighborhood and specialty shops in several fashionable shopping areas.

Shopping guides and suggestions can be found in most of the tourist magazines available in hotel rooms and lobbies. The New Orleans Tourist and Convention Commission office on Jackson Square (St. Ann St. side) also offers pamphlets on shopping.

Store hours are generally 10 AM to 5:30 or 6 PM, with shorter hours—noon to 5 PM—on Sundays. In areas with active nightlife, such as the French Quarter and the shopping malls, many stores stay open until 9 PM.

Sunday is a good shopping day in heavily trafficked areas, though some of the smaller shops and boutiques may not be open. Major credit cards are welcome in most stores, and traveler's and personal checks are often accepted, subject to the store policy. For smaller shops, it is always wise to check ahead on business hours and acceptable forms of payment.

The Central Business District

Canal Street is the anchor for a thriving shopping business located in the heart of Downtown. The local department stores, **D.H. Holmes** (819 Canal St., tel. 504/561–6611) and **Maison Blanche** (901 Canal St., tel. 504/566–1000), are located in the CBD with branches in the suburban shopping centers. Both carry designer labels, such as Liz Claiborne, Chaus, Ralph Lauren, Esprit, and OshKosh, as well as full lines of appliances and home furnishings.

In addition to these stores, there is the fashionable **Canal Place** with Saks Fifth Avenue, Guy Laroche, Gucci, Polo/Ralph Lauren, Brooks Brothers, and Benetton (1 Canal Pl., tel. 504/523–4158). The **New Orleans Centre** (600 Poydras St., tel. 504/568–0000), a new shopping complex located between the Superdome and the Hyatt Regency Hotel, houses Macy's and Lord & Taylor.

Riverwalk (1 Poydras St., tel. 504/522–1555), a Rouse development along the riverfront, features a half-mile-long marketplace with more than 200 nationally known shops, restaurants, and cafes. A shuttle bus takes you there from Canal Street.

Books **Deville Books and Prints** (Riverwalk, tel. 504/595–8916). This locally owned bookstore specializes in New Orleans books and collectibles. A second location is in Jackson Brewery in the French Quarter. The place for local literary memorabilia.

Clothing **Abercrombie & Fitch** (Riverwalk, tel. 504/522–7156). For the best in sportswear and casual clothes.
Banana Republic (Riverwalk, tel. 504/523–6843). The safari clothes and catalogs of this store are famous. Good place to buy casual and travel clothes and sportswear.
Benetton (Canal Pl., tel. 504/524–7656). Juniors delight in this fashionable designer line.
Brooks Brothers (Canal Pl., tel. 504/522–4200). For classic, tailored menswear.
The Gap (Riverwalk, tel. 504/529–4962). *The* place to shop for teenage and young adult fashions.
G.H. Bass (Riverwalk, tel. 504/522–3918). Classic styles in footwear for men and women.
Lord & Taylor (New Orleans Centre, tel. 504/568–0000). Fine designer clothes for men and women.

Macy's (New Orleans Centre, tel. 504/568–0000). New York–based department store with fashions for all ages.

Polo/Ralph Lauren (Canal Pl., tel. 504/561–8299). Fashions for men by the popular designer.

Rubenstein Brothers (102 St. Charles Ave., tel. 504/581–6666). Local, family-owned men's clothier. Carries Yves St. Laurent, Pierre Cardin, and others.

Terry & Juden Co., Ltd. (135 Carondelet St., tel. 504/522–7771). Custom-made shirts; stylish, traditional clothes for men.

Yvonne LaFleur Editions (Riverwalk, tel. 504/522–8222). For custom millinery, silk dresses, and the finest lingerie, Orleanian Yvonne LaFleur's shop is unsurpassed.

Food **D.H. Holmes** (819 Canal St., tel. 504/561–6611). A local institution, this department store has an excellent selection of local foods and delicacies, along with cookware and cookbooks.

Maison Blanche (901 Canal St., tel. 504/566–1000). Another locally owned department store carrying a large selection of New Orleans food specialties and cookbooks.

Riverwalk (1 Poydras St., tel. 504/522–1555). This several-block-long marketplace along the river features many local restaurants and food retailers. Among the best for local products are **Evans Creole Candies,** and **Creole Delicacies.**

Gifts **Rapp's Luggage and Gifts** (604 Canal St., tel. 504/568–1953). Locally owned variety store. Specializes in fine leather goods and unusual gift items.

F.A.O. Schwarz (Canal Pl., tel. 504/525–7092). For every conceivable game or toy, this renowned toy store has just the thing you are looking for.

Rhino (Place St. Charles, 200 St. Charles Ave., tel. 504/582–1173). Local handcrafts, including Mardi Gras masks. Features local artists and craftspeople.

Riverwalk (1 Poydras St., tel. 504/522–1555). Dozens of specialty shops feature a dazzling display of toys, crafts, cards, curios, and gift ideas. Look for **Natralee N'awlins, Masks and Make Believe, The Kite Loft, From Germany with Love, Books for Cooks,** and **Wicks 'N Sticks.**

Jewelry **Adler's** (722 Canal St., tel. 504/523–5292). Top-of-the-line jewelry, watches, and silver at this family-owned, local jeweler.

Hausmann's (732 Canal St., tel. 504/581–9581). Another locally owned jewelry store with branches in most major shopping centers. A tradition of quality.

Music **Canal Record Center** (1012 Canal St., tel. 504/523–3506). One of the city's largest record and tape stores. Specializes in Dixieland, historical jazz, and rhythm and blues.

Werlein's for Music (605 Canal St., tel. 504/524–7511). This historic, locally owned music store has a complete selection of records and tapes, as well as musical instruments. Salespeople are in the know about the local music scene.

Time Out **Bailey's,** located in the Fairmont Hotel, has the same elegance as the rest of the Fairmont, but in a more contemporary setting. Open 24 hours a day, this is a favored spot among locals that serves consistently good food (burgers and fries to seafood and local specialties) at reasonable prices ($6.75 for a club sandwich with fresh fruit salad). Be sure to take a look at the Sazerac Bar just down the lobby. This bar is notable not only for its alcoholic concoctions, but also for its art deco murals and ceiling design. *The Fairmont Hotel, located one-half block from Canal St. at University Pl., tel. 504/529–7111. AE, DC, MC, V.*

The French Quarter

The old French Quarter is the place to find dozens of shops, boutiques, and galleries housed in historic, balconied buildings. Narrow streets and quaint patios add a romantic tinge to the Southern hospitality of shopkeepers. The charm of this area and its fascinating merchandise should be enjoyed at a leisurely pace, with time to savor the unique character of the French Quarter. If you tire or find yourself overcome by the infamous New Orleans humidity, there's always a cafe or bistro nearby for a brief rest. Following is a selective list of the best shops and galleries.

Antiques The French Quarter is well known for its fine antique shops, which are located mainly on Royal and Chartres streets. One of the quickest ways to become familiar with the Quarter's antique market is to take a guided tour with Macon Riddle (tel. 504/899–3027), local antique expert who gives half- and full-day shopping tours. She visits the best shops and gives informed advice on styles, values, and prices.

French Antique Shop (225 Royal St., tel. 504/524–9861). Large selection of European furniture. Some Creole and local designs.

Lucullus (610 Chartres St., tel. 504/528–9620). Collection of fine Continental and English 17th- to 19th-century furniture, art, and cookware.

Manheim Galleries (403–409 Royal St., tel. 504/568–1901). Largest collection in the city of antique English, Continental, and Oriental furnishings, porcelains, paintings, silver, and jade. Agents for Boehm Birds.

Moss Antiques (411 Royal St., tel. 504/522–3981). Fine French and English furnishings, paintings, bric-a-brac. Large selection of antique and estate jewels.

M.S. Rau, Inc. (630 Royal St., tel. 504/523–5660 or 800/544–9440). American, French, English, Oriental furniture, china, glass, silver, ornamental iron, and American cut glass.

Parvizian Oriental Rugs (612 Bienville St., tel. 504/522–1200). Authentic antique hand-knotted Persian and Oriental rugs in all sizes.

Rothschild's Antiques (two locations: 241 Royal St. and 321 Royal St., tel. 504/523–5816). Large collection of furniture, silver, jewelry, mantels, and clocks from 18th to 20th century.

Royal Antiques (two locations: 307–309 Royal St. and 715 Bienville St., tel. 504/524–7033). Specializes in French and English 18th-century furnishings.

Waldhorn Company (343 Royal St., tel. 504/581–6379). Oldest antique store in New Orleans, established in 1881. Stocks English furniture, Victorian and Early American jewelry, and antique English porcelain and silver.

Art The French Quarter is known for its many art galleries, which are located mainly on Royal Street.

French Quarter Shopping

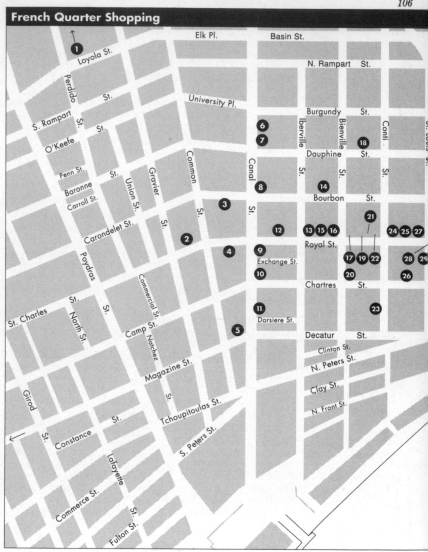

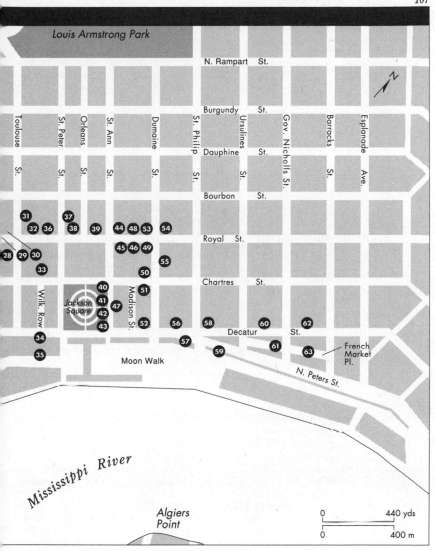

Louis Armstrong Park

N. Rampart   St.

Burgundy   St.

Dauphine   St.

Bourbon   St.

Royal   St.

Chartres   St.

Decatur   St.

Moon Walk

French
Market
Pl.

N. Peters St.

Jackson
Square

Wilk. Row

Madison St.

Mississippi River

Algiers
Point

0   440 yds
0   400 m

Toulouse   St.
St. Peter   St.
Orleans   St.
St. Ann   St.
Dumaine   St.
St. Philip   St.
Ursulines   St.
Gov. Nicholls St.
Barracks   St.
Esplanade   Ave.

Bergen Galleries (three locations: 308 Royal St., 730 Royal St., and Jackson Brewery, tel. 504/523–7882). Large selection of collectibles and the city's largest display of posters by local artists.
Circle Gallery (316 Royal St., tel. 504/523–1350). Paintings, sculptures, and graphics by internationally known artists including Vaskely, Lebadang, and Peter Max. Jewelry by Erté and drawings by Walt Disney also available.
The Crabnet (929 Decatur St., tel. 504/522–3478). A large collection of wood carvings, most by Louisiana carvers and wildlife artists. Known for wooden ducks and decoys.
Dynasen Gallery (433 Royal St., tel. 504/523–2902). Dynamic, modern gallery. Comprehensive collection of Erté's sculpture, lithographs, and serigraphs. Features art by Paul Wegner, Martinique, and Sasonne.
Hansen Gallery (229 Royal St., tel. 504/566–0816). Contemporary master graphics and originals by internationally known artists as well as some local artists. Features Miró, Calder, Tamayo, Neiman, among others.
Kurt E. Schon, Ltd. (523 Royal St., tel. 504/523–5902). Classic art from the 17th to 20th centuries. Stunning collection of landscapes and portraits. Staff is very knowledgeable.
Persian Boy Gallery (612 Royal St., tel. 504/524–2038). Publishes and distributes many New Orleans prints. Fine collection of posters, silk screens, and limited editions by local artists.
Reinike Gallery (300 Dauphine St., tel. 504/522–0470). Established in the Quarter in 1930. Fine contemporary watercolors and mixed media works by locally and internationally recognized artists.
Southern Expressions (521 St. Ann St., on Jackson Sq., tel. 504/525–4530). Regional paintings, prints, and watercolors by local artists.

Books Cookbooks and local history books are available in gift shops throughout the Quarter. Fun for any collector are the various musty used-book shops that proliferate in this area.

Librairie (823 Chartres St., tel. 504/522–4003). The Quarter's largest selection of local lore in books, old posters, and postcards. These shelves hold some real finds for the persistent browser.
Old Books (811 Royal St., tel. 504/522–4003). Owned by the same shopkeeper as the Librairie, this store has three floors of old and rare books, postcards, and photographs. The staff in both shops is very knowledgeable and helpful in locating titles.

Clothing **Cole/Vanderbilt Studio** (1222 Decatur St., tel. 504/522–5552). Award-winning silk masters Ray Cole and Jay Vanderbilt paint local scenes on silk dresses and scarves. Look for the red beans and rice dress!
Fleur de Paris (712 Royal St., tel. 504/525–1899). Innovative and elegant women's apparel shop. Designer dresses, custom hats, and silk lingerie.
Hats in the Belfry (Jackson Brewery, tel. 504/523–5770). The last word in headwear for men and women. The most complete line in New Orleans, and a fun place to visit.
Wehmeier's Belt Shop (719 Toulouse St., tel. 504/525–2758).

Large selection of finely crafted alligator and exotic leather goods. Belts, wallets, handbags, boots, and shoes.

Foods and Gift Packages

Café du Monde Shop (1039 Decatur St., tel. 504/581–2914). The delicious Creole coffee served at this French Quarter landmark is available here for retail in 15-oz. cans. Also available is the mix for Café du Monde beignets, the French doughnuts that accompany the coffee. The shop will ship anywhere in the country.

Farmer's Market (N. Peters St., tel. 504/522–2621). Open-air market where Louisiana's farmers sell their produce in town. Variety of local fruits and vegetables in season includes pecans, sugar cane, mirlitons, Creole tomatoes, and okra. Garlic wreaths hang from the rafters of the building where the great chefs of New Orleans shop for their kitchens.

Gumbo Ya-Ya (219 Bourbon St., tel. 504/522–7484). This is the only Cajun Country food and gift shop in the Quarter. Stock includes pralines, spices, and cookbooks.

Laura's (115 Royal St., tel. 504/525–3880). Homemade candies; pralines made fresh daily. Wonderful selection of hand-dipped chocolates. Creole spices and other local favorites.

Louisiana Products (507 St. Ann St., on Jackson Sq., tel. 504/524–7331). An entire store devoted to Cajun and Creole foods, Mardi Gras beads, local crafts, and novelties. Gift boxes filled with your choice of food items, from $5 to $15, can be shipped anywhere.

Vieux Carré Wine and Spirits (422 Chartres St., tel. 504/568–WINE). Wine by the glass, with frequent wine tastings. Large selection of imported and domestic beers, wines, spirits, and cheeses. Gift baskets available.

Jewelry

The Acorn (736 Royal St., tel. 504/525–7110). Estate, contemporary, and elephant-hair jewelry. Good selection of gift items.

Joan Good Antiques (809 Royal St., tel. 504/525–1705). Jewelry, including beautiful garnets, cameos, blue topaz, and marcasite pieces. Fine collection of Japanese Netsuke, Ojime, and Enro.

Nancy Kittay Jewels (617 Chartres St., tel. 504/524–1379). Specializes in antique jewelry.

The Quarter Stitch (509 Conti St., tel. 504/524–9731). Select from estate jewelry or have Ken Bowers create a piece from your own design.

Masks

The decorative masks worn at Mardi Gras in New Orleans are popular as gifts, souvenirs, and decorative pieces. Be careful of cheap imitations; the better hand-crafted, locally made masks bear the artist's insignia and are higher priced than the mass-produced ones. A good ceramic or feather mask starts at around $10 and can run as high as $300, depending on the materials and size of the mask.

Rumors (513 Royal St., tel. 504/525–0292). Large selection of top-of-the-line ceramic masks. Each mask here is a work of art. Priced from $17.

Tim Steele Masks (1023 N. Peters St., tel. 504/529–1548). Local mask designer and artist Tim Steele has won many awards for his innovative and whimsical creations. He works mostly in leather and feathers. Full-face molded leather masks are spectacular. Prices range from $20 to $300. His work is displayed in the open-air section of the French Market, or you can contact him directly.

Ye Olde Ship Store (831 Decatur St., tel. 504/522–9158). You would never guess from this store's name that it carries an excellent selection of feather masks. An extensive array of ornate Mardi Gras headdresses is on display here.

Music **Record Ron's** (1129 Decatur St., tel. 504/524–9444). If it's pressed in plastic, this shop has it or can locate it for you. Large selections of new releases and oldies. Good selection of local music.

Novelties and Gifts **Community Flea Market.** Open-air market with dozens of tables displaying everything imaginable: jewelry, antiques, clothing, leather goods, and local crafts. *The French Market at Gov. Nicholls St., tel. 504/566–7789. Open every weekend Fri.–Sun. 9 AM–6 PM.*

The Idea Factory (838 Chartres St., tel. 504/524–5195). This shop stocks one-of-a-kind gifts, ingenious custom-made, wooden toys, handmade jewelry. Owners George and Peg Bacon create many of the designs themselves.

New Orleans Cat House (840 Royal St., tel. 504/524–5939). A store devoted to cat-lovers with every imaginable gift for felines and masters. Many items feature a local accent (New Orleans Cathouse T-shirts and mugs).

Nostalgia (607 Dumaine St., no phone). Large shop crammed with American memorabilia and obsolete novelties. Great gift ideas at moderate prices.

Sigle's Historic New Orleans Metal Craft (935 Royal St., tel. 504/522–7647). Original cast-iron wall planters, handcrafted since 1938; frequently seen on Quarter balconies and patios.

Perfumes **Bourbon French Perfume Co.** (525 St. Ann St., tel. 504/522–4480). This shop has been custom blending fragrances for 150 years. Established line of over 30 women's and men's fragrances.

Hové Parfumeur, Ltd. (824 Royal St., tel. 504/525–7827). Creates and manufactures fine fragrances for men and women. Oils, soaps, sachets, and potpourri made to order on the premises. Local family-run business since 1932.

La Belle Epoque (Jackson Brewery, tel. 504/522–1650). Creators of Can-Can, New Orleans's own perfume. Glass perfume bottles and kaleidoscopes also available.

Toys **Hello Dolly** (815 Royal St., tel. 504/522–9948). Has one of the largest collections of dolls in the South. The locally made Gambina doll is a specialty here.

Le Petit Soldier Shop (528 Royal St., tel. 504/523–7741). Whole armies of hand-painted toy soldiers command attention in this unique shop. The toys are beautifully crafted to become heirlooms.

The Little Toy Shoppe (Two locations: 900 Decatur St. and 513 St. Ann St. on Jackson Sq.; tel. 504/522–6588). Largest Downtown selection of children's toys, books, and posters. Features beautiful, locally produced Gambina dolls, also Madame Alexander dolls. Many regional items for children of all ages.

Pontalba Historical Puppetorium (514 St. Peter St., on Jackson Sq.; tel. 504/522–0344). Largest selection of puppets and ventriloquistic dolls in the United States. Be sure not to handle the merchandise—the staff here is very fussy.

Time Out **The Napoleon House** is the perfect spot to take a refreshment break from shopping and at the same time soak up local history and tradition. The landmark building was reportedly offered as a refuge to Napoleon Bonaparte, but he died before the rescue plan could be completed. The building today has an ambience reminiscent of French Revolutionary times. Try the muffuletta sandwich, a large round Italian roll with several kinds of lunch meats and cheeses topped with an olive relish and served hot. It's a meal in itself and one can be shared by two people. *500 Chartres St., corner of Toulouse and Chartres Sts.; tel. 504/524 -9752. Closed Sun. AE, MC, V.*

Magazine Street

Magazine Street is one of the oldest and most diverse shopping districts in New Orleans. Named for the French word for shop —*magasin*—this street runs parallel to St. Charles Avenue, but several blocks closer to the river, and passes through old, established neighborhoods. Along its five miles, Magazine Street sports dozens of antique shops, bric-a-brac vendors, used clothing and furniture stores, several art galleries, and a number of businesses specializing in furniture restoration, interior decorating, and landscaping. Name it and it will probably be somewhere on Magazine Street.

The main stretch of shops begins at the intersection of Melpomene and Magazine streets. The Magazine Street bus runs there from Canal Street, and the St. Charles streetcar stops within blocks of this shopping district. The best and safest way to shop on Magazine Street is by taxi, as there are areas in certain neighborhoods between shops that are often deserted.

Macon Riddle (tel. 504/899–3027), a local antique expert and enthusiast, offers a guided antique shopping tour of Magazine and Royal streets by van. This is a super way to see the best shops and judge selection, quality, and price.

Antiques **Accent Antiques** (2855 Magazine St., tel. 504/897–9466). Large selection of American and European antiques, light fixtures, paintings, and prints.
Antiques Unlimited (2929 Magazine St., tel. 504/891–9948). Specializes in large cupboards and chests, mid-19th-century Irish and English pine. Also carries brackets, cornices, and stained glass.
As You Like It (3929 Magazine St., tel. 504/897–6915). Victorian and art deco flatware. Also complete sets of art nouveau sterling silver flatware.
British Antiques (5415 Magazine St., Tel. 504/895–3716). Great showplace of 18th- and 19th-century English antiques. Oriental and English porcelain.
Collector Antiques (3102 Magazine St., tel. 504/897–0905). Vintage linens, lace curtains, bedspreads, and tablecloths at good prices.
Jon Antiques (4605 Magazine St., tel. 504/899–4482). The place to go for English furniture, porcelain, mirrors, lamps, tea caddies, and other bric-a-brac.
Leon Irwin Antiques (1800 Magazine St., tel. 504/522–5555). Two stories of some of the finest 18th- and 19th-century French and English furniture.
Nina Sloss (6008 Magazine St., tel. 504/895–8888). Large as-

sortment of English and Continental pieces from the 18th and 19th centuries. Owner Nina Sloss is a nationally known decorator.

Wirth More Antiques (5723 Magazine St., tel. 504/897–9727). Carefully selected 18th- and 19th-century country furniture from France. One of Magazine Street's most popular stores.

Art **Carmen Llewellyn Gallery** (3901 Magazine St., tel. 504/891–5301). Specializes in choice contemporary Latin-American art.

Carol Robinson Gallery (4537 Magazine St., tel. 504/895–6130). A good place to discover regional and New Orleans artists; wide selection.

Davis Gallery (3964 Magazine St., tel. 504/897–0780). Rare African, pre-Columbian, and ethnographic art. Supplies collectors and museums.

Gallery for Fine Photography (5423 Magazine St., tel. 504/891–1002). Exhibits leading American photographers, past and present. Rare 19th- and 20th-century photos, books, posters, and postcards.

Books **George Herget Books** (3109 Magazine St., tel. 504/891–5595). Thousands of rare books including many regional titles, along with rare postcards, records, sheet music, and Civil War memorabilia. A treasure shop.

Magazine Street Bookshop (4222 Magazine St., tel. 504/899–6905). Rare and antique books, including many on regional subjects, old and new comic books.

Clothes **Perlis** (6070 Magazine St., tel. 504/895–8661). Home of the trademark Louisiana crawfish embroidered on shirts and ties. Top-quality men's and women's clothing. Personalized service; a New Orleans institution.

Second Hand Rose (3110 Magazine St., tel. 504/899–2098). Wonderful selection of antique clothing for men and women. Good place to look for costumes and unusual accessories.

Music **Sound Warehouse** (5500 Magazine St., tel. 504/891–4026). Outstanding record shop with large selection of local and regional music; knowledgeable staff.

Novelties and Gifts **Queen Flea** (3955 Magazine St., tel. 504/891–0481). Furniture, brass, copper, china, and glassware. Many oddities bought at local estate sales. Great place to rummage.

The Quilt Cottage (801 Nashville St., off Magazine St., tel. 504/895–3791). New and antique quilts and handmade gift items. Quilting service available.

Renaissance Shop (1101 First St., corner of Magazine St., tel. 504/529–2286). The place to find the unique gift item. Stock includes porcelain, small furniture, antiques.

Sixpence Antiques and Gifts (4904 Magazine St., tel. 504/895–1267). Imports from France and England. Lots of bric-a-brac and gift items.

Time Out Shops on Magazine Street are stretched along a five-mile route. About midway is a laid-back restaurant and bar frequented by merchants and workers from the neighborhood called **Joey K's.** The menu here consists of hot lunches, soups, salads, sandwiches, and full-course meals. *3001 Magazine St., tel. 504/891–0997. No credit cards. Closed Sun.*

Magazine St. / St. Charles Ave. Shopping

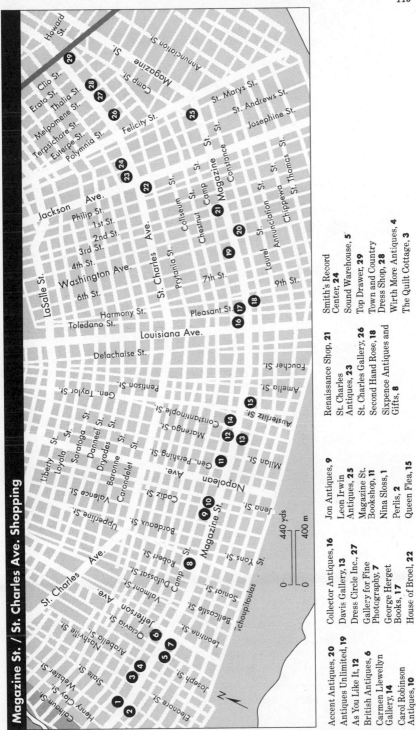

Accent Antiques, **20**

Antiques Unlimited, **19**

As You Like It, **12**

British Antiques, **6**

Carmen Llewellyn Gallery, **14**

Carol Robinson Antiques, **10**

Collector Antiques, **16**

Davis Gallery, **13**

Dress Circle Inc., **27**

Gallery for Fine Photography, **7**

George Herget Books, **17**

House of Broel, **22**

Jon Antiques, **9**

Leon Irwin Antiques, **25**

Magazine St. Bookshop, **11**

Nina Sloss, **1**

Perlis, **2**

Queen Flea, **15**

Renaissance Shop, **21**

St. Charles Antiques, **23**

St. Charles Gallery, **26**

Second Hand Rose, **18**

Sixpence Antiques and Gifts, **8**

Smith's Record Center, **24**

Sound Warehouse, **5**

Top Drawer, **29**

Town and Country Dress Shop, **28**

Wirth More Antiques, **4**

The Quilt Cottage, **3**

Maple Street/Riverbend

There's an old-fashioned aura in this area where most of the shops are housed in turn-of-the-century cottages. On Maple Street the shops run for six blocks, from Carrollton Avenue to Cherokee Street; in Riverbend, they dot the streets surrounding the Winn-Dixie Shopping Center on Carrollton Avenue. To reach both areas from Downtown, ride the streetcar until St. Charles Avenue becomes Carrollton Avenue, then get off at the first stop. This stop deposits you at the corner of Maple Street and Carrollton Avenue.

Antiques   **O'Keefe's Gallery Interiors** (700 Dublin St., tel. 504/861–7514). A selection of 18th-century English antiques, including breakfronts, drop-leaf tables, and linen presses that go for up to $3,000. Fabrics, wall coverings, trims, carpeting, and Oriental rugs are also found here, as well as brass, china, porcelain, and silver gift items starting at $15. Shipping is arranged.

Arts and Crafts   **Alartco** (7808 Maple St., tel. 504/865–8501). This shop takes the work of local artists on consignment; they can order quality prints of the masters and other known artists. A good selection of prints, posters, and postcards is also available.
Best of Both Worlds (7916 Maple St., tel. 504/866–7157). One-of-a-kind, handmade creations, most by Louisiana artists and craftsmen. Mediums include glass, pottery, textile, and wood. Handmade jewelry and clothing are also available.
Blue Roof Pottery (8133 Hampson St., tel. 504/866–0243). Functional pottery from about 30 of the finest potters across

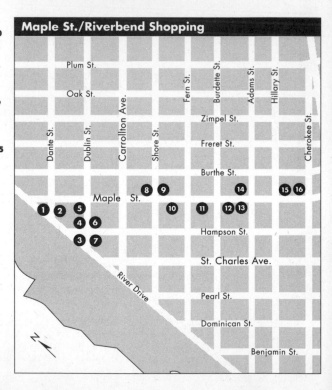

Maple St./Riverbend Shopping

the country. Another feature is the "design your own jewelry" table.

The Sun Shop (7722 Maple St., tel. 504/861–8338). For more than 20 years the proprietor has been traveling from Alaska to Peru on a regular basis, personally selecting the handcrafted works of native Americans. These include handwoven rugs, blankets, and wall hangings; pottery; jewelry; and a collection of hand-carved Indian masks.

Weavers Workshop Ltd., A Contemporary Crafts Gallery (716 Dublin St., tel. 504/866–0820). American crafts with a sense of humor. The shop carries mirrors and cabinets, wind sculptures, feather collars, and jewelry. They also have a selection of handwoven scarves, shawls, and throws.

Books   **Maple Street Book Shop** (7523 and 7529 Maple St., tel. 504/866–4916). The original location of a locally owned store that has branched out throughout the metropolitan area. Housed in Victorian cottages, the store includes the main shop with six rooms of books to browse through, **The Rare Book Shop,** which also stocks prints and records, and **The Children's Bookshop.**

Clothing   **Fiasco's Accessories** (7913 Maple St., tel. 504/861–8761). Filled with belts, bows, buckles, and buttons. If it's bold, bright, or the latest trend, they have it.

Gae-Tana's (7732 Maple St., tel. 504/865–9625). Casual, contemporary, and designer-label clothing at 30% to 50% discounts.

Jordan Bradley Women's Apparel (7933 Maple St., tel. 504/861–4174). Traditional styles and elegant designer clothing. A small shop that offers shoppers personal attention; appointments can be made if desired.

Yvonne La Fleur (8131 Hampson St., tel. 504/866–9666). Innovative custom-design fashions, French lingerie, and a full array of shoes and accessories (including a spectacular selection of hats).

Food   **P.J.'s Coffee & Tea Co.** (7713 Maple St., tel. 504/866–9963). Imported coffee beans and exotic teas. Pastries can be purchased in the cafe and enjoyed at umbrella-covered tables on the patio with cups of freshly brewed coffee or tea.

Gifts   **Cache Pót** (733 Dante St., tel. 504/861–2667). A delightful gift shop that shares an old house with **The Rose and The Ring,** a shop that features women's and children's clothing. Each type of gift in the Cache Pót has its own room in the house: baskets, candles and candlesticks, silk and dried flowers, French table linens, etc. There's also a year-round Christmas room and a room of ribbons and gift wraps.

The Squirrel Cage (7507 Maple St., tel. 504/866–5423). Gifts, with a special New Orleans section that features beignet mix, Café du Monde coffee, inexpensive cookbooks, Hurricane mix, jambalaya and gumbo mixes, notecards, prints, bags of red beans and rice, and unusual streetcar paraphernalia. Customers can choose items and have them packed in a harvest gift basket.

Time Out   **Dante Street Deli** has outdoor cafe seating year round on its flower bedecked patio. Enjoy light fare such as soups and sandwiches, or try the creative seafood and pasta salads. Hot specials daily and tempting homemade desserts: $7.50 is the

highest price on the menu! *736 Dante (in Riverbend), tel.
504/861–3634. Closed Sun. and Mon. MC, V.*

The Rink

There are only a few shops in The Rink, but if you want to
combine a shopping jaunt with a trek into an area filled with
New Orleans history, this is the place. For starters, The
Rink was built in 1884 as the South's first roller-skating rink.
The Behrman Gym, across the street on Washington Avenue,
houses the South's first indoor pool, which is still in use to-
day. This gym is also famed for being the training site of John
L. Sullivan when he fought Gentleman Jim Corbett. On
Washington Avenue stands Lafayette Cemetery, which dates
to the 1820s when this section was the town of Lafayette.
At the corner of Fourth Street and Prytania, the "other"
cornstalk fence (the first is in the French Quarter) surrounds
an 1880s mansion, and up the street a block on Washington
Avenue is the famous Commander's Palace Restaurant.

To reach The Rink by streetcar, exit at Washington Avenue and
walk toward the river. Shops in The Rink are open 10 AM–6 PM;
closed Sun. The address for every shop listed in this section is
2727 Prytania Street.

Antiques **Estella's Ltd.** (tel. 504/897–2966). A potpourri of carefully selected antiques, fine linens, and gifts. Handmade Dhurri
pillows are just one of the many eye-catchers in this shop.

Art **J. Raymond Samuel Ltd.** (tel. 504/891–9061). Fine prints
and paintings, rare books, antique maps, and historical documents. Mr. Samuel also has an outstanding collection of
famous autographs, which he buys and sells on a regular basis.

Books **Maple Street's Garden District Book Shop, Inc.** (tel.
504/895–2266). A well-stocked branch of **The Maple Street Book
Shop.** Festive wine and cheese autograph parties for local and
national authors are frequently held at this location.

Gifts **Kendall Kollection II** (tel. 504/891–7571). A wonderful selection of traditional gifts, highlighted by beautiful crystal and
porcelain pieces.

St. Charles Avenue

Some of the city's oldest and most prestigious shops line St.
Charles Avenue for a distance of 10 blocks from Clio St. to Jackson Avenue. Several elite dress shops are in this area, as well as
antiques, art, and children's clothing. There's an elegance to
shopping on the avenue that dates to another era.

Antiques **St. Charles Antiques** (2125 St. Charles Ave., tel. 504/524–0243).
An 1880s Victorian mansion lends itself well to displaying a collection of 18th-century English pieces, which include
sideboards and bureau bookcases in a price range of
$4,000–$9,000. Affordable Oriental porcelains.

Art **St. Charles Gallery** (1720 St. Charles Ave., tel. 504/581–9300).
The place for the serious art collector. The shop specializes in
original English watercolors and old master drawings of the
18th and early 19th centuries.

Clothing **Dress Circle Inc.** (1520 St. Charles Ave., tel. 504/523–3197). A small, sophisticated shop that's been on the avenue since 1933. A stunning collection of evening gowns and Joanie Char streetwear, light and packable cotton fashions great for traveling.
House of Broel (2220 St. Charles Ave., tel. 504/522–2220). Known for its wedding-gown collection, it also has an impressive selection of ball gowns, including antebellum styles, and cocktail dresses.
Town and Country Dress Shop (1432 St. Charles Ave., tel. 504/525–9572). A New Orleans classic, it carries everything, except shoes, for a lady of any age.

Music **Smith's Record Center** (2019 St. Charles Ave., tel. 504/522–7969 or 504/522–4843). One of the city's best collections of Dixieland jazz and rhythm-and-blues recordings. Special orders accepted: it ships anywhere in the world.

Shopping Centers

These are a few of New Orleans's better shopping centers not previously discussed in this chapter. These centers are open Mon.–Sat. 10 AM–9 PM, Sun. 12:30–5:30 PM.

Esplanade Mall (1401 W. Esplanade Ave., Kenner, tel. 504/468–6116). Besides housing impressive department stores such as Macy's and D.H. Holmes, this mall features locally owned shops such as Paradise (gift shop), Kamma's Imports (Indian boutique), Footloose 'n Fanci (jewelry and accessories), Yvonne LaFleur (elegant women's fashions), and a branch of Café du Monde.
Lakeside Shopping Center (3301 Veterans Memorial Blvd., Metairie, tel. 504/835–8000). This large center is one of the oldest malls in the country. Here you will find J.C. Penney, B. Dalton Bookseller, D.H. Holmes, Hausmann's Jewelers, five cinemas, Ruby Tuesday's restaurant, and Popeye's Fried Chicken, in addition to the more typical mall shops.
The Plaza at Lake Forest (5700 Read Blvd., tel. 504/246–1500). Besides an ice-skating rink, the Plaza is where you'll find D.H. Holmes, Maison Blanche, Sears, Hausmann's Jewelers, and plenty more to let you shop till you drop.
Uptown Square (200 Broadway, tel. 504/866–4513). This is one of the finer shopping centers outside the Downtown area. Among the many locally owned shops here are the Maple Street Book Shop, Pour Moi (expensive gifts), Imagine (gifts and games), and J. Carvin (a local version of Crabtree & Evelyn). There are also two cinemas and the Complete Wine Cellar restaurant and Keswany's (for Indian cuisine).

6 Sports and Fitness

Participant Sports and Fitness

Bicycling Rentals are available at **Bicycle Michael's,** *618 Frenchman St., tel. 504/945–9505. Cost: $3.50/hr, $12.50/day.*

City Park also rents bicycles for use within the park's boundaries. Minimum age is 16; only one rider per bike. *Dreyfous Dr., tel. 504/483–9371. Cost: $2.50 hr (2-hr minimum). Daily 9–4.*

Boating In New Orleans Lake Pontchartrain awaits the boating enthusiast. **Sailboats South** rents monohulls (9'–36'), catamarans (14'–36'), sailboards, and powerboats (16'–18') for use on the lake, as well as rowing shells and skiffs for the bayous. *300 Sapphire St., 70124, tel. 504/288–7245. No rentals Nov.–Feb.*

Pedal boats, rowboats, and canoes are available at **City Park.** *Dreyfous Dr., tel. 504/483–9371. Cost for pedal boats: $6.50/hr.; rowboats and canoes: $5/hr. Daily 9–5.*

Bowling Bowling lanes are located throughout metropolitan New Orleans. The two **Don Carter's All Star Lanes** are open 24 hours, every day of the year. *901 Manhattan Blvd., Harvey, tel. 504/361–7991, and 3640 Williams Blvd., Kenner, tel. 504/ 443–5353.*

Canoeing **Canoe and Trail Adventures** offers a schedule of overnight canoe trips and moonlight paddles. Reservations are a must and can be made up to six months in advance. Canoes and equipment can be rented for personal use. *2020 Veterans Blvd., Metairie, 70002, tel. 504/822–9541.*

City Park rents canoes for exploring the network of semitropical lagoons that wind through the park's 1,500 acres. *Dreyfous Dr., tel. 504/483–9371. Cost: $5/hr. Daily 9–5.*

Fishing and Hunting Nonresident visitors intending to fish or hunt in the New Orleans area must purchase the necessary licenses. Seven-day licenses are issued separately for saltwater (which includes Lake Pontchartrain) and freshwater fishing; these are required whether fishing from shore or from a boat. For hunting there is a three-day license. Certain types of crabbing and shrimping also require a license; crawfishing does not. For $1.50 City Park issues one-day permits (sunup to sundown) that allow fishing from the shore in the stocked streams of the park. A state license is required for this as well. To obtain a license or inquire about fishing and hunting regulations, season dates, and archery and trapping information, contact the **Louisiana Wildlife and Fisheries Dept.** (400 Chartres St., French Quarter, tel. 504/568–5616).

Golf The public can golf at the following courses in the New Orleans area:

Audubon Park, 18-hole course. *473 Walnut, tel. 504/861–9511. Greens fees $6 weekdays, $9 weekends.*
Brechtel, 18-hole municipal course. *3700 Behrman Pl., Westbank, tel. 504/362–4761. Greens fees $4.75 weekdays, $6 weekends.*
City Park, 4 18-hole courses. *1040 Filmore, tel. 504/483–9396. Greens fees $5–$6.75 weekdays, $7–$8.75 weekends.*
Joe Bartholomew Golf Course, Pontchartrain Park, 18-hole

course. *6514 Congress Dr., tel. 504/288–0928. Greens fees $5.75 weekdays, $8 weekends.*

Plantation Golf Course, 18-hole, par 69 course. *1001 Behrman Hwy., Westbank, tel. 504/392–3363. Greens fees $5 weekdays, $8 weekends.*

Hiking The Bartaria Unit of **Jean Lafitte National Historical Park** has several trails that explore Louisiana's Delta Wetlands and important archaeological sites. *Located about an hour's drive from New Orleans near Lafitte, tel. 504/348–2923 or 504/-589–2636.*

Canoe and Trail Adventures has a regular schedule of backpacking trips that vary from overnight to a week in length; reservations are necessary. The firm also rents a complete line of equipment for individuals to camp or backpack on their own. *2020 Veterans Blvd., Metairie, tel. 504/833–9541.*

Louisiana Nature and Science Center also plans hiking and backpacking excursions into areas around New Orleans. *11000 Lake Forest Blvd., New Orleans East, tel. 504/246–9381.*

Horseback Riding **Cascade Stables** in Audubon Park rents horses for riding within the boundaries of the park. Located east of the zoo, off a one-way side road that runs into Magazine Street, the stables are hard to find the first time, but most anyone in the area will be happy to give directions. *6500 Magazine St., tel. 504/891–2246. Cost: $20 for 45-min ride.*

Jogging **Audubon Park,** between St. Charles Avenue and Magazine Street, has a two-mile jogging path that passes several scenic lagoons as it encircles the golf course. Exercise stations parallel the trail. The **Mississippi River levee** and **City Park** are also popular jogging places. Several organized running events are held in New Orleans that are open to the public (*see* Spectator Sports).

Tennis **Audubon Park** has 10 new courts, located at the back of the park, off Tchoupitoulas Street. *Tel. 504/865–8638. Cost: $5. Daily 8–dark.*

City Park has 39 lighted courts that are open 7 AM until 10 PM weekdays and 7 AM until 6 PM weekends. *Dreyfous Dr., tel. 504/483–9383. Cost: $2.25–$5.*

Stern Tennis Center has 8 lighted courts, open 8 AM until 8 PM weekdays and 8 AM until 5 PM weekends. *4025 S. Saratoga, tel. 504/891–0627. Cost: $2.75 weekdays, $3.75 weekends.*

Spectator Sports

Baseball New Orleans has no major or minor league teams, but in the spring top-flight collegiate teams play at both **Tulane University** and **University of New Orleans.**

Basketball The **Sugar Bowl Basketball Tournament** is held at the Superdome the week preceding the annual football classic. The Superdome is also the site of the NCAA Final Four when it's played in New Orleans. The University of New Orleans plays NCAA Division I Competition; other schools, including Delgado Junior College, Dillard, Xavier, and Southern University, also have teams that play home games at gyms and field houses on their respective campuses.

Bowling The **Professional Bowler's Tour** periodically schedules competition during the last week of January at Don Carter's All Star Lanes on the Westbank. *901 Manhattan Blvd., Harvey, tel. 504/361-7991.*

Boxing Every Tuesday professional boxing, world-class, takes place at Bud Olister's Riverboat Hallelujah. Seating is theater style and tickets are available at city outlets. *3615 Tulane Ave., 70119, tel. 504/484-7868.*

The Superdome also hosts publicized boxing events from time to time.

Football The Louisiana Superdome is the place for football. On Sundays the **New Orleans Saints** of the National Football League play their home games; on Saturday afternoons you can usually catch **Tulane University's** home games. The famed LSU–Tulane game is played at the Superdome in odd-numbered years. Grambling and Southern universities renew their annual rivalry in the **Bayou Classic** each November. On New Year's Day the Superdome hosts the **Sugar Bowl.** Every four years the BIG one comes to town; the next **Super Bowl** at the Superdome is schedule for 1990. *Saints tickets tel. 504/522-2600; Tulane tickets tel. 504/861-3661.*

Golf In April the nation's top professional golfers come to New Orleans to compete in the USF&G at English Turn, the new Jack Nicklaus golf course that opened in September 1988. *Hwy. 406, East Canal, Westbank, tel. 504/394-5294.*

Horse Racing There is year-round Thoroughbred racing in New Orleans. At **The Fair Grounds,** third-oldest racetrack in the nation, the season opens Thanksgiving Day and runs through mid-April. Big races include the New Orleans Handicap for older horses and the Louisiana Derby for three-year-olds, a major prep for the Kentucky Derby. Both of these are run in March. *1751 Gentilly Blvd., tel. 504/943-2200. Post time 1 PM, Fri. 3 PM. Closed Mon. and Tues., mid-Apr.–Thanksgiving.*

Jefferson Downs Race Track has night racing and clubhouse dining from mid-April to mid-November. Located in Kenner on Lake Pontchartrain. *Williams Blvd., exit off I-10 West to the Lakefront, tel. 504/466-8521. Post time 7:15 PM. Closed Mon. and Tues., mid-Nov.–mid-April.*

Running Many organized runs take place in New Orleans every year. These include the **Crescent City Classic** in April, the **Mississippi River Bridge Run** in late August, **Witches Moonlight Run** the night before Halloween, the **Thanksgiving Day Classic,** and the **Corporate Run** in December. For further information on these and other running events, contact Greater New Orleans Runners Association (tel. 504/454-8247 or 504/340-7223).

Tennis New Orleans became a Virginia Slims City in 1984. The tournament is hosted each year at the UNO Lakefront Arena and is usually scheduled in September or October. *Tel. 504/286-7222.*

7 Dining

Introduction

*by Lisa Le
Blanc-Berry*

*The "Urbane
Gourmet" food
critic for* Gambit
*newspaper, Lisa
LeBlanc-Berry
gives weekly
restaurant
reviews on New
Orleans's radio
station WWIW.
She is currently
the editor of*
Where Magazine
in New Orleans.

New Orleans usually means excellent dining. The Big Easy is recognized almost as much for its hot and spicy culinary delights as it is for its hot and steamy jazz. Louisiana styles of cooking are becoming increasingly popular worldwide, but what is a fad elsewhere is a tradition here.

As a general rule, expect to tip from 15% to 20%. Most establishments do not automatically add a service charge.

Apart from K-Paul's and Galatoire's, where people stand in line to be served on a first-come basis, you are strongly advised to make reservations and to book well in advance for weekends, particularly during holiday periods or conventions.

Most of the more pricey restaurants adhere to a moderate dress code—jackets for men, and in some places, a tie. New Orleans is a conservative city; dining out is an honored ritual, and people are expected to dress the part. A man in faded jeans and sports coat may not be turned away, but he may not feel terribly comfortable either. Credit cards are accepted in most, but not all, dining establishments; it's wise to check in advance.

Lunch hours are 11:30 AM to 2:30 PM. Dinner is almost always served from 6 to 10 PM, although some restaurants will close an hour earlier or later depending on volume of business and season.

The following terms will appear frequently throughout this section:

andouille (an-*dooey*)—Cajun sausage made with ham and garlic.
boudin (boo-*dan*)—hot, spicy pork with onions, rice, and herbs stuffed in sausage casing.
bananas Foster—a dessert of bananas sautéed with butter, sugar, and cinnamon, flambéed in brandy, and served on ice cream.
barbecue shrimp—large shrimp baked in the shell and covered with a butter and pepper sauce.
court bouillon (coo-boo-*yon*)—a spicy stew made from fish fillets, tomatoes, and onions.
crawfish (pronounced as spelled)—also known as "mud-bugs," because they live in the mud of freshwater streams. They resemble miniature lobsters and are served in a great variety of ways.
etouffee (ay-to-*fay*)—a sauce of tangy tomatoes and crawfish or shrimp, served over rice.
filé (fee-*lay*)—ground sassafras, used to season gumbo and many other Creole specialties.
grillades (gree-*yads*)—squares of broiled meat, usually served for breakfast with grits.
gumbo—a hearty soup prepared in a variety of combinations (okra gumbo, shrimp gumbo, chicken gumbo, to name a few).
jambalaya (jum-bo-*lie*-yah)—a rich stew made of tomatoes, rice, ham, chicken, shrimp, onions, and lots of spicy seasonings.
muffuletta—a large, round loaf of bread filled with cheese, ham, and salami smothered in a heavy, garlicky olive salad.

French Quarter Dining

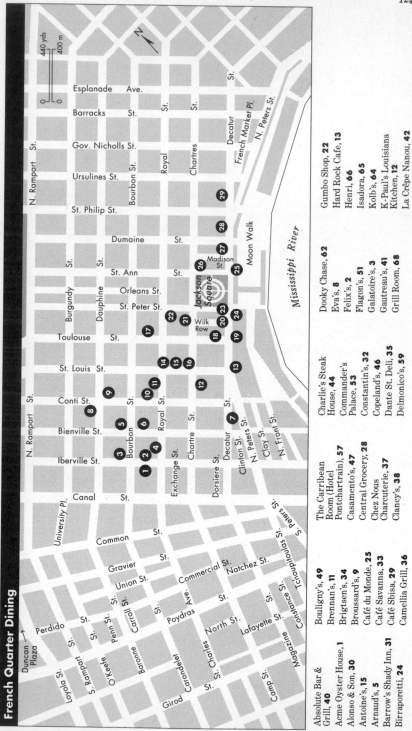

Absolute Bar & Grill, **40**
Acme Oyster House, **1**
Alonso & Son, **30**
Antoine's, **15**
Arnaud's, **5**
Barrow's Shady Inn, **31**
Birraporetti, **24**

Bouligny's, **49**
Brennan's, **11**
Brigtsen's, **34**
Broussard's, **9**
Café du Monde, **25**
Café Savanna, **33**
Café Sbisa, **29**
Camellia Grill, **36**

The Carribean Room (Hotel Pontchartrain), **57**
Casamento's, **47**
Central Grocery, **28**
Chez Nous Charcuterie, **37**
Clancy's, **38**

Charlie's Steak House, **44**
Commander's Palace, **53**
Constantin's, **32**
Copeland's, **46**
Dante St. Deli, **35**
Delmonico's, **59**

Dooky Chase, **62**
Eva's, **8**
Felix's, **2**
Flagon's, **51**
Galatoire's, **3**
Gautreau's, **41**
Grill Room, **68**

Gumbo Shop, **22**
Hard Rock Cafe, **13**
Henri, **66**
Isadora, **65**
Kolb's, **64**
K-Paul's Louisiana Kitchen, **12**
La Crêpe Nanou, **42**

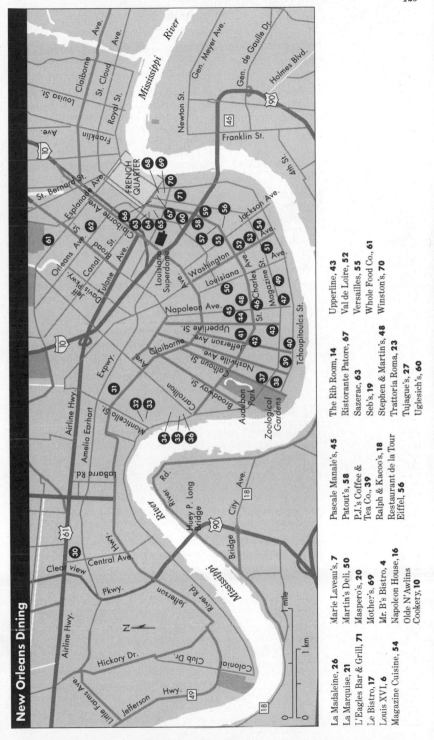

125

New Orleans Dining

La Madaleine, **26**
La Marquise, **21**
L'Eagles Bar & Grill, **71**
Le Bistro, **17**
Louis XVI, **6**
Magazine Cuisine, **54**

Marie Laveau's, **7**
Martin's Deli, **50**
Maspero's, **20**
Mother's, **69**
Mr. B's Bistro, **4**
Napoleon House, **16**
Olde N'Awlins
Cookery, **10**

Pascale Manale's, **45**
Patout's, **58**
P.J.'s Coffee &
Tea Co., **39**
Ralph & Kacoo's, **18**
Restaurant de la Tour
Eiffel, **56**

The Rib Room, **14**
Ristorante Patore, **67**
Sazerac, **63**
Seb's, **19**
Stephen & Martin's, **48**
Trattoria Roma, **23**
Tujague's, **27**
Uglesich's, **60**

Upperline, **43**
Val de Loire, **52**
Versailles, **55**
Whole Food Co., **61**
Winston's, **70**

remoulade—a cold dressing that accompanies shrimp or crabmeat, made up of green onions, celery, catsup, and hot Creole mustard.

praline (praw-*leen*)—candy patty most commonly made from sugar, water, and pecans.

New Orleans is renowned for *Creole* cuisine. A Creole, by definition, is a person of French or Spanish ancestry born in the New World. However, Creole is also a word of elastic implications,and in culinary terms, Creole refers to a distinctive cuisine indigenous to New Orleans that has its roots in European dishes enhanced by the liberal usage of local seasonings such as *filé*. The French influence is also strong, but the essence of Creole is in sauces, herbs, and the prominent use of seafood.

In recent years the term *Nouvelle Creole* has been popularized by local restaurateurs. Instead of gumbo or jambalaya, a nouvelle menu might include hickory-grilled items, seafood served with pasta, or smoked meats and fish. There has also been a strong Italian influence in Creole cuisine in the last decade, creating yet another marriage of styles.

The initial restaurant listings here are divided into five Creole categories: *Classic Creole*, those restaurants devoted to traditional Louisiana cuisine with minimal French overtones; *French Creole*, indicating a more expansive Continental accent; *Italian Creole*, Creole with an Italian flair; *Soul Creole*, black cuisine of Creole origin; and *Creole-Inspired*, meaning the newer breed of cooking styles that incorporate Nouvelle Creole dishes, new American cooking, and classic Creole. Please note that the above categories often overlap; it is not unusual to find a blend of varying Creole cuisines on any given menu.

Cajun cuisine was brought from Nova Scotia to the bayou country of Louisiana by the Acadians over 250 years ago. Cajun cooks generally use less expensive ingredients than their Creole counterparts, and they are heavy-handed on the herbs and spices.

Cajun cuisine is rarely served in its purest form in New Orleans, and it is often blended with Creole to create what's known as "New Orleans–style" cooking. There is a difference, though, between the two: Creole is distinguished by its rich and heavy sauces, Cajun by its tendency to be spicy and hot.

The most highly recommended restaurants in each price category are indicated by a star ★.

Category	Cost*
Very Expensive	$35 and up
Expensive	$25–$35
Moderate	$15–$20
Inexpensive	under $15

*per person without tax (9% in New Orleans), service, or drinks

The following credit card abbreviations are used: AE, American Express; CB, Carte Blanche; DC, Diners Club; MC, MasterCard; and V, Visa.

Cajun-Inspired

Expensive
★ **Brigtsen's.** Chef-owner Frank Brigtsen trained with Paul Prudhomme, so it is no wonder that his small restaurant has attracted a great following. Some of his signature dishes are panfried speckled trout, duck boudin with honey-pecan gravy, cream of oyster Rockefeller soup, and rabbit tenderloin with sautéed spinach and Creole mustard sauce. Brigtsen's blending of Cajun and Creole styles, dubbed "modern Louisiana city food" by the management, is a less traditional form of Cajun cuisine than that offered at K-Paul's. The menu changes daily. *723 Dante St., Uptown, tel. 504/861–7610. Dress: informal; no jeans or cutoffs. Reservations required; weekend reservations should be made a week in advance. AE, MC, V. Closed Sun. and Mon.*

K-Paul's Louisiana Kitchen. In a class by itself, K-Paul's has redefined Cajun cooking in New Orleans. Author of a best-selling cookbook, chef Paul Prudhomme is a national celebrity who has done more than any other single individual to popularize Cajun cooking. A cheery man of ample girth, Prudhomme is a purist when it comes to spices and seasonal uses of seafood; he strongly opposes crawfish breeding to lengthen the harvest period. He made blackened redfish so famous that a commercial fishing ban had to be levied in early 1988 and restaurateurs can no longer acquire it. Instead of redfish, K-Paul's now serves blackened yellowfin tuna. The blackened steak available at K-Paul's has an equally distinctive taste, as do the thick sauces. For an expensive restaurant K-Paul's offers little in the way of ambience: Strangers often share tables, martinis are served in jelly jars, no reservations are accepted, and customers must wait outside in long lines. Food, not creature comforts, is what attracts the crowds here; K-Paul's is a shrine to the popular concept of Cajun cooking. Aside from the blackened dishes, the menu changes daily. *416 Chartres St., French Quarter, tel. 504/942–7500. Dress: informal. No reservations. AE. Closed Sat. and Sun.*

★ **Patout's.** Chef Alex Patout has established a distinctive culinary style in New Orleans. The original Patout's is in New Iberia, the heart of Cajun country; there are two others, one in Los Angeles and one in Dallas. The elegant atmosphere lends a sophisticated touch to Cajun cuisine. Chicken Lizzy—smoked breast of chicken enhanced with crabmeat or crawfish in a creamy sauce—is a wonder. For a sampling of crawfish in season, try the crawfish Yvonne. Also excellent is the shrimp and tasso pasta, and the tournedos topped with crawfish and a cream sauce. *1319 St. Charles Ave., Uptown, tel. 504/524–4054. No jeans. Weekend reservations advised. AE, MC, V.*

Moderate
★ **Copeland's.** With handsome cafe decor, this is a neighborhood-oriented chain restaurant that is rapidly expanding. A saucy range of appetizers is offered, and the menu is extensive. It is possible to order taster portions here, such as a serving of jambalaya for under $2, coupled with appetizers, soups, or salads. The entree selection is vast. Portions are generous, and the food is very spicy. Some of the best-known appetizers are Cajun popcorn (batter-fried shrimp and crawfish), Huey's

Jerry + Wilma
25/8/89
? 215 Royal St

Andouille (smoked and poached sausage served on a bed of collard greens with a buttermilk biscuit), and the onion mum (a large onion cut into the shape of a chrysanthemum before it is deep-fried). The duck, rabbit, and fish entrees are the best choices. California wines and specialty drinks like hurricanes and mint juleps are served. Copeland's is the least expensive of the Cajun restaurants. Best dessert: the mile-and-a-half-high pie for two. *4338 St. Charles Ave., Uptown, tel. 504/897–2325; 1001 S. Clearview Pkwy., Metairie, tel. 504/733–7843; 701 Veterans Blvd., Metairie, tel. 504/831–9449; 1700 Lapalco Blvd., Gretna, tel. 504/364–1575. Dress: informal. No reservations. AE, MC, V.*

Olde N'Awlins Cookery. Inspired by K-Paul's, but with more accent on atmosphere, this restaurant is adorned with quaint photographs of New Orleans and gently cooled by slow-spinning ceiling fans. There are several undistinguished dishes, and a few that are consistently good. After trying a belt-bender Cajun martini, the alligator sausage gets you off to a steady start. Predictably, there are a couple of blackened dishes on the menu. Segue into the main course with the prime rib, cooked with spices on an open grill. Finish with sweet potato pie. Lunch specials change daily. *629 Conti St., French Quarter, tel. 504/529–3663. Dress: informal. No reservations. No credit cards.*

Classic Creole

Expensive **Arnaud's.** The restaurant had degenerated into a sorry state
★ until the present owners took over in 1978, restoring it to its 1918 grandeur. Beveled glass, ceiling fans, and tiled floors contribute to the aura of traditional Southern hospitality. The Sunday jazz brunch is a classic New Orleans experience. Shrimp Arnaud is the best version of shrimp remoulade in the city. Pompano *en croute*, veal Wohl, and fillet Charlemond topped with two sauces are savory entree selections. There is little on the Arnaud's menu that isn't excellent. Lunch specials change weekdays; weekend brunch. For dessert, the crêpes Suzette Arnaud rivals the bananas Foster. Café brulot (an after-dinner coffee-and-liqueur drink), prepared at tableside, is the finest in New Orleans. *813 Bienville St., French Quarter, tel. 504/523–5433. Jackets. Reservations required. AE, MC, V.*

The Caribbean Room. Located in the famed Pontchartrain Hotel, this is a charming establishment long frequented by Uptown families. Rose-colored walls are warmed by gas chandeliers that hang above an exquisite fountain. Seafood is the real draw here, but the steaks are commendable, too. Gone is the popular pompano Pontchartrain; its replacement is trout Eugene, topped with crabmeat and shrimp in a simple butter sauce. Another well-appointed, simple dish: oysters *en brochette*. The restaurant is famed for its mile-high pie, a heap of peppermint, chocolate, and vanilla ice cream, meringue, and chocolate sauce, the entire concoction measuring about eight inches high. There's a Sunday brunch buffet with live classical music. *Pontchartrain Hotel, 2031 St. Charles Ave., Uptown, tel. 504/524–0581. Jackets required for dinner. Reservations advised for weekends. AE, MC, V. Closed Sat. lunch.*

Moderate **Delmonico's.** Popular with Uptowners and CBD professionals, Delmonico's is an old-line Creole establishment replete with antiques. A bevy of New Orleans Creole classics is offered on the menu. Recommended is the trout plate with crawfish etouffee sauce, the soft-shell crab in season, the seafood gumbo, and the redfish with shrimp and crabmeat toppings. Best desserts are the fluff (vanilla ice cream, chocolate sauce, almond and coconut toppings) and the egg custard with rum sauce. *1300 St. Charles Ave., Uptown, tel. 504/525–4937. Dress: informal. Reservations advised for weekends. AE, CB, DC, MC, V. Closed Sat.*

★ **Galatoire's.** Operated by the fourth generation of the Galatoire family, this restaurant is a tradition in New Orleans. Creole specialties are served in a large, brightly lit room graced with mirrors on all sides. Lunch is served all afternoon, and the food is superb and reasonably priced (by New Orleans standards), which explains why it's so difficult to get a table (expect lines from 11:30 AM to 1:30 PM). Start with oysters Bienville, shrimp remoulade, or the oysters *en brochette*. When crawfish are in season, try the crawfish etouffee. The pompano meuniere amandine is excellent. Two recommended crab dishes: Yvonne and Ravigote. Bouillabaisse for two can be ordered in advance, and there's also a choice of omelets and Creole egg dishes, like Benedict and Sardou. The strong coffee is unbeatable. Waiters do much of the food preparation in the kitchen. *209 Bourbon St., French Quarter, tel. 504/525–2021. Dress: informal. No reservations. No credit cards. Closed Mon.*

Marie Laveau's. Named after the 19th-century voodoo queen, Marie Laveau's is not only an interesting dining spot, but also a favorite bar hangout of locals. There's also a stage in the rear where musical comedies are performed Friday and Saturday nights. The food is distinctive—a blend of Creole and a bit of Cajun. Try the Creole crab cakes, filé gumbo, quail, and alligator soup. You can request large or small portions of almost anything on the menu. The seafood platter can be arranged in a variety of combinations. *329 Decatur St., French Quarter, tel. 504/525–9655. Dress: informal. Reservations advised Fri. and Sat. nights. AE, MC, V.*

Tujague's. This 150-year-old French Quarter institution has the only neon sign on Decatur Street, aside from Jax Brewery. One of the dining rooms is decorated with memorabilia of Madame Begue, the late and legendary restaurateur who had a restaurant housed at the same spot as Tujague's. A balcony upstairs, off the Governor Noe Room, overlooks the bustling French Market activity. The six-course dinner menu includes shrimp remoulade, soup du jour, boiled beef brisket, a choice of three entrees, vegetables du jour, and a terrific bread pudding. The best chicken entree is the chicken grande, a huge platter of chicken with raw tomatoes, peppers, and enough garlic to spice three legs of lamb. *823 Decatur St., French Quarter, tel. 504/525–8676. Dress: informal. Reservations advised for dinner. AE, MC, V.*

Inexpensive **Gumbo Shop.** Standard Creole cuisine is served in an 18th-century building. You enter the restaurant through a small courtyard, where lines form on the weekends. Inside, red-checked tablecloths and large murals set the tone. The gumbo, sad to say, is inconsistent. Order the combination plate for a taste of New Orleans's classics: shrimp Creole, jambalaya, and red beans. Decent po-boys. *630 St. Peter St., French Quarter, tel. 504/525–1486. Dress: informal. No reservations. AE, MC, V.*

[handwritten margin note:] mixed recommendation 8/89

French Creole

Very Expensive **Antoine's.** Founded in 1840 by Antoine Alciatore, this is the oldest independently owned restaurant in the United States. Managed by fifth-generation proprietors, this restaurant has a rich 19th-century Creole ambience. Dining rooms are chock-full of memorabilia, and the menu is entirely in French. The menu has changed little since the 1940s, when Chateaubriand for two was $3.75 (it's $43.50 today). Antoine's is one of the city's most expensive restaurants, but it is also one of the most interesting. Request to be seated in the Large Annex—one of 15 dining rooms—which is filled with photographs of the restaurant. Waiters are particularly adept at enlightening diners about the specialties of the house. The locals who frequent the restaurant enter at a special side entrance, and everyone has a regular waiter. The best way to order here is to tell the waiter what you're in the mood for, and he will suggest accordingly. Recommended appetizers are the oysters Rockefeller, the crawfish etouffee in season, and the crab Ravigote. Entrees like the *poulet bonne femme* (allow 40 minutes), fillet tips Medicis, and pompano amandine are dependably good. Best dessert: baked Alaska. Finish off with café brulot, then tour the restaurant; the wine cellar houses the city's largest collection of wine. *713 St. Louis St., French Quarter, tel. 504/581–4422. Jacket required for dinner; no blue jeans. Reservations advised weekends. AE, DC, MC, V.*

★ **Brennan's.** Opened in 1956, Brennan's is one of the city's premier dining establishments. Breakfast at Brennan's is a tradition unto itself—"1,000 served daily" in one of a dozen intimate dining rooms or on the lush patio. The eggs Benedict, Sardou, and Houssarde are rich, creamy, and consistently good. Here one should never be shy of ordering a breakfast dessert: the famed bananas Foster, flamed with liqueur in a tableside ritual. Weekend brunch begins earlier than at most restaurants, at 8 AM. The turtle soup is superb and the oysters Rockefeller magnificent—no spinach is used, which is different from most recipes. For dinner, the bountiful tournedos Chanteclair, three prime cuts each with a different sauce, is representative of one of the strong suits of the restaurant: excellent French sauces with a Creole stamp. Recipient of numerous awards, Brennan's has an outstanding wine cellar. *417 Royal St., French Quarter, tel. 504/525–9711. No jeans. Reservations advised. AE, DC, MC, V.*

★ **Commander's Palace.** Housed in a renovated Victorian mansion, this elegant restaurant offers an excellent sampling of old Creole cooking prepared with a combination of American and French styles. There's always something original coming out of the kitchen, like Gulf fish and fresh quail stuffed with crabmeat. Whatever you order can be counted upon to be fresh daily from local farms or the sea. Start with the soups, particularly the turtle, and the many oyster appetizers. Best entrees: veal chop Tchoupatoulas, trout with roasted pecans, and tournedos. Among the best desserts is the one-of-a-kind bread-pudding soufflé. Jazz brunch is served weekends with lots of Creole egg dishes; best enjoyed in the Green Room overlooking the patio. *1403 Washington Ave., Garden District, tel. 504/899–8221. Jackets required. Reservations required. AE, DC, MC, V.*

★ **Le Ruth's.** The food here is a vigorous selection of modern Creole cuisine. Popular with visiting heads of state, Le Ruth's is housed in a charming Victorian building. A remarkable art collection hangs in two of the dining rooms. Specialties are the chef's steak, a two-pound sirloin strip charred under a broiler, and the roast duck with green peppercorns. French bread and ice cream are homemade. The desserts are dramatic. Ladies' seating arrangements include footstools. Service is casual. *636 Franklin, Gretna, tel. 504/362–4914. Dress: informal. Reservations advised. AE, MC, V. Closed Sun. and Mon.*

Expensive **Broussard's.** A popular old restaurant that features traditional Creole cuisine with French overtones. Three dining rooms face a patio of lush greenery. Broussard's hors d'oeuvre selections, called "A Taste of New Orleans," include escargots; mushrooms stuffed with crawfish, soft-shell crab, and oysters; and classic oyster dishes. It's best to avoid the trout, which can be dry. The quail and the rack of lamb with mint sauce are deftly seasoned. *819 Conti St., French Quarter, tel. 504/581–3866. Jackets required. Reservations required. AE, CB, DC, MC, V.*

Christians. The building that houses this restaurant was converted from a church, making Christians a unique establishment. Cushioned pews line the walls, and the room glows with light that shines through the stained-glass windows. The only negative point is that the tables are too close together. Creole and Continental dishes mark the diverse menu. The wine selection is strong on California chardonnay and cabernets. Recommended appetizers are the escargots and the smoked soft-shell crab. Fresh Norwegian salmon is a specialty here, and the bouillabaisse is well prepared. Dependable sweetbreads and filet mignon. *3835 Iberville St., Mid-City, tel. 504/482–4924. Dress: informal. Reservations advised. AE, MC, V. Closed Sun.*

Seb's. This new restaurant, which overlooks the Mississippi River, has a strong emphasis on fish—right down to the decor. Mardi Gras artist Joe Barth's school of carefully crafted fish dot the walls, depicting the 13 different fish on the dinner menu. It is possible to sample a variety of dishes in taster portions. A recommended appetizer is the cold taster: shrimp remoulade Royal, crabmeat Decatur, and seafood seviche. *Jackson Brewery Millhouse, 5th floor, 600 Decatur St., French Quarter, tel. 504/522–1696. Dress: informal. Reservations advised weekends. AE, MC, V. Closed Sat. for lunch.*

★ **La Lousiane.** La Lousiane recently reopened under new ownership with all the grandeur of its former life and a menu that blends imaginative new dishes with some old classics. The historic building dates back to the early 19th century, and it is one of the Quarter's best examples of French-Spanish architecture. Shimmering Bacarat crystal chandeliers illuminate Italian silk wall coverings in the main dining room. The Garden Room overlooks a small courtyard, and there is a private dining room for 12, complete with a buzzer for service. The cuisine is French-Creole, and the service is classic New Orleans style. Herbed crawfish on toast is a delicate starter, served in a small casserole with a light, garlic sauce. The best entree offerings are usually the daily specials, particularly the pompano and salmon. *725 Iberville St., French Quarter, tel. 504/523–4664. Dress: informal. Reservations advised. AE, MC, V. Closed Sun. and Mon. and for lunch on Sat.*

Moderate   **Berdou's.** Proprietor George Berdou founded the restaurant 33
★   years ago and still does much of the cooking. The ambience is
casual and the prices are low for food comparable to that of the
finest Creole restaurants in town. It is worth the trip to Gretna
for a slice of local color. Mr. Berdou supervises the preparation
of each pompano *en papillote* by his chef of 12 years. The Creole
gumbo, crawfish etouffee and crawfish bisque (in season),
chicken Clemenceau, and trout amandine are recommended.
All seafood items are prepared fresh in season. Service is
friendly. *300 Monroe St., Gretna, tel. 504/366–2401. No jeans.
No credit cards. Closed Sun. and Mon.*

Cafe Savanna. A small, casual cafe with a tropical patio in the
rear of the restaurant. An interesting array of seafood specialties are served; the grilled fish is usually the best selection.
Sunday brunch changes weekly, and a blackboard serves as the
menu. Good po-boys. *8324 Oak St., Uptown, tel. 504/866–3223.
Dress: informal. No reservations. MC, V.*

Chez Pierre's. Chef Perry Fuselier and his family offer fine Creole and French cuisine in a casual setting. For starters, try the
crabmeat St. Pierre or the oysters Casino. There are some
good trout dishes and a seafood fettuccine that changes daily.
The chef prides himself on homemade ice cream and bread. *3
Westbank Expressway, West Bank, tel. 504/362–6703. Dress:
informal. Reservations advised. MC, V. Closed for lunch Sat.;
closed Sun.*

Feelings. A small, pleasant restaurant with a leafy courtyard
set in a historic building in the popular Bywater section. A pianist performs weekends, and cocktails and appetizers are
served in the courtyard. A five-course dinner is offered for an
extra $10 over the price of entrees. Veal Florentine is a best-
seller. Best peanut butter pie around. The food is modest but
well prepared. *2600 Chartres St., Faubourg Marigny, tel.
504/945–2222. Dress: informal. Reservations advised weekends for dinner. AE, MC, V. Closed for lunch Sat.–Tues.*

★   **Gautreau's.** This small cafe (converted from an old pharmacy) is
one of the most popular restaurants in the Uptown area. The
food is straightforward, imaginative, and comfortably Creole.
Lunches are light and include soups, salads, and entrees. The
dinner menu consists entirely of specials; perhaps the best of
those regularly appearing are the various renderings of filet
mignon, but the fish and veal are also consistent winners. For
dessert try the chocolate corruption. One problem here is overly lively acoustics. *1728 Soniat St., Uptown, tel. 504/899–7397.
Dress: informal. Reservations advised. MC, V. Closed for
lunch Sat.; closed Sun.*

Recommended →
3/89

Creole-Inspired

Expensive   **Cafe Sbisa.** Especially popular with local writers and artists,
★   Cafe Sbisa was one of the first restaurants in the city to revive
the mesquite grill. It has served as a training ground for some
of the city's finest young chefs. The cuisine is a mixture of classic Creole, French, and new American. Seafood is the specialty
here. The grilled swordfish is unbeatable, and the mussels in
absinthe and cream is delicate and delicious. Duckling is also
prepared with flair. Musical entertainment evenings and for
Sunday brunch. *1011 Decatur St., French Quarter, tel.
504/561–8345. Dress: informal. Reservations advised for
weekends. AE, MC, V.*

Clancy's. This is an old neighborhood bar that has become one of the city's most adventuresome nouvelle restaurants. The kitchen's centerpiece is a mesquite grill, which is used in preparing shrimp, duck, and lamb dishes. The rest of the menu sallies into some previously uncharted territory; the results are of inconsistent quality, but the hits are unforgettable. Especially good: oysters Bienville or Rockefeller, the sausage *en croute*, the angel-hair pasta with shellfish in season, and the smoked soft-shell crab. *6100 Annunciation St., Uptown, tel. 504/895–1111. Dress: informal. Reservations advised for weekends. AE, DC, MC, V. Closed Sun.*

Flagon's A Wine Bar & Bistro. Originally a wine bar that served light hors d'oeuvres, Flagon's became a full-scale restaurant rivaling the city's better nouvelle-cuisine establishments. The dining rooms, with their sleek art-deco lines, are elegant and understated. Besides housing one of the few caviar bars in town, Flagon's also claims to offer the largest selection of wine by the glass in the South. A rich appetizer is the roast duck leg stuffed with andouille dressing; the chilled shrimp in basil-lime vinaigrette and pasta carbonara are equally superb. Recommended entrees are veal grillades and hominy grits, served at the Sunday jazz brunch, and grilled shrimp with fettuccine and tasso. The bistro menu offers a choice of appetizer, entree, and dessert at a more affordable price. Complimentary valet parking. *3222 Magazine St., Uptown, tel. 504/895–6471. Dress: informal. Reservations advised for weekends. AE, MC, V.*

Moderate **Bouligny.** The building this restaurant occupies was once a fire station. One wall of the engine room was removed, making way for an airy dining room with large paintings, plants, modern sculpture, and lots of sunshine. Nouvelle cuisine is the style here. The grilled fish, veal Magazine, and roasted grilled duck are signature dishes. There is an inexpensive lunch menu weekdays and brunch on Sunday. *4100 Magazine St., Uptown, tel. 504/891–4444. Dress: informal. Reservations advised. AE, MC, V.*

★ **Constantin's.** This bright new star, located in a building that was once Lee Barnes Cooking School, is the most nouvelle of all Uptown restaurants. The entrance is through a walkway with latticework decorated with tiny white lights. The inside is austere. Hardwood floors and not much on the walls, but it's stately. The husband and wife team (she's the chef) who run Constantin's have put together a very interesting menu. Great sandwiches and daily specials are offered for lunch. The dinner menu is completely different, and much more elaborate. Order the brie wrapped in spinach and pepper jelly (deep fried) as an appetizer. The creamy rabbit soup is spiced with lots of ginger. There's a nice oyster dish, breaded and served on steamed artichoke leaves with a spicy lemon beurre blanc sauce with tasso. Friendly and attentive service. *8402 Oak St., Uptown, tel. 504/861–2111. Dress: informal. Reservations advised for dinner. AE, MC, V. Closed Sat. for lunch; closed Sun.*

★ **L'Eagles Bar and Grill.** One of the finest new restaurants to surface in New Orleans. A European country decor creates an intimate environment, with lovely antique prints hanging on the deep coral walls. According to chef James Braddock, L'Eagles offers Southern regional cuisine. The first course is ample and creative. Fresh herbs are always used. The crabmeat and ratatouille is a hearty melange. The crawfish fettuccine, served cold, has cream, herbs, and a piquant twist.

There are usually four or five fresh fish specials daily; some are prepared on a mesquite grill. The swordfish and the mixed grill are immaculate. Provimi veal and steaks also have character. Desserts include the excellent chocolate Bourbon pie with pecans and spirits—sinfully enticing. Some of the kitchen staff are Vietnamese, and they influence the chef's use of herbs. This is becoming a trend in many distinguished New Orleans kitchens. Lunch is a bargain for $5.95, which includes an entree and soup or salad. *545 Julia St., Central Business District, tel. 504/529–2271. Dress: casual. Reservations not accepted at lunch for fewer than 4 people; reservations advised for dinner. AE, DC, MC, V. Closed for lunch Sat. and Sun.*

Flagon's in the Jackson Brewery. This wine bar and bistro is an offshoot of the original Flagon's, the result of a partnership breakup. Located in the Jax Brewery Millhouse, the dining rooms are fairly small with a nice view of the Mississippi River. It's a good place to meet friends for wine by the glass and hors d'oeuvres. The menu offers regional dishes. Try the grilled Gulf fish and shrimp or the Southern buttermilk chicken. *Jackson Brewery Millhouse, 600 Decatur St., French Quarter, tel. 504/524–5494. Dress: informal. Reservations accepted. MC, V.*

★ **Gee & Lil's.** Jamaican Creole cuisine has arrived in New Orleans. Once a neighborhood seafood eatery, this new restaurant is tucked away on Hayne Boulevard, facing the levee. It has a plain brown facade and neon sign, circa 1950. Inside, low ceilings, small tables, and a long bar create a casual, down-home atmosphere. This is some of the spiciest and most imaginative food north of the Caribbean Sea. The chef-owner, a Jamaican, was formerly sous-chef at Willy Coln's, the German restaurant on the West Bank. He grows his own peppers and herbs in his backyard. He has Creolized and Europeanized traditional Jamaican dishes, like the jerk chicken (which, instead of being grilled, is sautéed in a demi-glacé sauce), and the steamy pepper soup. Limited but interesting and moderately priced wine list. Not recommended for someone on a salt- and pepper-restricted diet. *7204 Hayne Blvd., Lakefront, tel. 504/242–7570. Dress: informal. Reservations advised for dinner. AE, MC, V. Closed Sun. and Mon.*

★ **Mr. B's Bistro.** The younger generation of the Brennan family that owns Commander's Palace have branched out into the French Quarter with this classy and innovative bistro. The specially designed hickory- and pecan-log fire roasts fish and steak offerings, which add a wonderful aroma to the entrance on Royal Street. The shrimp Chippewa and hickory-grilled fish are highly recommended, and the gumbo ya-ya is first-rate. The wine list is solid, with some very good wines available by the glass at the bar. Lively weekend jazz brunch with New Orleans classic egg dishes. *201 Royal St., French Quarter, tel. 504/523–2078. Dress: informal. Reservations advised. AE, MC, V.*

Upperline. When chef-owner Jason Clevenger left his family-run restaurant for new horizons, Tom Cowman, former chef of Jonathan's, took his place at Upperline. Cowman has brought with him some of his best signature dishes. This neighborhood Uptown bistro is casual and elegant, offering luscious oysters with five sauces, liver with orange, cold trout mousse with dill mayonnaise, and fine charcoal-grilled items. Wonderful desserts. *1413 Upperline St., Uptown, tel. 504/891–9822. Dress: informal. Reservations advised. AE, MC, V.*

Italian Creole

Expensive ★ **Frank Occhipinti's.** This large and popular suburban Italian Creole place is probably the best restaurant in Metairie. Start with oysters Diablo, the fine artichoke soup, and the memorable salad with house dressing. The steaks are prime and broiled; the several veal dishes use excellent white veal. Good seafood and chicken dishes as well. For dessert, sample the rich pineapple fluff with a bottom layer of pecans and a topping of vanilla pudding, and the banana shortcake with homemade whipped cream. Occhipinti's has a little bit of everything and good service. *2712 N. Arnoult Rd., Metairie, tel. 504/888-1131. Dress: informal. Reservations advised. AE, MC, V. Closed for lunch Sat.; closed Sun.*

★ **Mosca's.** One of New Orleans's great restaurants, Mosca's is also among the hardest to find. Approximately 15 minutes from Downtown, Mosca's is located in Waggaman, past the Huey P. Long Bridge, and only becomes visible upon arrival. Large platters of Italian Creole food are served in the stark dining room. Garlic is the prevalent seasoning. The best dish at Mosca's is the Italian oysters, baked in a casserole with sauce and bread crumbs. The Italian sausage is homemade. The crab salad marinated in shells is a highly recommended first course. Chicken à la grandee, game birds, and filet mignon are also excellent. Service is casual. *4137 U.S. 90, Waggaman, tel. 504/436-9942. Dress: informal. Reservations advised. No credit cards. Closed Sun. and Mon.*

New Victoria Train Station. Formerly part of a chain, this restaurant now is owned and operated independently by locals. Train cars with booths are the dining rooms, and there's a large bar at the entrance with live weekend entertainment. The head chef was formerly with La Louisiane, the stately Italian Creole restaurant that closed in 1987. The steak and seafood menu has been expanded with rich, garlicky appetizers and a few good Italian lunch items. Although lobster is supposed to be a specialty here, it isn't. Stick to the seafood appetizers, steaks, and prime rib. Delicious barbecue shrimp, and a fine, rich bread pudding that comes flaming to the table in whiskey sauce. The food is better than the less than elegant surroundings. *111 Iberville St., French Quarter, tel. 504/523-7793. Dress: informal. Reservations accepted. AE, MC, V.*

★ **Pascal Manale's.** Family-owned since 1913, this is the home of the original barbecue shrimp. A terrific appetizer is the combination remoulade, crabmeat, and shrimp topped with a ring of spicy cocktail sauce. Steaks, veal, Italian dishes, and seafood entrees are the offerings here. Lunch is very popular, and so is the old-time oyster bar, which serves a New Orleans tradition: ice-cold oysters on the half shell (meant to be eaten standing up). It is common to have to wait in the bar for a table when it's crowded, sometimes for as long as 45 minutes. Service is casual. Ribs are provided for the barbecue shrimp. You can get good po-boys at the bar for lunch. *1828 Napoleon Ave., Uptown, tel. 504/895-4877. Dress: informal. Reservations advised for dinner. AE, MC, V. Lunch and dinner. Closed for lunch Sat.; closed Sun.*

Stephen & Martin's. Off St. Charles Avenue, this is a popular and attractive neighborhood restaurant serving solid Creole and Italian dishes. An oyster bar connects the main dining room to the **4141 Club,** a chic bar and disco, which adjoins a second restaurant, the Grill Room. In the more casual **Grill Room** you can get the delicious soups and desserts offered in the main dining room of Stephen & Martin's, as well as grilled chicken, fish, and baby-back ribs. The main room features rich pasta dishes, such as capellini and meatballs, and other fine entrees, including the superbly rich veal Reginald. Cream sauces abound. The Grill Room overlooks St. Charles Avenue. *1613 Milan St., Uptown, tel. 504/897–0781. Dress: informal. Reservations accepted. AE, MC, V.*

Soul Creole

Moderate **Chez Helene.** Stuffed bell peppers, fried chicken, Creole gumbo, and smothered okra are just some of the fine recipes of Helene Howard, whose nephew, Austin Leslie, opened the second Chez Helene at 316 Chartres Street (de la Poste Hotel, French Quarter, tel. 504/525–6130). The popular television series *Frank's Place* is based on Leslie and his soulful, soul-food establishment. Leslie's soul and Cajun specialties are marked by spiciness and fresh herbs; he uses no bottled, dried, or dehydrated condiments. This is rich New Orleans cooking. The Creole jambalaya and crawfish etouffee are among the city's simplest and best. The fresh corn bread is a joy. *1540 N. Robertson St., Mid-City, tel. 504/947–1206. Dress: informal. Weekends until 1 AM. Reservations accepted. AE, MC, V.*

★ **Dooky Chase.** When they opened the doors in 1941, Leah and Dooky Chase began a neighborhood restaurant that has become one of the most popular in New Orleans. The dining room features artwork by several nationally known black artists. Although the clientele is mixed, Dooky Chase is a key lunch place for black politicians, community leaders, and businessmen. The menu offers a wide variety of spicy Creole dishes and good steaks. The delicious gumbo is made with a good roux, crab, shrimp, oysters, chicken, sausage, ham, and seasoning, and is finished with filé. Recommended is the breast of chicken à la Dooky, stuffed with oyster dressing and baked in a marchand du vin sauce, accompanied by sweet potatoes. Shrimp Creole, Dooky's seafood platter, and grillades with jambalaya are popular dishes here. *2301 Orleans St., Downtown, tel. 504/821–2294. Dress: informal. Reservations accepted. AE, MC, V.*

Inexpensive **Eddie's Restaurant & Bar.** Nestled in a working-class black
★ neighborhood of the Seventh Ward, this down-home tavern is a popular political hangout and an inexpensive family restaurant. Eddie Bacquet specializes in Creole gumbo (with everything imaginable in it), red beans with sausage, and fried chicken. The best entree is the pork-chop plate with oyster dressing. Like a good politician, Eddie makes the rounds to chat with guests. The place is difficult to find, as Law Street does not cross any major thoroughfares; it passes under their bridges. The best way to get there is to head toward Lake Pontchartrain via Elysian Fields Avenue, make a U-turn under the bridge at the I–10 junction, double back and turn right on Law Street. It's four blocks west on the right-hand side of the street. *2119 Law St., Seventh Ward, tel. 504/945–2207. Dress: informal. No reservations. No credit cards. Closed Sun.*

International Cuisines

Chinese
Expensive
★

Trey Yuen. This is the new Trey Yuen and most popular location. The restaurant is situated in the Jackson Brewery, and its decor is authentic Chinese, elegantly and tastefully appointed. Trey Yuen has a menu of average to great Chinese food, mostly Cantonese, but a little of everything. The incorporation of Louisiana seafood with Chinese culinary techniques makes for marvelous ethnic dining. Some of the specials, particularly those involving seafood, are remarkable, as is the Chinese feast for eight or more, which you must book well in advance. Fresh local specialties include alligator with mushrooms, crawfish with spicy lobster sauce, and the Trey Yuen soft-shell crab topped with Tong-Cho sauce. The Jackson Brewery location has a view of the Mississippi River. *Jackson Brewery, 620 Decatur St., 5th fl., French Quarter, tel. 504/588-9354; Causeway Blvd., Mandeville (about 30 mi from New Orleans), tel. 504/626-4476. Dress: informal. Reservations advised. AE, MC, V.*

Continental
Very Expensive
★

26/8/89 RM
good / expensive
$150 + tip

Grill Room. Housed in the elegant Windsor Court Hotel, the Grill Room is furnished with antiques, original art, and fresh flowers. The sophisticated ambience is enlivened on weekends when a symphonic harpist performs. Ask to be seated near the picture windows. Chef John Carey bills the cuisine here as New American, although there are strong Continental overtones. Begin with baked oysters Peacock or the steak tartare. Especially recommended are the steamed halibut with Beluga caviar and the saddle of red deer with red currant sauce. The grill provides good blackened shrimp. Salads are marvelous. The wine cellar houses an extensive, fairly priced collection. *Windsor Court Hotel, 300 Graviar St., Central Business District, tel. 504/523-6000. Dress: informal. Reservations advised. AE, MC, V.*

★ **The Rib Room.** Large windows afford a generous view of pedestrians, musicians, and the rest of the active street life in the Vieux Carré. Inside, the restaurant's rustic brick walls and glowing rotisseries provide a hearthlike aura, which is particularly pleasant in the winter. Meat is the specialty here; the anchor item is a succulent beef prime rib served with a baked potato and Yorkshire pudding (be sure to use a dash of horseradish on this one). When available, try the lobster stuffed with a blend of shrimp and crabmeat. For the finale, a bevy of tantalizing desserts is rolled out on a tiered silver cart. Also note: The luncheon menu, including the New Orleans oyster poboy, is reasonable. This is a favorite hangout for local politicians. *Royal Orleans Hotel, 621 St. Louis St., French Quarter, tel. 504/529-7045. Dress: informal. Reservations advised for dinner. AE, MC, V.*

★ **Winston's.** This hotel restaurant was recently renovated, and a fresh menu concept was created, featuring dishes that represent the freshest ingredients of each season; the menu changes four times a year. The hotel restaurant scene is very competitive in New Orleans, and Winston's is one of the best. The only drawback is the surroundings; although elegant and beautifully decorated, Winston's is housed on the second floor of the Hilton Hotel lobby in an open space. The most impressive appetizers are the hot ones, such as the smoked Alaskan salmon with pasta. From the grill comes a selection of prime, aged beef, like the Porterhouse. Best signature dishes: lobster Savoy and the roast squab. Desserts are magnificent. *2 Poydras St., Central Business District, tel. 504/561–0500. Jackets required. Reservations advised. AE, MC, V.*

Moderate **Isadora.** A swank art-deco-style restaurant named after Isadora Duncan, the artistic sensation who reached her creative
★ height with interpretive dance during the 1920s. A stunning bar is the restaurant's centerpiece, where locals gather for cocktails after hours. Jazz wafts through the room and onto the street. Seating 90, Isadora serves some of the most imaginative cuisine in New Orleans. Three talented chefs (two are from Acadiana) create visual and flavorful masterpieces. The style is nouvelle Continental/American with a Cajun twist to the seasoning. Start with the sautéed pâté, oysters Lafayette, and rabbit Wellington. The Isadora salad is excellent. For entrees, order the smoked salmon en croute with artichoke crab sauce, the English mixed grill, and the tournedos with crawfish Sabayon and sauce Rouennaise. Nice dessert truffles. *1111 Lafayette Mall in the Energy Center, Central Business District, tel. 504/585–7787. Jackets required. Reservations accepted. AE, MC, V. Closed Sun.*

French **Le Chateau.** Traditional haute cuisine served in an ambience of
Very Expensive simple elegance. Beluga caviar, smoked salmon, and foie gras
★ de Strasbourg are good primers, paving the way for some of chef-owner Denis Rety's fine French cooking. He artfully prepares bouillabaisse à la Marseillaise, scampi Provençale, saumon en croute in a beurre blanc sauce, and a sumptuous Chateaubriand bouquetiere (for two). A nice side dish is the champignons sautéed in shallots. The Grand Marnier soufflé for two is highly recommended; you must order this when you order your entree. *1000 Behrman Hwy., Gretna, tel. 504/392–4690. Dress: informal. Reservations accepted. AE, MC, V. Lunch and dinner. Closed for lunch Sat., Sun.*

★ **Henri.** This stunning gourmet restaurant in Le Meridien Hotel welcomes consultant Marc Haeberlin of Auberge de l'Ill restaurant (in Alsace, France) twice annually to fashion seasonal specialties for Henri. The quality of cuisine here is almost as spectacular as the parent French establishment. Henri inherited the famed signature dishes, like the dense and flavorful salmon mousse, a marvelous creation covered with a frothy fish mousse and white-wine sauce. The foie gras trufee rivals the best found in Strasbourg and in Paris during the Christmas season. For a taste of this, order the duckling salad. A combination of sweetbreads and rabbit is artful. The venison with grand veneur sauce is deep and gamey. The best dessert is a visual masterpiece: the cake and chocolate mousse with pistachio ice cream, perfectly inscribed with treble clefs. Courses are pleasantly paced. *Le Meridien Hotel, 614 Canal St., Central Business District, tel. 504/527–6708. Jackets required. Reservations advised. AE, MC, V.*

La Provence. Chef-owner Chris Kerageorgiou combines local ingredients such as mierlitons, oysters, and crawfish in French Provençale recipes. The decor is reminiscent of an intimate roadside cafe in the French provinces. Kerageorgiou delights in explaining dishes to diners, and clearly enjoys the compliments he receives from clientele. Begin with panache des poissons Scandinaves, an array of various smoked North Sea fish; the chilled salad of artichoke and crawfish (in season); or the soup du jour. The best entrees are the sweetbreads, duck, and leg of lamb. Presentations are simple and straightforward. *U.S. 190, Lacombe (35 mi from downtown New Orleans, across Lake Pontchartrain), tel. 504/626–7662. Dress: informal. Reservations advised. AE, MC, V. Closed Sun.–Tues.*

★ **Sazerac.** A large, charming, and expensively furnished room with red velvet-covered walls, soft lights, and a strolling accordionist during dinner hours—in a word, romantic. At lunch, local politicos can be seen. French haute cuisine, nouvelle cuisine, and classic Creole dishes are offered on the diverse menu. For dinner, start with the crab vermicelle, Louisiana lump crabmeat, and pasta wrapped in Boston lettuce leaf and served with a Venetian sauce. An order of caviar is rolled to the table on a huge ice carving—everything is dramatically presented here. The young partridge in white burgundy wine is a first-class entree. The desserts are the tour de force; order the chocolate domino. The Sazerac has an elaborate collection of postprandial liqueurs and Jamaican cigars. *University Pl., Central Business District, tel. 504/524–8904. Jackets required for dinner. Reservations advised for dinner. AE, MC, V. Closed Sat. and Sun. for dinner.*

Versailles. The restaurant serves predominantly French cuisine, enhanced by Continental and Creole dishes, prepared by a German chef-owner. The dining room overlooks tree-lined St. Charles Avenue. Start with escargot bourguignonne en croute. The shrimp curry with hearts of palm and pimentos is fairly nice, as are the stuffed quails roasted with cranberries. The desserts are always interesting. The service is occasionally stuffy. Decent wine list. *2100 St. Charles Ave., Uptown, tel. 504/524–2535. Jackets required. Reservations accepted. AE, MC, V. Dinner. Closed Sun.*

Expensive **Crozier's.** A delightful French couple, Eveline and Gerard Crozier, work as a team to create a warm, intimate atmosphere where diners enjoy simply prepared, elegant haute cuisine. The daily specials are always exciting. Veal sweetbreads sautéed in lemon butter win superlative ratings from local diners. A classic coq au vin, simmered in red wine with mushrooms, bacon, and pearl onions, is offered. Veau à la Crozier is superb —morsels of veal and shrimp combined in a light cream sauce, served with rice (available Saturday only). Service is amiable. *7033 Read La., New Orleans East, tel. 504/241–8220. Dress: informal. Reservations accepted. MC, V. Closed Sat.–Mon. for lunch; Sun.; Mon. for dinner.*

★ **Louis XVI.** The restaurant moved to the St. Louis Hotel three years ago. The new proprietors and executive chef are French. The dining rooms, which overlook a pretty courtyard, are appointed with elegant art-deco designs. A pianist performs nightly at a black grand in the bar. (You can eat at the bar if the dining rooms are full.) The menu is devoted largely to Gallic cuisine. There are a few Creole appetizers, but the strength of the menu is in the French classic dishes, like the rack of spring lamb, the foie gras, smoked salmon, and the signature dish, Chateaubriand for two. The duck with peppercorns and the steak au poivre are commendable. The desserts are strong, in the French tradition. Top ratings go to the Louis XVI cake, a feather-light wisp of a dessert. Service can sometimes be a bit slow when the restaurant is crowded. *730 Bienville St., French Quarter, tel. 504/581–7000. Reservations required weekends. Jackets required. AE, MC, V.*

Restaurant de la Tour Eiffel. The 1986 arrival of this architectural marvel capped a mini-epic. In 1981, the French government closed the Eiffel Tower's second-level restaurant because of structural cracks. Meticulously disassembled into 11,000 boxes, the restaurant was shipped first to New York, then to New Orleans, and finally resurrected into a wondrous structure resembling a giant kaleidoscope. The French cuisine is reasonably priced and generally quite good. Many Creole dishes have been added to the menu. Breakfast is elaborate. For lunch, there are light offerings like salade Niçoise and crudités, as well as a full-scale assembly of appetizers, soups, and entrees. The oyster Rockefeller soufflé is tops. Shrimp tout Paris is one of the chef-owner's signature dishes. *2040 St. Charles Ave., Uptown, tel. 504/524–2555. Dress: informal. Reservations recommended. AE, CB, DC, MC, V.*

Moderate **Le Bistro.** This small, elegant restaurant has a 1900 Parisian ★ bistro decor with beveled glass mirrors, red leather banquettes, and delightful Impressionist-style paintings. The cuisine is a blend of Mediterranean and Provençal styles. The eggplant caviar appetizer is superb: It is roasted; chilled; seasoned with garlic, olive oil, and basil; and served in ramekins alongside a hearty tapenade. Try a glass of 1873 Graves Château de Malle along with your appetizer. The spinach salad with sautéed oysters and the grilled shrimp are recommended, as are the daily pasta dishes. A sampling of appetizers is a good way to experience the range of chef Susan Spicer's culinary talents. A miniature courtyard behind the restaurant is a fitting spot to linger over desserts and coffee. Le Bistro seats only 40 people, and the tables are close together, but it ranks at the top of New Orleans's restaurants. *733 Toulouse St., French Quarter, tel. 504/528–9206. Dress: informal. Reservations advised. AE, MC, V. Closed Sun. for lunch.*

Val de Loire. A new restaurant in the Rink. The French chef-owner previously owned five restaurants in Washington, DC, and recently moved to New Orleans to open Val de Loire. The restaurant resembles some of the finer bistros in Paris. Windows overlook Washington Avenue, and pastries are displayed at the bar, a tempting sight. The only ingredients this restaurant stocks that aren't fresh here are the canned tomato paste and the hearts of palm. The chef makes liberal and distinctive use of fresh herbs in the sauces, which are excellent. The anchovy butter and fresh dill butter that accompany the hot bread are a nice touch. Best bets are the daily specials. The crawfish bisque has crème fraîche and fresh tarragon. The crawfish mousse is artful: A bouquet of plump crawfish is tucked inside a dome-shaped mousse, topped with fresh mint. The duckling breast is tender. None of the meat is overcooked here. A complimentary glass of champagne ends each meal. *2727 Prytania St., Uptown, tel. 504/891–1973. Dress: informal. Reservations advised for dinner. AE, MC, V. Closed Sat. for lunch; closed Sun.*

Inexpensive **Café Degas.** This charming little open-air cafe is named for Edgar Degas, the French Impressionist who once lived 10 blocks away. Several of his paintings hang in the nearby New Orleans Museum of Art. The 50-seat restaurant is adjoined by a small bar. The best time to come is during a rainstorm, which makes a dramatic impact on the tin roof. Classical music and French-speaking waiters create the ambience here. The menu offers predominantly French classics, although there are a few Creole overtones, especially for Sunday brunch, which is popular. The onion soup is a disappointment. The salade Niçoise is better sampled elsewhere. The smoked salmon with capers is the best appetizer. Seafood and chicken specials are offered daily; among the best are the shrimp Pernod and the chicken Cassis. The wine list contains 15–20 good choices from France and California. *3127 Esplanade Ave., Esplanade Ridge (near City Park), tel. 504/945–5635. Dress: informal. AE, MC, V. Closed Sun. for dinner.*

La Crêpe Nanou. What used to be a small and simple creperie is now a full-scale, reasonably priced French restaurant. There's a charming little patio flanking the main dining room (where you can see them making the crepes). The place has a feeling of a small French country inn. Light lunches with good daily specials, dinner, and Sunday brunch (which begins as early as 9:30 AM) are served. Fresh mussels Provençale is a good starter. Baked oysters à la Creole is prepared with andouille sausage and mushroom, strongly flavored by aioli. The crisp green salad is tossed at the table with vinaigrette in a large wooden bowl. The lamb is exceptional and modestly priced. Crepes still abound, both as entrees and desserts. *1410 Robert St., Uptown, tel. 504/899–2670. Dress: informal. Reservations accepted. MC, V.*

German
Moderate

Kolb's. The main dining room has quaint belt-operated ceiling fans that were purchased at the 1884 Cotton Centennial Exposition. Popular with CBD professionals. Some of the waiters are multilingual. A national historic landmark, Kolb's is now located on the site of the original Jockey Club. German food is the strong suit, although Creole and Continental dishes are available too. Good turtle soup, barbecue shrimp, and a fresh seafood salad for lunch. Try the Kolb schnitzel, crabmeat on top of pannéed veal. The dessert specialty is cheesecake strudel. Personalized service. They live it up for Oktoberfest, with oom pah bands and a special menu. During Carnival, Kolb's charges special rates for parade nights and Mardi Gras day, complete with buffet and open bar. *125 St. Charles Ave., Central Business District, tel. 504/522–8278. Dress: informal. Reservations accepted. AE, MC, V. Closed Sun.*

Willy Coln's. Housed in a building that resembles a Swiss chalet, this pretty, rustic restaurant has several dining rooms, each with its own character and a cozy bar, which is usually empty unless there's a line for tables. A strolling accordionist plays and sings at appointed times. Chef-owner Coln serves a mixed menu of German, Creole, Caribbean, and French food. Start with the hearty, spicy black-bean soup or the smoked salmon. The fresh fish of the day is always a winner. A house specialty is the roast veal shank for two, tender meat that is carved at tableside and served au jus with an assortment of vegetables. The Black Forest cake is feather light. There's a May winefest and a full-blown German Oktoberfest. *2505 Whitney Ave., Gretna, tel. 504/361–3860. Dress: informal. Reservations advised. AE, MC, V. Closed Sun. and Mon.*

Italian
Expensive
★

Andrea's. Roberto De Angelis and Andrea Apuzzo have created a dining environment of tasteful elegance that showcases the rich tradition of Italian dining. It is possible to have a light lunch here for those on the run, but the best way is to linger over several courses. The menu selections are gourmet northern Italian. There's a delightful array of antipasto displayed at the entrance. Start with antipasto, then move on to a pasta course, the Capelli d'Angelo Andrea (angel hair tossed with salmon, flamed with vodka in a light cream sauce and topped with caviar). A delicate middle course is the homemade caciota cheese. The Ossobuco Milanese is the best in town. Recommended is the marvelous Filetto di Manzo Andrea, prime tenderloin of beef butterflied, flamed with brandy, sautéed with assorted peppers and mushrooms, and finished in a light demi-glace sauce. For dessert, order the layered sponge cake filled with mascarpone cheese and the espresso coffee. Sunday brunch is replete with live Italian music and balloons. Discounts are offered at dinner before 7 PM. *3100 19th St., Metairie, tel. 504/834–8583. Dress: informal. Reservations advised. AE, MC, V. Closed Sat. for lunch.*

La Riviera. Everything is fresh, even the pasta, which is made by a creative chef-owner whose dishes are more northern Italian than is ordinarily seen in seemingly all-Sicilian New Orleans. Especially good is the appetizer of crabmeat ravioli; the veal and the trout entrees and steak pizzaiola are the best entrees. *4506 Shores Dr., Metairie, tel. 504/834–8583. Dress: informal. Reservations advised. AE, MC, V. Closed Sun.*

Ristorante Patore. A quaint, understated Italian restaurant offering a fairly extensive menu of northern classics. The fried calamari makes good finger food for groups. The ravioli in brodo is served in a rich, steaming broth. Among the best pasta choices is the gnocchi pomodoro, a regional delicacy made with potato flour. Good jumbo shrimp brochette topped with crabmeat. Service is casual. *301 Tchoupitoulas St., Central Business District, tel. 504/524–1122. Dress: informal. Reservations advised for dinner. AE, MC, V. Closed Sat. for lunch; closed Sun.*

Trattoria Roma. A charming two-story restaurant with chandeliers, small tables, and Italian music on stereo. Upstairs there's a bar where postprandial liquors can be enjoyed. The menu changes with the seasons. Homemade pasta dishes like the linguine Puttanesca (pasta with capers, olives, cherry tomatoes, mushroom, and garlic), and the semolina and spinach noodles with prosciutto, mushrooms, and white sauce are recommended. Rigatoni with four cheeses is a house specialty. There's a nice porterhouse, plump lamb chops, and interesting rabbit dishes, particularly the cacciatore. Good Italian wines. *611 Decatur St., French Quarter, tel. 504/523–9814. Dress: informal. Reservations advised for dinner. AE, MC, V. Closed Mon.*

Moderate **Birraporetti.** A chain restaurant that began in the posh River Oaks area of Houston. The decor is much more distinguished than the food. The hand-rubbed mahogany bar serves locals after hours. Housed on the fourth floor of the Jax Brewery Millhouse, Birraporetti offers a sweeping river view. Casual food with a heavy emphasis on pizza. Don't bother with the stuffed mushroom caps, crab cakes, or fettuccine. Good lasagna and cheesecake. *640 Decatur St., Jackson Brewery Millhouse, French Quarter, tel. 504/525–9191. Dress: informal. Reservations accepted. AE, MC, V.*

Tony Angello's. This is the best version of Sicilian cooking in New Orleans. This casually appointed, extremely popular restaurant is known for its slogan "let Tony feed me," which means you can tell the waiter how hungry you are and he'll produce a meal accordingly. Lots of rich red sauces (a bit on the sweet side), breaded veal, redfish with crabmeat on top, oyster-artichoke soup, eggplant rolls, cannelloni, and manicotti—all quite good. Sicilian cuisine is the most common style of Italian cooking in town. *6262 Fleur de Lis Dr., Lakeview, tel. 504/488–0888. Dress: informal. Reservations accepted. AE, MC, V. Closed Sun. and Mon.*

Eva's Restaurant. A little hole in the wall, close enough to Downtown to get heavy lunch trade, Eva's serves arguably the best lasagna in town. The other Italian specialties are of no greatness; Eva's also features very cheap lunch specials and sandwiches. *337 Dauphine St., French Quarter, tel. 504/523–8534. Dress: informal. No reservations. No credit cards. Closed Sun.*

Napoli. This is the lunch version of Tony Angello's, operated by one of his former managers, and serving similar food along with good versions of New Orleans lunchtime staples. *1917 Ridgelake Dr., Metairie, tel. 504/837–8463. Dress: informal. Reservations accepted. AE, MC, V. Closed Sat. and Sun.*

Back to Basics

Seafood
Moderate
★

Casamento's. The two rooms sparkle from floor to ceiling, with tiled walls and floors that lend themselves to producing an echo effect. Trophies on the walls were won by the muscular chef, the proprietor's nephew. Casamento's specializes in oysters: raw at the bar, fried to order on a platter, or in a sandwich. Other entrees of note are the fried dishes of whatever other seafood they may happen to have that day. Po-boys are made with thick pan bread. A very consistent Uptown favorite. *4330 Magazine St., Uptown, tel. 504/895–9761. Dress: informal. No reservations. No credit cards. Closed Sun. and Mon; closed throughout the summer months.*

★ Drago's. An interesting Yugoslavian seafood restaurant and bar that serves well-spiced, imaginative food. Popular with locals. The extensive menu has bountiful seafood offerings, well apportioned. The seafood platter is enormous. A rich, abundant dish is the seafood pasta—angel hair with shrimp, crawfish, crabmeat, and a cream sauce. There's an excellent redfish filet, thick and succulent, with crabmeat stuffing. For a taste of Yugoslavian fare, order the Yugo platter, which is a combination of three specials (like moussaka, skewered lamb, and grilled lamb sausage). Casual ambience. *3232 N. Arnoult Rd., Metairie, tel. 504/888–9254. Dress: informal. Reservations accepted. AE, MC, V. Closed Sun.*

Felix's. The restaurant was recently expanded, taking over the next-door neighbor's property (Tony's Spaghetti House), which shortened the awful wait at the entrance. The oyster bar puts out some of the best cold ones in town. Good grilled or barbecue shrimp, trout almondine, soft-shell crabs, and frog's legs. Aside from seafood, the lengthy menu includes sandwiches, spaghetti dishes, steaks, chicken, salads, and omelets. Open later than most seafood restaurants—until midnight weekdays and until 1:30 AM on weekends. Diner-style service. *739 Iberville St., French Quarter, tel. 504/522–4440. Dress: casual. Reservations accepted. No credit cards.*

Ralph and Kacoo's. There are two locations in town of this large and popular seafood chain. Each of the many dining rooms has a theme, like Carnival or hunting. The extensive menu is categorized by the different types of shellfish and fish. Particular attention is focused on crawfish and catfish in season. Complimentary hush puppies begin every meal. The portions are enormous, the food fairly spicy, and the sauces overly rich. The fried crawfish are tiny and understated; the crab dishes are better. Also good are the grilled items, particularly the shrimp. A silver tray of home-style desserts is presented after the meal. *519 Toulouse St., French Quarter, tel. 504/522–5226; 601 Veterans Blvd., Metairie, tel. 504/831–3177. Dress: informal. Reservations accepted. AE, MC, V.*

Inexpensive **Acme Oyster House.** Opened in 1907, the Acme is one of the old-
★ est oyster bars in town. Tiled floors, small tables, and a long oyster bar sets the mood for this New Orleans classic. The oysters are cold, and the draft beer even colder. You order your own sandwiches from the cooking station, where you can see the chefs frying the oysters. The wait can be aggravating if it's a crowded day, but it's worth it. The front dining room overlooks the street, and the rear one has a long mirror on the back wall. A recent addition is a very limited salad bar. Most of the po-boys are excellent. Delicious gumbo. You can eat oysters on the half shell at table, although this isn't the normal style of the natives. *724 Iberville St., French Quarter, tel. 504/523–8928. Dress: informal. No reservations. No credit cards. Closes early for dinner: Mon.–Thurs. at 8:30 PM, Fri. at 10 PM, Sat. at 8 PM, and Sun. at 6 PM.*

Alonso & Son. This neighborhood restaurant has a rather dingy appearance, but offers good po-boys and several fried seafood items. It's a popular lunch spot for locals. Try the oyster sandwich, the roast beef, and the fried fish. *587 Central Ave., Jefferson, tel. 504/733–2796. Dress: informal. No reservations. No credit cards. Closed Sun.*

Barrow's Shady Inn. Opened in the 1940s, the restaurant serves only catfish, with casual homecooked stews, hash, and roast beef as afterthought. The catfish is some of the best in these parts, freshly fried to a golden brown, accompanied by potato salad and lettuce and tomatoes. *7214 Mistletoe St., Uptown, tel. 504/482–9427. Dress: informal. No reservations. No credit cards. Closed for lunch Sun.–Wed.; closed for dinner Sun. and Mon.*

Steaks **Crescent City Steak House.** Among the first purveyors of quali-
Expensive ty beef in New Orleans. The chef uses butter excessively, but the steaks are succulent. Recommended is the filet mignon and the T-bone. The large porterhouse is cut to serve two, three, or four people. Good side dishes of broccoli au gratin, spinach, and onion rings. *1001 N. Broad St., Mid-City, tel. 504/821–3271. AE, MC, V.*

★ **Ruth's Chris Steak House.** Ruth's is the leading steak house in New Orleans. The Broad Street location was renovated, and it's now full of light. The clientele is still mostly male—businessmen talking big deals—but there are now more women at lunch, probably due to the new valet parking and lighter additions on the menu. Two-fisted cocktails are served, along with two-fisted cuts of meat. U.S. Prime is bred and corn-fed in the Midwest, aged in dry refrigeration, then cut to order and broiled in sizzling butter. The heavenly barbecue shrimp are peeled with tails on. There's a nice veal chop that's a newcomer; also recommended is the Maine lobster, Alaskan king crab, and thick salmon steaks. The vegetables are mediocre, except for the potatoes. You can spend quite a lot at dinner: lunch is the better deal. *711 N. Broad St., Mid-City, tel. 504/486–0810; 3633 Veterans Blvd., Metairie, tel. 504/888–3600. Dress: informal. Reservations advised. AE, MC, V.*

Moderate **Charlie's Steak House.** A simple and casual Uptown steak house that caters to neighborhood patrons. The prices are high for the surroundings, but the portions are enormous. Pools of butter coat each cut of meat. Typical steak-house side dishes; among the best are the onion rings. Friendly service. *4510 Dryades St., Uptown, tel. 504/895–9705. Dress: informal. Reservations accepted. AE, MC, V. Closed Sun.*

Grills and Coffee Shops **Absolute Bar & Grill.** The main dining room, situated on 3,000 square feet, overlooks a patio with tables. The large bar at the *Moderate* entrance, replete with a waterfall in the center and a large-screen TV in the corner, houses a pianist five nights a week. Patrons' dress runs the gamut from jogging suits to mink coats. Tables are well spaced at this popular new Uptown spot in the Riverside Marketplace. Early-bird breakfast has simple offerings, elaborate omelets, and sandwiches. Sunday brunch is fancier. You can get eggs at all hours here. There are 27 sandwiches listed on the menu, and the best are the specialty sandwiches. The "bar delight" appetizers are interesting, particularly the phyllo munchies. Good pasta dishes daily specials. You can get everything from a peanut-butter-and-jelly sandwich to fried seafood and filet mignon. All grill items are recommended. Great desserts. *Riverside Marketplace, on Tchoupitoulas St., tel. 504/899–7008. Reservations accepted. AE, MC, V. Closed for dinner Sun.*

Hard Rock Cafe. A chain restaurant devoted to rock 'n' roll music. There's always a line at the T-shirt booth, and roughly one-third of the annual sales are said to come from the shirts, pins, and other keepsakes on sale here. Covering 8,000 square feet of prime, riverfront real estate, the Hard Rock is more a cultural experience than a restaurant. The walls are covered with guitars, posters, memorabilia, and artifacts of popular musicians. Fats Domino's grand-piano lid, John Lennon's fingerprints, and Elvis Presley's Christmas postcards are displayed, among other collectibles. The bar is a handsome fiberglass guitar sculpture. If you can tolerate blasting rock, you can try the good hamburgers, nachos with avocado dip and salsa, and grilled lime chicken. A recommended specialty is the Baby Rock watermelon ribs with barbecue sauce. Prices are high for the caliber of the food. Waitresses are decked out in 1950s polyester uniforms and bobby socks. *418 N. Peters St., 3rd fl. of the Jackson Brewery, French Quarter, tel. 504/529–5617. Dress: informal. No reservations. AE, MC, V.*

Inexpensive **A & G Cafeteria.** This is home cooking served cafeteria style. The gumbos and fried fish are savory, and there's a choice of 15 to 20 salads, soups, breads, and desserts. Miniplates of smaller portions cost about $3, which includes an entree and two vegetables. On Wednesdays and Fridays, shrimp or crawfish etouffee is served, depending on the season. It's a good place to let your eyes grow larger than your stomach. *Lakeside Shopping Center, Metairie, tel. 504/834–5951; Clearview Shopping Center, Metairie, tel. 504/885–5951. No credit cards. Closed Sun. for dinner.*

★ **Camellia Grill.** Located at the corner of St. Charles Avenue and Carrollton, Camellia Grill is a sparkling clean grill with a bustling ambience and maître d'. You can watch the cooks preparing the food—they always manage a joke with waiters. Perch on a swivel stool and wait for your order of old-fashioned lunch-counter food to be dished up. The omelets are the best in town, particularly the ham, cheese, and onion—huge and fluffy. Good red beans and rice on Monday. Great hamburgers, pecan pie, cheesecake, and banana cream pie. The chocolate freezes are also popular. Long lines on weekends for breakfast. *626 S. Carrollton Ave., Uptown, tel. 504/866–9573. Open Mon. –Sat. 8 AM–1 PM, Fri.–Sun. 8 AM–2 PM.*

Maspero's. Long lines of people waiting for overstuffed sandwiches at reasonable prices can be seen daily in front of the restaurant. Deli-style corned beef, turkey, and pastrami are among the best selections. No po-boys here; sandwiches come on a bun, and, with an added appetizer or a steaming bowl of chili, they're large enough to satisfy two people. Don't bother with the overcooked hamburgers. *601 Decatur St., French Quarter, tel. 504/523–6250. No credit cards.*

Mother's. Recently acquired by new proprietors, Mother's is known for its huge po-boys and gumbo. Order the Verdi, a combination of meats freshly baked on the premises. Breakfast, which is popular with the CBD blue-collar workers, begins early. Red beans and rice are spicy and delicious. *401 Poydras St., Central Business District, tel. 504/523–9656. No credit cards. Open 5 AM–3 PM. Closed Sun. and Mon.*

★ **Napoleon House.** An antiquated bar serving a limited menu in an old-world setting. The tables in the front room open onto the street, and there's a charming courtyard in the back. The very short menu offers several po-boys (mostly Italian), appetizers (cheese board, jambalaya, antipasto salad, and gumbo), a salad bar for lunch, and a few desserts. The dish that draws people here is the muffuletta, one of the best in town: The bread is warmed and isn't overly thick, the meat layers are generous, and the olive salad is perfect. The popular drink is still Pimm's cup, cool and light with a slice of cucumber. The second floor, named "L'Appartement de l'Empereur," was recently renovated for private parties. The classical music and mellow ambience make this an alluring spot for repose. Very popular with locals. *500 Chartres St., French Quarter, tel. 504/524–9752. AE, V, MC. Open 11 AM–1 AM. Closed Sun.*

★ **R & O Pizza Place.** The name is deceptive, since the menu is hardly limited to pizzas, although the ones they make are pretty good. You can see the chefs making the pizzas through a window inside the R & O, which recently moved from a hole-in-the-wall location to this larger location. Mounted ducks still hang on the walls, but the menu has been spiffed up. The best po-boys in New Orleans are served here. Huge, messy, and hot from the oven, they are made with opulent Greek bread topped with sesame seeds. One of the best po-boys is the combo, made with a full-bodied Italian sausage, sliced meatballs, melted cheese, and homemade red sauce—the same sauce that is used on the pizzas, spaghetti, and lasagna. The roast beef, smothered in a deep brown gravy, comes second to this. Good muffulettas. Don't bother with the fettuccine or the gumbo. Good fried and boiled seafood. The marinated crabs (halved) are very popular (be sure to get there early, as they often run out by evening's end). *210 Hammond Hwy., Metairie, tel. 504/ 831–1248. No credit cards. Closed for lunch Sun.*

Ted's Frostop Restaurant. An old-fashioned hamburger joint that serves good burgers, shakes, and waffle fries. The spicy red beans and rice is a good daily special. The Yatwich combo of roast beef, ham, and cheese makes a hefty sandwich. Another daily special is the thin fried catfish. Very inexpensive and ample breakfast. The South Claiborne location has the daily specials and a more interesting menu than the other locations. *6303 S. Claiborne Ave., Uptown; 2900 Canal St., Mid-City; 600 Decatur St. in the Jackson Brewery, French Quarter. No credit cards.*

Uglesich's. You can tell someone's been to Uglesich's if he smells like a fried oyster. The restaurant's dingy, run-down appearance is deceptive. Uglesich's po-boys are some of the tastiest in town, and the best are the seafood. Try the soft-shell crab po-boy, which has legs dangling out of the French bread—an odd sight, but delicious nevertheless. *1238 Baronne St., Uptown, tel. 504/523–8547. No credit cards. Closed Sat. and Sun.*

Deli and Fast Food
Inexpensive

Central Grocery. One of the largest purveyors of Italian groceries and specialty items in New Orleans. The only thing served here is the muffuletta, an enormous Italian sandwich with many layers of meat, cheese, and olive salad. *923 Decatur St., French Quarter, tel. 504/523–1620. No credit cards.*

Chez Nous Charcuterie. This take-out deli, located in an old home, offers fresh homemade daily specials that come packed in single-serving sizes: seafood gumbo, crawfish etouffee, and quiche. Good wine selection; homemade salad dressings, sauces, and dips. *5701 Magazine St., Uptown, tel. 504/899–7303. MC, V. Closed Sat.*

★ **Dante St. Deli.** This small deli, next to the levee and flanked by an open-air cafe, has two small dining rooms. Cold meats and lots of other goodies are available. You can order anything on the menu to go. The soups are recommended, especially the corn shrimp chowder and the artichoke. Everything is served on paper plates, except the soups, which come in coffee cups. The specialty sandwiches are the best, never heavy on the mayonnaise. Best-bet daily special is the salmon mousse with duck pâté. The deli also stocks an assortment of pastries and chocolates, and a fair selection of wine and other gourmet items. This is a health-conscious approach to a deli, without being overly so. *736 Dante St., Uptown, tel. 504/861–3634. MC, V. Closed Sun. for dinner.*

Magazine Cuisine. The specials in this pleasant restaurant are in the exotic vein: vegetable lasagna, shrimp and hearts of palm remoulade, crabmeat-stuffed eggplant. You can eat in at the few small tables, or take out meats, pâtés, cheeses, pastries, chocolates, fresh herbs, and daily specials. The wine is mostly Californian. Good croissants. *3242 Magazine St., Uptown, tel. 504/899–9453. AE, MC, V. Closed for breakfast weekends.*

Martin's Deli. Known for its imaginative variety of sandwiches, the deli part of Martin's Wine Cellar is a popular lunch spot for locals on the run who don't mind dining at a small counter on bar stools. When you buy four sandwiches you get a bonus fifth sandwich for free! A glass of wine at Martin's costs 25 cents. There's a tremendous assortment of cheeses and several good pâtés. Also available are baked meats, party sandwiches and trays, fresh breads and croissants, fresh pasta, smoked salmon, and a decent frozen-food department. Gourmet items abound. This is the city's biggest wine store, and its specials are usually good deals. *3827 Baronne St., Uptown, tel. 504/899–7411. AE, MC, V.*

★ **Popeye's.** This is a home-grown fried-chicken place that has gone nationwide on the merits of its very spicy chicken and delicious, freshly baked buttermilk biscuits. If spicy is not for you, it also prepares a mild chicken. Red beans and rice is quite good, and you can opt for the red beans or "dirty" rice instead of fries with your order of chicken. Cajun popcorn (fried shrimp) and chicken tacos are big sellers. The biscuits, served at select locations, are popular with the breakfast set on the run. *Various locations around town. No credit cards.*

★ **Whole Food Company.** Two locations: One on Esplanade Avenue is a grocery store with a deli; one on Riverwalk is a deli with dining tables. Both have bakeries and an assortment of cold meats, cheese, pâtés, gourmet items, and daily specials. Riverwalk offers imaginative "Great River Specialties," unusual varieties of combo sandwiches, breakfast pastries from its German bakery, and a wine bar with wine by the glass, bottle, or case. Another plus is free delivery to anywhere in the CBD. *3135 Esplanade Ave., Mid-City, tel. 504/943–1626; Riverwalk Shopping Complex, Central Business District, tel. 522–5534. AE, MC, V.*

Cafes/Coffeehouses

New Orleans's weather generally goes directly from requiring air-conditioning to requiring heating; the humidity makes alfresco dining uncomfortable on all but a very few lucky days a year. There are very few outdoor cafes but the number is growing each year. However, there is one longstanding alfresco tradition here: finishing off the evening at one of the two French Market coffeehouses, one of which, ironically, is no longer within 10 miles of the French Market.

Inexpensive

Café du Monde. This New Orleans institution is still located where it's always been, at the Uptown extreme of the French Market in the French Quarter, with a small dining room and a large canvas-covered outdoor section. The coffee is café au lait, the famous New Orleans dark-roasted, chickory-blend coffee, far too strong to be drunk without the hot milk poured with the coffee into the cup. Beignets, little leaden fried squares of sour dough, dusted with powdered sugar that will probably wind up dusting you, are served with your coffee. *Decatur St. and St. Ann St., French Quarter, tel. 504/525–4544. Open 24 hrs daily. No credit cards.*

[handwritten: Good 1989 Fountain closed off 8/89 and a bit run down coffee etc AOK]

Morning Call. A far cry from the French Quarter, this cafe serves the same items as Café du Monde, but in a slightly better and more consistent form in the much less atmospheric setting of an antiseptic suburban-strip shopping center. The 60-year-old furnishings of the French Quarter premises were moved some years ago into Morning Call's present stark space. *3325 Severn Ave., Metairie, tel. 504/885–4068. Open 24 hrs daily. No credit cards.*

La Marquise. A fine little French pastry shop run by two very talented French chefs, just off Jackson Square. There are a few tables inside and on the patio, and there is much coffee drinking done here. *625 Chartres St., French Quarter, tel. 504/524–0420. Open 9 AM–5 PM Thurs.–Fri. No credit cards.*

La Madeleine. This cafe is a nice-size French pastry shop overlooking Jackson Square. It offers sandwiches, soups, salads, quiche, and a large variety of freshly baked breads and croissants. The strawberry, peach, and kiwi tarts are delicious, and the coffee is exactly like the grand crèmes of Paris. *547 St. Ann St., French Quarter, tel. 504/568–9950. No credit cards.*

PJ's Coffee & Tea Co. is a pleasant coffeehouse popular with students. PJ's serves coffees, teas, and a variety of pastries. Classical music adds to the ambience in this low-key place. *7713*

Maple St., Uptown, tel. 504/866–9963; 5432 Magazine St., Uptown, tel. 504/895–0273. No credit cards.

Dessert

With the exception of the Oriental restaurants, most New Orleans eateries have serious dessert menus. One of the most popular items is bread pudding, which is very unlike the item served elsewhere under that name. New Orleans bread pudding is usually custardy, raisiny, and moistened with this or that version of whiskey or rum sauce. Fancier but also a local staple is bananas Foster, made by flaming bananas in brandy and banana liqueur with cinnamon, butter, and sugar, and serving them over ice cream.

Pralines—the classic New Orleans candy of caramelized sugar and nuts—are available just about everywhere and in the French Quarter in particular. However, New Orleans does have some confection specialists. Two of them—**Evan's** and **Aunt Sally's**—are near each other in the French Market (800 block of Decatur St.) and are set up so you can watch pralines being manufactured. Also good are **Leah's** (714 St. Louis St.) and **Laura's** (115 Royal St.). Despite the fact that all these places are extremely touristy, the pralines are pretty good. But for the best pralines anywhere, **Evelyn's Pralines** can be found at the **Landmark Hotel's Gift Shop** (2601 Severn Ave., Metairie). Made from an old Cajun recipe, these wonderful confections are a combination of whipping cream, roasted pecan halves, butter, and sugar. These pralines have received considerable attention in the national media. Evelyn's sells pralines in one- and two-pound gift boxes with lace doilies, gold ribbons, and enclosures; you can order them through the mail. (Evelyn's Pralines, 209 Chevis St., Abbeville, LA 70150).

There are some popular local ice-cream stands, if you develop a craving: **Haagen-Dazs** has three locations: Uptown, Metairie, and the French Quarter; **Baskin Robbins** has many outlets around town (look in the telephone book for the nearest one).

There is one local ice-cream parlor that has become a local institution, **Angelo Brocato's** (214 N. Carrollton Ave., Mid-City, tel. 504/488–1465; 537 St. Ann St., French Quarter, tel. 504/525–9676). Everything here is homemade, and the biggest sellers are the spumoni and cannoli (made with vanilla and chocolate ricotta cheese, pistachio nuts, and powdered sugar). Among the many flavors of ice cream, the torroncino and cassata (with cake and crystallized fruit in it) are the most popular. The fresh seasonal ices, in flavors like strawberry and lemon, are great. There are Italian cookies, candies, and good cappuccino. *Open 9:30 AM–10 PM daily. No credit cards.*

8 Lodging

Introduction
by Nancy Ries

Visitors to New Orleans have a wide variety of accommodations to choose from: posh high-rise hotels, antique-filled antebellum homes, Creole cottages, old slave quarters, or the more familiar hotel chains.

When planning a stay in New Orleans, try to reserve well in advance, especially during Mardi Gras or other seasonal events. Frequently, hotels offer special packages at reduced rates, but never during Mardi Gras, when almost every accommodation raises its rates higher than listed here. Many chain or associated hotels and motels offer the additional convenience of advance reservations at affiliated hostelries of your choice along your route.

Hotels and motels located in the Central Business District, French Quarter, and Garden District are listed alphabetically for each area. Guest houses are listed for the French Quarter and Garden District. National chains, bed-and-breakfasts and hostels have their own separate categories.

Each hotel's price range is indicated at the end of its review. Hotels will add an 11% tax to all accommodation bills in Orleans Parish (County). Our ratings are flexible and subject to change. Dollar amounts overlap slightly because of the range of accommodations available in given hotels.

We have also provided toll-free numbers for making reservations when available. If you need assistance in choosing a place to stay, contact the Housing Bureau (tel. 504/566–5021) or the New Orleans Tourist and Convention Commission (tel. 504/566–5011).

The selections provided here are varied in price and have been chosen on the basis of good value and service for your money.

The most highly recommended properties in each price category are indicated by a star ★.

Category	Cost*
Very Expensive	Over $120
Expensive	$90–$120
Moderate	$50–$90
Inexpensive	under $50

double room; add 11% tax

The following credit card abbreviations are used: AE, American Express; CB, Carte Blanche; DC, Diners Club; MC, MasterCard; V, Visa.

Hotels

Central Business District Staying in the Central Business District will appeal to visitors who prefer accommodations in luxurious high-rise hotels. All the hotels listed here are located within walking distance of the

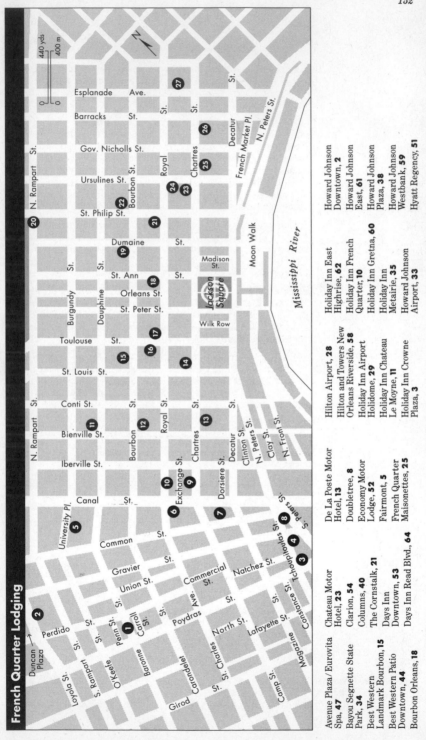

152

French Quarter Lodging

440 yds
400 m

N

Esplanade   Ave.

Barracks   St.

Gov. Nicholls St.

Ursulines St.

St. Philip St.

Dumaine   St.

St. Ann   St.

Orleans St.

St. Peter St.

Toulouse   St.

St. Louis St.

Conti St.

Bienville St.

Iberville St.

Canal   St.

Common   St.

Gravier   St.

Union St.

Commercial St.

Natchez St.

Poydras   St.

North St.

Lafayette St.

Girod   St.

Perdido   St.

Duncan Plaza

Mississippi River

Moon Walk

Jackson Square

Madison   St.

Wilk Row

French Market Pl.

N. Peters St.

Decatur   St.

N. Front St.

Clay St.

N. Peters St.

Clinton St.

Dorsiere St.

Exchange St.

St. Peters St.

Tchoupitoulas St.

Constance St.

Magazine   St.

Camp St.

St. Charles   St.

Carondelet   St.

Baronne   St.

O'Keefe   St.

S. Rampart   St.

Loyola St.

N. Rampart   St.

Burgundy   St.

Dauphine   St.

Bourbon   St.

Royal   St.

Chartres   St.

St.   St.

University Pl.

Carroll   St.

Penn St.

153

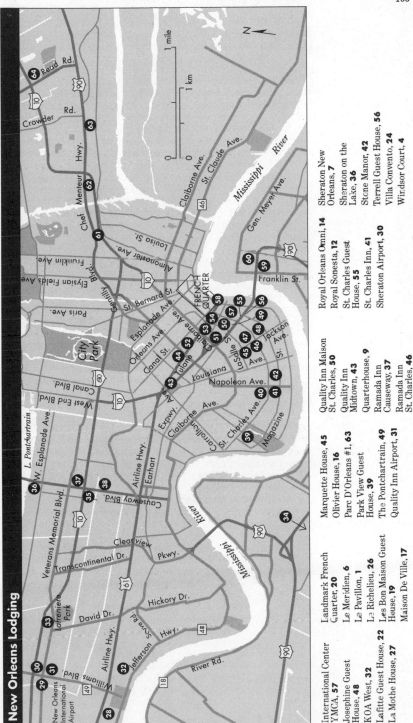

New Orleans Lodging

Royal Orleans Omni, **14**
Royal Sonesta, **12**
St. Charles Guest House, **55**
St. Charles Inn, **41**
Sheraton Airport, **30**

Sheraton New Orleans, **7**
Sheraton on the Lake, **36**
Stone Manor, **42**
Terrell Guest House, **56**
Villa Convento, **24**
Windsor Court, **4**

Quality Inn Maison St. Charles, **50**
Quality Inn Midtown, **43**
Quarterhouse, **9**
Ramada Inn Causeway, **37**
Ramada Inn St. Charles, **46**

Marquette House, **45**
Olivier House, **16**
Parc D'Orleans #1, **63**
Park View Guest House, **39**
The Pontchartrain, **49**
Quality Inn Airport, **31**

Landmark French Quarter, **20**
Le Meridien, **6**
Le Pavillon, **1**
Le Richelieu, **26**
Les Bon Maison Guest House, **19**
Maison De Ville, **17**

International Center YMCA, **57**
Josephine Guest House, **48**
KOA West, **32**
Lafitte Guest House, **22**
La Mothe House, **27**

French Quarter, but shuttles, taxis, buses, and the streetcar are available if your feet hurt.

Clarion Hotel. The lobby is exceptionally large with conversation areas grouped both here and on the mezzanine. Rooms are not exceptional in size or style, but the rates are good for the CBD (this is one hotel that does not raise its rates for Mardi Gras). Easy access off I–10 and about a 10-minute walk to the French Quarter. *1500 Canal St., 70112, tel. 504/522–4500 or 800/824–3359. 736 rooms; 23 suites with wet bars. Facilities: restaurant, lounge, 24-hour deli, outdoor pool, hot tub, fully equipped exercise room, self-serve laundry, free shuttle to Bourbon St. and the Rivergate, valet parking. AE, CB, DC, MC, V. Moderate.*

Doubletree Hotel. The small, comfortable lobby is graced with flower arrangements and decorative bowls of potpourri. Decor is country French and rooms have an open, airy feeling with matching pastel draperies and spreads and light-colored furniture. Rooms ending in 05 are larger and the eighth floor is nonsmoking. The hotel is located close to the river, and a short walk from the French Quarter. The staff at this hotel is exceptionally helpful. *300 Canal St., 70140, tel. 504/581–1300 or 800/528–0444. 363 rooms; 15 suites. Facilities: restaurant, lounge, mezzanine bar, outdoor pool, laundry, valet parking. AE, CB, DC, MC, V. Expensive.*

Economy Motor Lodge. This well-kept motel is on the edge of CBD, close to LSU and Tulane Medical Centers. Rooms in the main building are larger and closer to the pool, but traffic noise is more noticeable. Although quilted spreads and framed prints add some hominess, furnishings are motel modern. Complimentary breakfast of eggs, grits, toast, coffee, and juice is served 7–9:30 AM. Tropical plants enhance the pool area. *1725 Tulane Ave., 70112, tel. 504/529–5411. 150 rooms, 3 suites. Facilities: restaurant, outdoor pool, cable TV, free parking. AE, CB, DC, MC, V. Inexpensive.*

★ **Fairmont Hotel.** The Fairmont is one of the oldest grand hotels in America. The red and gold Victorian splendor of the massive lobby evokes a more elegant and gracious era. The hotel is composed of three separate buildings. The Baronne and University sections have spacious rooms. Rooms in the Shell section, however, are small and require a hike as there is no elevator service in this building. Decorating varies from room to room and is a continuous project. Special touches in every room include four down pillows, electric shoe-buffers, and a bathroom scale. Impressive murals depicting life in the South enliven the walls of the famed *Sazerac Bar; the Sazerac Restaurant* offers a romantic elegance not to be missed (herbs used in the restaurants are grown on the rooftop and delivered fresh to the kitchens). *The Blue Room,* the oldest supper club in the country, featuring dining, dancing, and big-name entertainment six nights a week, is also a must. *University Pl., 70140, tel. 504/529–7111 or 800/527–4727; telex 8109516015. 685 rooms, 50 suites. Facilities: 4 restaurants with bars, heated outdoor pool, 2 lighted tennis courts, beauty salon, gift shop, newsstand, florist, jewelry store, public stenographer, valet parking. AE, CB, DC, MC, V. Very Expensive.*

Hyatt Regency New Orleans. Multilevel public areas are complex and dark. Fountains, indoor gardens, and a skylight try to dispel the gloom but to little avail. Go for a corner room where two walls of windows give a sense of space and sometimes a good view. Every room in the Lanai Building faces the pool and has a private patio or balcony. Special rooms for women travelers are larger, close to the elevators, and come with hair dryers and makeup mirrors. The revolving *Top of the Dome Restaurant* offers a great view of the city. A glass atrium connects the hotel with the recently opened New Orleans Centre shopping mall and the Superdome. *500 Poydras Plaza, 70140, tel. 504/ 561–1234 or 800/228–9000; telex 584229. 1,196 rooms, 100 suites. Facilities: 3 restaurants, lounge, deli, Sun. jazz brunch, VIP floor, heated outdoor pool, beauty salon, gift shop, valet laundry, parking. AE, CB, MC, V. Very Expensive.*

★ **Le Meridien New Orleans.** Marble, gleaming brass, beveled mirrors, and stunning displays of fresh flowers create contemporary elegance at this French luxury hotel. The hotel faces Canal Street across from the French Quarter; the motor entrance is at 609 Common Street. Deluxe corner rooms offer the best views. Le Meridien houses a complete Nautilus health club including masseuse and a business center with multilingual service. Dixieland bands play nightly at the *Jazz Meridien*. *614 Canal St., 70130, tel. 525–6500 or 800/543–4300. 497 rooms, 5 bilevel suites. Facilities: 2 restaurants, nightclub, Sun. jazz brunch, nonsmoking floor, business center, health club, aerobics classes, heated outdoor pool, sauna, gift shop, jewelry store, laundry, valet parking. AE, DC, MC, V. Very Expensive.*

★ **Le Pavillon Hotel.** Magnificent chandeliers grace the European-style lobby of this historic hotel (built in 1905). Another pièce de résistance is the marble railing in *Le Café Trianon*, originally from the Grand Hotel in Paris. High-ceiling rooms boast hand-carved furnishings; try to get one of the 36 rooms with a bay window. *833 Poydras St., 70140, tel. 504/581–3111 or 800/535–9095. 220 rooms, 8 suites. Facilities: 2 restaurants, lounge, rooftop pool, and sundeck, 2 nonsmoking floors, valet laundry, parking. AE, CB, DC, MC, V. Moderate.*

★ **Windsor Court Hotel.** Exquisite, gracious, elegant, eminently civilized—these words frequently are used to describe Windsor Court, but all fail to capture the wonderful quality of this hotel. From *Le Salon's* scrumptious high tea, served each afternoon in the lobby, to the unbelievably large rooms, this is one of *the* places to stay in New Orleans. Plush carpeting, canopy and four-poster beds, stocked wet bars, marble vanities, oversized mirrors, dressing areas—all contribute to the elegance and luxury of the Windsor Court. Located across from the Rivergate and four blocks from the French Quarter. *300 Gravier St., 70140, tel. 504/523–6000 or 800/262–2662. 58 rooms, 266 suites. Facilities: 2 restaurants, lounge, entertainment, Olympic-size outdoor pool, health club, Jacuzzi, steam bath, sauna, gift shop, shoe shine, valet laundry, parking. AE, DC, MC, V. Very Expensive.*

French Quarter Since most people who visit New Orleans stay in the Quarter, the 96-square-block area abounds with every type of guest accommodation. The selections that follow are all quality establishments chosen to provide variety in location, atmosphere, and price. Reservations are usually a must.

★ **Bourbon Orleans.** Entering the lobby of this historic hotel is like being received in a grand French drawing room: A wall of French doors overlooks Orleans Street, conversation areas are tastefully arranged, and cocktails are served at an intimate bar. A grand piano, and magnificent spiral staircases that lead to the Orleans Ballroom on the third floor complete the picture. The 1815 ballroom, now restored to its original beauty, was the site of innumerable masquerade and quadroon balls. The large guest rooms have Queen Anne furnishings and most of the king-size beds have canopies. Bathrooms are fitted with telephones and mini-TVs. Even-numbered rooms face a beautiful courtyard. The suites are bilevel and have two entrances. *717 Orleans St., 70116, tel. 504/523–2222 or 800/521–5338; telex 5101012685. 164 rooms, 47 suites. Facilities: restaurant, lounge, entertainment, outdoor pool, secretarial service, valet service, parking. AE, CB, DC, MC, V. Very Expensive.*

Chateau Motor Hotel. Simple, friendly, and filled with historic charm, this moderately priced hotel (only a few blocks from Jackson Square) is a real find. The original carriageway leads to the guest rooms, which vary in size and decor. Some rooms are furnished with antiques, but most are traditional or contemporary; many have balconies and a few open directly onto the courtyard that houses the only silo in the Vieux Carré. (The silo encloses a spiral stairway to the penthouse suites.) The restaurant's tiny cafe and old copper-topped bar are housed in the slave quarters with tables placed outside year-round. The only negative note to an otherwise delightful stay is that the bathtubs aren't full-sized. *1001 Chartres St., 70116, tel. 504/524–9636. 37 rooms, 5 suites. Facilities: restaurant, bar, outdoor pool, complimentary valet parking. AE, CB, DC, MC, V. Moderate.*

The Cornstalk Hotel. The historic cast-iron "Cornstalk Fence" surrounds this 1816 Victorian-style Vieux Carré landmark. Antique mirrors reflect the glow of crystal chandeliers in the plush entrance hall. Each room is unique and has a sitting-room atmosphere of another era. Furnishings include armoires, canopy or four-poster beds, marble-top tables or nightstands, stained-glass windows, oriental rugs, and fireplaces. Guests can enjoy a complimentary Continental breakfast either on the balcony overlooking Royal Street, or outside on the gallery or patio. Parking is available on the grounds. *915 Royal St., 70116, tel. 504/523–1515. 14 rooms. AE, MC, V. Moderate–Expensive.*

De la Poste Motor Hotel. The French Quarter's *Chez Helene Restaurant* adjoins the small, functional lobby of this hotel. Most rooms are located in the main building, a few are in the back; some have French doors that open directly onto the courtyard. The location is great if you want to be close to Jackson Square, Bourbon Street, and Canal Street. Stately flags mark the entrance, making it easy to spot on a busy section of Chartres Street. *316 Chartres St., 70130, tel. 504/581–1200 or 800/448–4927. 92 rooms, 8 suites. Facilities: restaurant, lounge, outdoor pool, valet service, parking. AE, CB, DC, MC, V. Expensive.*

★ **Hotel Maison de Ville.** This small, romantic hotel lies in seclusion amid the hustle and bustle of the French Quarter. Tapestry-covered chairs, a fire burning in the sitting room, and antique-furnished rooms all contribute to a 19th-century atmosphere. Some rooms are in former slave quarters in the courtyard; others are on the upper floors of the main house. Fully-stocked minibars and robes are provided for all guests.

The complimentary Continental breakfast is served with a rose on a silver tray. Other meals can be enjoyed at a small adjacent restaurant called *The Bistro*, where the garlic soup is a must. Visitors who seek a special hideaway will love the hotel's cottages—located off the street in a private, enclosed area, each with kitchen and individual patio—two blocks from the hotel. *727 Toulouse St., 70130, tel. 504/561–5858 or 800/634–1600. 14 rooms, 2 suites, 7 cottages. Facilities: restaurant, outdoor pool at cottage location, valet service, parking. No children under 12. AE, CB, MC, V. Expensive—Very Expensive.*

Landmark French Quarter Hotel. The Landmark is located in the outer Quarter, across from Armstrong Park. French doors open to the pool area from a small restaurant that serves a buffet breakfast and sandwiches at lunch. Beyond the pool an exquisite tropical courtyard surrounds a splashing fountain. The best rooms are in the back buildings facing the patio. *920 N. Rampart St., 70116, tel. 504/524–3333 or 800/535–7862; telex 78–4080. 100 Rooms. Facilities: restaurant, lounge, outdoor pool, free parking. AE, CB, DC, MC, V. Moderate.*

★ **Le Richelieu in the French Quarter.** Tucked in a corner of the French Quarter, close to the old Ursuline Convent and the French Market, Le Richelieu combines the friendly, personal atmosphere of a small hotel with amenities usually associated with a luxury high rise—all at a moderate rate. Some rooms have mirrored walls as well as large walk-in closets, many have refrigerators, and all are adorned with brass ceiling fans. To be sure you don't get caught looking rumpled, each room also has a full-size ironing board. Balcony rooms are available at the same rates. There is an intimate bar and cafe off the courtyard with tables on the terrace by the pool. *1234 Chartres St., 70116, tel. 504/529–2492 or 800/535–9653; telex 9102404914. 71 rooms, 17 suites. Facilities: restaurant, lounge, outdoor pool, valet service, free parking. AE, CB, DC, MC, V. Moderate.*

★ **Olivier House Hotel.** Located half a block off Bourbon Street, this small hotel has 40 rooms in two 1836 town houses. The enormous hand-carved mirror gracing the entrance hall as well as the chandeliers are from the house's original furnishings. Room design and decor vary. Some have lofts, many have complete kitchens; baths in suites feature raised tub areas; gas-burning fireplaces are found throughout. Most are a comfortable mixture of antique and traditional; some have a tropical atmosphere with wicker furnishings and sunny colors. James and Kathryn Danner, the hospitable owners, point out that both children and pets are welcome. Collect calls for reservations are accepted. *828 Toulouse St., 70112, tel. 504/525–8456. 40 rooms. Facilities: pool; quiet, plant-shaded courtyard, elevator. AE, CB, DC, MC, V. Moderate–Very Expensive.*

Quarterhouse. Located a half block from Canal Street, these luxury time-shares are available on a nightly basis. Each has a sitting area, bedroom, and fully equipped kitchen. Many accommodations have exposed-brick walls; baths are fitted with whirlpool tubs. Since no pressure is exerted on overnight guests to purchase a unit, these are a refreshing alternative to hotel rooms. The size of the unit determines the rate. Avoid those facing Exchange Street—the view is Holiday Inn's parking garage. *129 Chartres St., 70130, tel. 504/523–5906. 36 units. Facilities: courtyard with small pool, individual security alarms. AE, MC, V. Expensive.*

★ **Royal Orleans Hotel (Omni).** This elegant, white-marble hotel, built in 1960 in the heart of the Vieux Carré, is said to be an exact replica of the grand St. Louis Hotel of the 1800s. Sconce-enhanced columns, gilt mirrors, fan windows, and three magnificent chandeliers brought from France all blend to re-create an aura that reigned in New Orleans more than a century ago. Rooms, though not exceptionally large, are well appointed with marble baths (telephone in each) and more marble on dressers and tabletops. Balcony rooms cost most. The well-known *Rib Room Restaurant* makes its home on the lobby level. The old New Orleans map that covers one wall of the lounge will fascinate anyone with an interest in history. *621 St. Louis St., 70140, tel. 504/529–5333 or 800/THE–OMNI; telex 588216. 350 rooms, 16 suites. Facilities: 2 restaurants, 3 lounges, rooftop heated pool, fully equipped exercise room, florist, gift shop, jewelry store, beauty salon and barber shop, valet service, parking. AE, CB, DC, MC, V. Expensive–Very Expensive.*

Royal Sonesta Hotel. Guests step directly from the revelry of Bourbon Street into the chandeliered, marble elegance of this renowned hotel's lobby, where a cool, serene atmosphere is embellished with a lush array of live plants. Most of the guest rooms are average size and furnished with light-colored antique reproductions. Many have French doors that open onto balconies or patios. The quietest rooms face the pool and courtyard; those facing Bourbon Street have a noise problem. Live entertainment is featured in both the *Mystic Den* cocktail lounge and the *Can-Can Cabaret*. There are occasional complaints that the staff here is not as helpful as it might be and that the rooms are small for the rates charged. *300 Bourbon St., 70140, tel. 504/586–0300 or 800/343–7170; telex 58336. 500 rooms, 35 suites. Facilities: 2 restaurants, 3 lounges, live entertainment, outdoor pool, concierge floor, valet parking. AE, CB, DC, MC, V. Expensive–Very Expensive.*

Garden District/ Uptown

Visitors to New Orleans who prefer accommodations away from Downtown will find the historic Garden District and Uptown area ideal. All are located on or close to fashionable, mansion-lined St. Charles Avenue, where the St. Charles Avenue streetcar runs (24 hours), making the CBD and French Quarter a mere 15–20 minutes away.

Avenue Plaza Hotel/EuroVita Spa. The Spartan lobby of this St. Charles Avenue accommodation belies the amenities found here. Public rooms include romantic lounge with dark wood panels from a French chalet and a small, intimate restaurant. The spacious rooms have generous dressing areas and kitchenettes with full-size refrigerators. Rooms are decorated in either traditional or art-deco styles, both equally appealing. Guests have complimentary use of the EuroVita Spa, which offers a Turkish steam bath, Swiss showers and a Scandinavian sauna, in addition to numerous personalized services at additional cost. The pool is in a pleasant courtyard setting; a sundeck and hot tub are on the roof. *2111 St. Charles Ave., 70130, tel. 504/566–1212 or 800/535–9575. 160 rooms, 80 suites. Facilities: restaurant, lounge, spa, outdoor pool, sundeck, valet service, on-site parking, 24-hr. security, shuttle to CBD. AE, CB, DC, MC, V. Moderate–Expensive.*

Columns Hotel. Expect both the good and the bad at this impressive white-columned, Victorian-style hotel on St. Charles Avenue. The wide veranda, set with cloth-covered tables for outdoor dining or cocktails, is very inviting, as are the two period-furnished parlors (one of which has coal-burning fireplaces). The dark and intimate lounge with two wood-burning fireplaces is a favorite with locals and visitors alike. One of the most impressive staircases you will ever climb leads to cold-looking, sparsely furnished, overpriced rooms without phones or TVs. However, for the budget-minded, one of the cheaper rooms with a shared bath on the third floor might fit the bill. Rooms with private baths are priced way out of line. Rates include Continental breakfast served either in the dining room or on the veranda. *3811 St. Charles Ave., 70115, tel. 504/899–9308. 10 rooms with private bath, 8 rooms with shared bath. AE, MC, V. Inexpensive–Expensive.*

★ **The Pontchartrain Hotel.** Maintaining the grand tradition is the hallmark of this quiet, elegant European-style hotel that has reigned on St. Charles Avenue for more than 60 years. From the canopied entrance, through the marble foyer, to the white-gloved elevator operator, the hotel's commitment to quality, service, and taste comes through clearly. Each room or suite is different in design or decor. The one common denominator is that all are lavish. The internationally known *Caribbean Room Restaurant* provides memorable dining. *2031 St. Charles Ave., 70140, tel. 504/524–6361 or 800/952–8092; telex 266068Pont. 50 rooms, 25 suites. Facilities: 2 restaurants, piano bar, 24-hr. concierge, limousine, valet service, parking. AE, CB, DC, MC, V. Very Expensive.*

St. Charles Inn. This small Uptown hotel features good-size modern rooms, each with a dressing area. Rooms in the front with a St. Charles Avenue view are best unless streetcar noise is a bother. Complimentary Continental breakfast and a newspaper are brought to your room each morning. The staff is friendly and accommodating. Hotel is adjacent to *Que Sera Restaurant*, a sidewalk cafe and lounge. *3636 St. Charles Ave., 70115, tel. 504/899–8888. 40 Rooms. AE, CB, DC, MC, V. Moderate.*

Stone Manor Hotel. This awesome Romanesque Revival stone mansion, built in the 1890s, opened its doors for the first time as a hotel during Mardi Gras 1988. An arriving visitor enters the hotel's lobby, a magnificent room large enough to host a gala ball or reception, with an adjacent parlor and dining room. Patterned parquet floors have been restored to their original beauty in these rooms and are especially intriguing. All of the guest rooms are large and in the process of being furnished with antiques. Some have balconies on St. Charles Avenue, which is ideal for parade-viewing at Mardi Gras. Six rooms on the third floor are graced with slanted ceilings and dormer alcoves, but share two baths. Continental breakfast is included and may be enjoyed on the veranda that faces St. Charles Avenue. *3800 St. Charles Ave., 70115, tel. 504/899–0600. 11 rooms. AE, MC, V. Moderate–Expensive.*

Guest Houses

Guest houses are for those who come to New Orleans with a desire to savor the old-world charm and atmosphere that is so proudly preserved in this city. All have a limited number of rooms, so it is advisable to make reservations well in advance of arrival—a full year is not an unreasonable amount of time.

French Quarter **French Quarter Maisonnettes.** The Maisonnettes, located in the
★ residential part of the Vieux Carré, are for those who want to

open a wrought iron gate, walk through a flagstone carriageway, and find themselves in the private courtyard of a past century. All of the maisonnettes (some with two and three rooms) open directly onto the courtyard. Homey furnishings, private baths, and TVs are included; private phones are not available. Mrs. Underwood, the chatelaine, offers a special brochure to guests that gives inside information on what to see and do in the area. She will organize individualized tours upon request. Children over 12 and well-trained pets are welcomed. *1120 Chartres St., 70116, tel. 504/524–9918. 1 room, 7 suites. No credit cards. Closed July. Inexpensive.*

Hotel Villa Convento. Lela Campo and her son Larry provide round-the-clock attention and service to guests in their three-story 1848 Creole town house. The guest house is located in a quiet end of the French Quarter, close to the old Ursuline Convent. Each morning guests can enjoy croissants and fresh-brewed coffee either in the cheery breakfast room or on the lush patio. Antique-furnished rooms with chandeliers or ceiling fans vary from inexpensive to moderate, based on location, size, and amenities. Some have balconies; all have private baths and phones. The elevator is padded with a tapestry, which creates a sensation not to be missed. *616 Ursulines St., 70116, tel. 504/522–1793. 22 rooms, 2 suites. AE, MC, V. Inexpensive–Moderate.*

Lafitte Guest House. A four-story, 1849 French manor house, Lafitte's is meticulously restored, with rooms individually decorated in period furnishings. Room 40 takes up the entire fourth floor and overlooks French Quarter rooftops. Complimentary Continental breakfast can be brought to your room, served in the Victorian sitting room, or enjoyed on the patio. Parking is available in a private lot at no extra charge. *1003 Bourbon St., 70116, tel. 504/581–2678 or 800/331–7971. 13 rooms, 1 suite. AE, DC, MC, V. Moderate–Expensive.*

★ **La Mothe House.** This white-columned 1849 town house, which rests on Esplanade Avenue at the edge of the French Quarter, radiates Southern grace and charm. A wide entrance hall, formerly a carriageway, and a sweeping staircase lead to the second-floor reception parlor and formal dining room. An array of antiques furnishes each room and lace curtains cover every window; baths are small and modern. Guests can choose to stay in the main house, slave quarters, carriage house, or a Creole cottage with its own patio. Complimentary Continental breakfast is served in the dining room or courtyard, and every afternoon guests can enjoy port or sherry in the parlor. Off-street parking is provided free of charge. *621 Esplanade Ave., 70116, tel. 504/947–1161 or 800/367–5858. 11 rooms, 9 suites. AE, MC, V. Moderate–Very Expensive.*

Les Bon Maison Guest House. Quaint accommodations lie within the gates of this 1840 town house, situated on the quiet end of Bourbon Street. Rooms off the courtyard in the slave quarters are pleasantly furnished with quilted spreads, ceiling fans, and fully equipped kitchenettes. Two large suites are located in the main house. No elevator—so lots of stair-climbing to upper floors. Host Butch Brown welcomes each guest with a complimentary cocktail. Breakfast is not included. *835 Bourbon St., 70116, tel. 504/561–8498. 3 rooms, 2 suites. MC, V. Inexpensive.*

Garden District **The Josephine Guest House.** This Italianate mansion,
★ built in 1870, has been perfectly restored to provide visitors

with the pleasures of the graceful lifestyle of an old New Orleans home. French antiques fill the rooms, and Oriental rugs cover gleaming hardwood floors. Four rooms and a parlor are in the main house; there are two smaller but spacious rooms in the garçonnier (quarters where the original owners' sons stayed). The bathrooms are impressive in both size and decor. A complimentary Creole breakfast of fresh-squeezed orange juice, café au lait, and homemade biscuits can be brought to your room (Wedgwood china on a silver tray) or served on the secluded patio. Phones can be installed in rooms upon request. *1450 Josephine St., 1 blk from St. Charles Ave., 70130, tel. 504/524–6361. 6 rooms. AE, CB, DC, MC, V. Moderate.*

Park View Guest House. Adjacent to beautiful Audubon Park, this historic Victorian guest house has graced St. Charles Avenue as an Uptown landmark since 1884. Rooms on the east side offer great views of the park. The general rule here is that you get either antiques or a view, but brass beds and ceiling fans adorn the "view" rooms. There is a lounge replete with a TV and fireplace. Complimentary Continental breakfast is served in a large bay-windowed dining room. *7004 St. Charles Ave., 70118, tel. 504/861–7564. 25 rooms (10 with shared bath). MC, V. Moderate.*

St. Charles Guest House. Simple, clean, and comfortable, this European-style pension is an affordable find located in four buildings one block from St. Charles Avenue. Rooms in the B and D buildings are larger. The small "backpacker" rooms share a bath and do not have air-conditioning. Guests receive a survival manual from proprietors Joanne and Dennis Hilton, which includes self-guided Garden District and streetcar tours. A pleasant surprise is the large swimming pool and deck. A Continental breakfast is served daily, and on occasion, Dennis and Joanne delight their guests with an impromptu crawfish boil or an introduction to New Orleans's red beans and rice. *1748 Prytania St., 70130, tel. 504/523–6556. 22 rooms (4 with shared bath). Facilities: common room, outdoor pool. AE, MC, V. Inexpensive.*

Terrell Guest House. This restored 1858 mansion is located in the lower Garden District, where a renovation project called "Operation Comeback" is in full swing. Some may feel the area is undesirable until they step inside the guest house's double parlors, which are furnished with period antiques, where guests gather each evening for a hospitality hour. A Waterford chandelier graces the formal dining area where a Continental breakfast is served each morning. Rooms in the carriage house and slave quarters face a large, fountain-enhanced patio, and each is equipped with a private security alarm. One room and a suite are in the main house. *1441 Magazine St., 70130, tel. 504/524–9859. 8 rooms, 1 suite. AE, MC, V. Moderate.*

National Hotel and Motel Chains

In addition to the many excellent independent hotels and motels throughout the area, there are also many that belong to national or regional chains. A major advantage of the chains is the ease of making reservations either en route or in advance. If you are a guest at a member hotel or motel one night, the management will be delighted to secure a booking at one of their affiliated hotels at no cost to you. Chains usually have toll-free lines to assist you. For directory information on toll-free numbers, dial 800/555–1212 and ask for the 800 number of the hotel you want to reach.

The main hotel and motel chains in metropolitan New Orleans are Best Western, Days Inn, Hilton, Holiday Inn, Howard Johnsons, Ramada Inns, Rodeway Inns, Sheraton, and TraveLodge. Other popular motel chains include Comfort Inn, Family Inns of America, La Quinta, Shoney's, and Superior Motor Inns.

There are numerous national chain accommodations in New Orleans, and many are properties that rank at the top of their line. Those selected for the alphabetical listings below provide a choice from luxury high rise to family motel in a variety of locations throughout the metropolitan area. Kenner and Metairie are west of the city, New Orleans East is exactly that, and Westbank is across the Mississippi River.

Central Business District

Best Western Patio Motel. 75 rooms, 1 suite, 2 outdoor pools, laundry facilities, nonsmoking rooms, cable TV, covered parking. *2820 Tulane Ave., 70119, tel. 504/822–0200 or 800/528–1234. AE, CB, DC, MC, V. Moderate.*

Days Inn Downtown. High rise with 20 executive guest rooms, 206 rooms, 8 suites, restaurant, lounge, outdoor pool, laundry facilities, free garage parking. *1630 Canal St., 70112, tel. 504/586–0110 or 800/325–2525. AE, CB, DC, MC, V. Moderate.*

★ **Holiday Inn Crowne Plaza.** Twenty-three stories of stunning glass architecture, with a concierge on the top floor. Four lounges, 437 rooms, 2 restaurants, nightly entertainment, outdoor pool, fully equipped exercise room, gift shop, car rental on premises, valet, self-parking. *333 Poydras St., 70130, tel. 504/525–9444 or 800/522–6963. AE, CB, DC, MC, V. Moderate –Very Expensive.*

Howard Johnson—Downtown. Located a few blocks from the French Quarter; close to the Superdome. 296 rooms, 4 suites, restaurant, lounge, rooftop heated pool, hydrospa, free indoor parking. *330 Loyola Ave., 70112, tel. 504/581–1600 or 800/654–2000. Telex 6821233. AE, CB, DC, MC, V. Moderate.*

Hilton and Towers—New Orleans Riverside. Two glass-enclosed passageways connect the hotel's 10-year-old high-rise building with its newer four-story Riverside section. Sprawling multilevel public areas tend to be confusing and, to make matters worse, each hotel section has a separate registration area. Try to book into the Riverside—the rooms are larger, the decor more appealing, and the views of the Mississippi unmatched. This is the home of Pete Fountain's nightclub and an official stop of the Riverfront streetcar. *Poydras St. at the Mississippi River, 70140, tel. 504/561–0500 or 800/HILTONS. 1602 rooms, 86 suites. Facilities: 5 restaurants, 6 lounges, nonsmoking floors, business center, 2 heated outdoor pools, outdoor hot tubs, 8 indoor and 3 outdoor tennis courts, racquetball, squash, outdoor jogging track, health club with sauna, steam bath, aerobics class, tanning and massage facilities, beauty salon, gift shops, valet service, self-park garage. AE, CB, DC, MC, V. Very Expensive.*

Quality Inn—Midtown. Too far to walk but only a short drive from the French Quarter. 102 rooms, restaurant, lounge, entertainment, outdoor pool, whirlpool, nonsmoking rooms, airport shuttle, free parking. *3900 Tulane Ave., 70119, tel. 504/486–5541 or 800/228–5151. AE, CB, DC, MC, V. Moderate.*

★ **Sheraton New Orleans.** On Canal Street, across from the

French Quarter. Lobby is large and user-friendly. A tropical atmosphere permeates the *Gazebo Lounge*, which features jazz nightly. *Café Promenade* encircles the second level. There's a $79 rate here that's not always available, but give it a shot and ask! Executive rooms on the top floors come with many special amenities. Expect top-quality service. *500 Canal St., 70130, tel. 504/525–2500 or 800/325–3535. 1,200 rooms, 84 suites. Facilities: restaurant, lounge, entertainment, river view, outdoor swimming pool with restaurant, gift shop, video checkout, nonsmoking rooms, valet service, and parking. AE, CB, DC, MC, V. Moderate–Very Expensive.*

French Quarter   **Best Western Landmark Bourbon Street Hotel.** Courtyard and balcony rooms. Rooms facing courtyard are quieter. 186 rooms, 4 suites, cafeteria-style cafe, sing-along piano bar, nightclub entertainment, outdoor pool, gift shop, valet parking. *541 Bourbon St., 70130, tel. 504/524–7611 or 800/535–7891. AE, CB, DC, MC, V. Moderate.*

★ **Holiday Inn Chateau Le Moyne.** Old-world atmosphere and decor; 8 suites located in slave quarters off a tropical courtyard. 160 rooms, 11 suites, restaurant, lounge, outdoor heated pool, valet parking. *301 Dauphine St., 70112, tel. 504/581–1303 or 800/HOLIDAY. AE, CB, DC, MC, V. Moderate–Expensive.*

Holiday Inn—French Quarter. Located close to Canal Street. 252 rooms, 56 suites, restaurant, lounge, indoor pool, coin-operated laundry, free garage parking. *124 Royal St., 70130, tel. 504/529–7211 or 800/HOLIDAY. AE, CB, DC, MC, V. Moderate–Expensive.*

Garden District   **Quality Inn Maison St. Charles.** Lovely property in five historic
★ buildings along St. Charles Avenue. Home of Alex Patout's fine restaurant. 121 rooms, 11 suites, lounge, outdoor pool, heated whirlpool, nonsmoking rooms, valet parking. *1319 St. Charles Ave., 70130, tel. 504/522–0187 or 800/228–5151. AE, CB, DC, MC, V. Moderate.*

Ramada Inn—St. Charles. Newly renovated hotel with good-size rooms and attractive lobby. 121 rooms, 6 suites, restaurant, lounge, free parking in secured lot. *2203 St. Charles Ave., 70140, tel. 504/566–1200 or 800/228–2828. AE, CB, DC, MC, V. Moderate.*

Kenner/Airport   **Hilton—New Orleans Airport.** A brand-new hotel is being constructed on the site of the former Hilton, directly across from New Orleans International Airport. Anticipated opening is early 1989. 315 rooms, restaurant, lounge, heated outdoor pool, tennis court, fitness center, business center, valet service, airport shuttle. *901 Airline Hwy., Kenner 70062, tel. 504/469–5000 or 800/HILTONS. AE, CB, DC, MC, V. Moderate–Expensive.*

Holiday Inn—Airport Holidome. Many of the rooms here face the dome-covered pool area. 301 rooms, 1 suite, restaurant, lounge, indoor pool, exercise room, sauna, Jacuzzi, airport shuttle, free parking. *I–10 and Williams Blvd., Kenner, 70062, tel. 504/467–5611 or 800/HOLIDAY. AE, CB, DC, MC, V. Moderate.*

Quality Inn—Airport. Free coffee and doughnuts served daily in the lobby. 126 rooms, 1 suite, restaurant, lounge, room service, heated pool, Jacuzzi, satellite TV, 24-hr. airport shuttle, free parking. *2125 Veterans Blvd., Kenner, 70062, tel. 504/464–6464 or 800/228–5151. AE, CB, DC, MC, V. Moderate.*

Sheraton—Airport. Easy access to I–10 West. 244 rooms, 3 suites, restaurant, oyster bar, disco lounge, outdoor pool, 2 lighted tennis courts, 24-hr. airport pickup service, free parking. *2150 Veterans Blvd., Kenner, 70062, tel. 504/467–3111 or 800/325–3535. Telex 804–686. AE, CB, DC, MC, V. Expensive.*

Metairie   **Holiday Inn New Orleans/Metairie.** Easy access to I–10; near Lakeside Shopping Mall. 194 rooms, restaurant, lounge, outdoor pool, free parking. *3400 I–10 Service Rd., Metairie, 70001, tel. 504/833–8201 or 800/HOLIDAY. AE, CB, DC, MC, V. Moderate.*

Howard Johnson—Airport/Metairie. Remodeled in 1988. 228 rooms, restaurant, lounge, outdoor pool, Jacuzzi, airport shuttle, free parking. *6401 Veterans Blvd., Metairie, 70003, tel. 504/885–5700 or 800/654–2000. AE, CB, DC, MC, V. Inexpensive.*

Howard Johnson Plaza. Formerly the Gateway Hotel. 191 rooms, 15 suites, restaurant, lounge, outdoor pool, executive floor, airport shuttle, free parking. *2261 N. Causeway Blvd., Metairie, 70001, tel. 504/833–8211 or 800/654–2000. AE, CB, DC, MC, V. Moderate.*

Ramada Inn Causeway. Located next to I–10 at Veterans Blvd.; close to Lakeside Shopping Mall. 118 rooms, 10 suites, restaurant, lounge, outdoor pool, airport shuttle, free parking. *2713 Causeway Blvd., 70002, tel. 504/835–4142 or 800/228–2828. AE, CB, DC, MC, V. Inexpensive.*

Sheraton-on-the-Lake. Part of a new glass office complex that towers beside Lake Pontchartrain. Art-deco-style lobby is decorated with marble mirrors and brass. Some rooms overlook the lake. 210 rooms, 2 restaurants, 2 lounges, entertainment, health club, tennis club, VIP lagniappe floor, nonsmoking rooms, beauty salon, free airport limo service, valet parking. *3838 N. Causeway Blvd., Metairie, 70002, tel. 504/836–5253 or 800/325–3535. AE, CB, DC, MC, V. Moderate–Expensive.*

New Orleans East   **Days Inn Read Boulevard.** All rooms in this high rise have a separate vanity area and private balconies. Located across from Lake Forest Shopping Mall. 143 rooms, restaurant, outdoor pool, playground, cable TV, free parking. *5801 Read Blvd., 70127, tel. 504/241–2500 or 800/325–2525. AE, DC, MC, V. Inexpensive.*

Holiday Inn East Highrise. Balcony rooms; easy access to I–10 East. 200 rooms, restaurant, lounge, outdoor pool, free shuttle to French Quarter and Lakefront Airport, free parking. *6324 Chef Menteur Hwy., 70126, tel. 504/242–2900 or 800/HOLIDAY. AE, CB, DC, MC, V. Moderate.*

Howard Johnson Motor Lodge East. Newly remodeled. 160 rooms, 24-hr. restaurant, lounge, 2 pools, shuttle to Lakefront Airport, free parking. *4200 Old Gentilly Rd., 70126, tel. 504/944–0151 or 800/654–2000. AE, CB, DC, MC, V. Inexpensive.*

Westbank   **Holiday Inn—Gretna.** Don't get confused—the address here is exactly the same as the Howard Johnson Westbank, but this hotel is located a few blocks farther along the expressway, on the opposite side of the expressway when coming off the Greater New Orleans Bridge. 313 rooms, restaurant, lounge, outdoor pool, free parking. *100 Westbank Expwy., Gretna, 70053, tel. 504/366–2361 or 800/HOLIDAY. AE, CB, DC, MC, V. Inexpensive–Moderate.*

Howard Johnson Westbank. Formerly the Sheraton; located just across the Greater New Orleans Bridge. 168 rooms, restaurant, lounge, outdoor pool, heliport, free parking. *100 Westbank Expwy., Gretna, 70053, tel. 504/366–8531 or 800/654–2000. AE, CB, DC, MC, V. Inexpensive.*

Bed-and-Breakfasts

Bed-and-breakfast means overnight lodging and breakfast in a private residence. Begin by writing or calling a reservation service and discussing price range, type of residence, location, and length of stay. The service in turn will provide you with descriptions of several choices of B&Bs that meet your criteria.

From these choices you'll make a decision and send a 20% deposit. You'll receive the address and other pertinent details before you arrive.

Bed & Breakfast, Inc.—Reservations Service. This service offers a variety of accommodations in all areas of New Orleans. Some homes are 19th-century, others are contemporary. Guest cottages, rooms, and suites are also available. Prices range from $40 to $110. *Write or call Hazel Boyce, 1360 Moss St., Box 52257, 70152, tel. 504/525–4640 or 800/228–9711–Dial Tone–184. No credit cards. Inexpensive–Expensive.*

New Orleans Bed & Breakfast. Among 300 properties citywide are private homes, apartments, and condos. Prices range from $35 to $150. *Contact Sarah-Margaret Brown, Box 8163, 70182, tel. 504/822–5046 or 504/822–5038. AE, MC, V. Inexpensive–Very Expensive.*

Hostels

International Center YMCA. Accommodations are for both men and women. Guests can use the weight room, gym, track, and pool. Rooms in Pratt Building are newer and have TVs. Hint for Mardi Gras: 20 of these rooms face St. Charles Avenue or Lee Circle and provide excellent parade views. There are bathrooms and showers on each floor. *936 St. Charles Ave., 70130, tel. 504/568–9622. 150 rooms, no private baths. Facilities: restaurant, gym, weight room, track, indoor pool, parking. MC, V. Inexpensive.*

Marquette House, New Orleans International Hostel. This is the fourth largest youth hostel in the country, run by Steve and Alma Cross. It is located in a 100-year-old lower Garden District home, one block from St. Charles Avenue and the streetcar. There are bunk beds in dorms, and private rooms with double beds are also available. *2253 Carondelet St., 70130, tel. 504/523–3014. 80 beds, 5 private rooms, no private baths. Facilities: 2 lounge areas with TV (1 nonsmoking), 2 equipped community kitchens, dining room, coin-operated laundry and lockers, garden patio with picnic tables. AE, MC, V. Inexpensive.*

9 The Arts

The performing arts are alive and well in New Orleans, where a number of small companies offer an impressive variety of fare. You must keep in mind, however, that the stage in New Orleans —although generally good—can't and shouldn't be compared to New York, although it is entertaining and reasonably priced. For current productions and performances, consult the daily calendar in *The Times-Picayune* and "Lagniappe," the Friday entertainment section. *Where* and *Gambit* are two free publications (distributed in restaurants and other public places) that also have up-to-date entertainment news.

Theater

Le Petit Théâtre (616 St. Peter St., tel. 504/522–9958) is the oldest community theater in the United States. Located in a historic building in the French Quarter, it has a children's corner to complement its usual adult plays.
Bayou Dinner Theatre (4040 Tulane Ave., tel. 504/486–4545) is in the downtown area.
The Contemporary Arts Center (900 Camp St., tel. 504/523–1216) features two theaters that offer exciting experimental works and plays by local playwrights.
Chianti's Upstairs Dinner Theater (4241 Veterans Hwy., tel. 504/885–PLAY) usually has musicals.
Rose Dinner Theater (201 Robert St., tel. 504/367–5400) is located across the river in Gretna.
The Saenger Performing Arts Center (Canal at N. Rampart St., tel. 504/524–0876), a splendidly restored theater, brings national and international talent to the New Orleans stage. The Saenger is on the national theater circuit for Broadway revivals and road shows.

Concerts

The city has several major concert facilities including the **Louisiana Superdome,** the **Theatre for the Performing Arts,** the **Municipal Auditorium,** the **Saenger Performing Arts Center,** and the **Lakefront Arena** of the University of New Orleans. For a current schedule of concerts in these facilities check *The Times-Picayune.*

Free year-round musical events are held in the city's parks and universities. The **New Orleans Symphony** has had a rocky existence in the past few years; it folded in winter 1988, but there are constant attempts to revive it. The symphony's home, the Orpheum Theater (129 University Pl.), was restored to its original magnificence by the symphony, and provided a beautiful environment for concerts; its future use is in doubt.

Opera

New Orleanians have had a long love affair with opera, but unfortunately the city has not had an opera house since the French Opera House was destroyed by fire in 1919.

The **New Orleans Opera Association** now performs a number of operas each season in the Theatre for the Performing Arts (tel. 504/529–2278).

Xavier University (tel. 504/486–7411) has an opera school in its music department, and it stages occasional student productions.

Dance

The **New Orleans City Ballet** (tel. 504/522–0996) is the only major professional ballet company in the city. It performs in the Theatre for the Performing Arts.

Film

The city has many cinemas showing a range of movies. Art films and less well-known works are usually screened at the **Prytania** (5339 Prytania St., tel. 504/895–4513). Loyola University also has a **Film Buffs Institute** (tel. 504/865–2152), which offers an excellent selection of art and foreign films during the school year. Both of these institutions publish schedules of upcoming films, available by request.

10 Nightlife

Introduction

It has been said that if one drops dead of cirrhosis of the liver in New Orleans, it's considered death by natural causes. Drinking accompanies almost every recreational activity in this city, particularly those that take place after dark. Some major events, like Mardi Gras or the Jazz Festival, take on truly bacchanalian proportions with regards to imbibing.

The city's enthusiastic interest in dining presents additional opportunities for clinking glasses. In fact, restaurants remove much nightclubbing from the streets; Orleanians tend to think of dinner as an entire evening's activity, rather than the beginning or end of it.

In any case, if you want to have a drink, you can get one in New Orleans no matter what the time of day. The bars rarely close—not even on Election Day. Things do slow down considerably on Ash Wednesday, following the Mardi Gras splurging, but that happens only once a year.

The liveliness (and livelihood) of a club often depends on the live music or the array of characters in the club that evening. However, there are some local specialties you should know about. Up and down Bourbon Street you will see many places touting the Hurricane. This is a creation of Pat O'Brien's and really should be sampled in his bar. The Hurricane is four and a half ounces of dark rum with a variety of fruit juices served in a tall, curved glass—yummy but lethal! Many bartenders will tell you the mint julep is *not* a good drink—they say this when they are out of mint. In reality, the drink can be very refreshing, and has the old-fashioned taste of bourbon, mint, and quinine.

The best of the local drink specialties is the Ramos gin fizz, invented at the Sazerac Bar but now done best in the Royal Orleans's Esplanade Lounge. It's gin with cream, egg white, orange-flower water, and soda. Not as rich as it sounds, it makes a nice before-dinner cocktail or pick-me-up in the summertime. Finally, there is the Sazerac itself, which, it is claimed by the Sazerac Bar staff, is the original cocktail. It's a bit of bourbon and bitters in a glass coated with absinthe substitute. It's not for lightweights.

The main attraction in the way of nightlife for anyone visiting New Orleans is live music. There is plenty of it, ranging from the very oldest and most authentic Dixieland jazz to rock and modern jazz. The best places for music tend to be rather old, slightly run-down, and crowded; clubs offering more familiar amenities, like prompt service and comfortable seating, are few and far between. Dancing space in New Orleans clubs is almost always at a premium.

Everyone winds up on Bourbon Street sooner or later. While there is a little bit of everything and much of interest to look at, the street is largely dominated by seedy operations: T-shirt stores, porn theaters, bad fast-food places, etc.

Six blocks from Canal Street, the block between St. Ann Street and Dumaine Street features the largest number of gay clubs in the city. There are other gay bars along North Rampart in the Armstrong Park area and in the Marigny section just east of the Quarter. As in any large city, exert caution in the neighborhoods, particularly at night.

All bars in New Orleans are allowed unlimited hours. In the French Quarter, closing is rarely earlier than 2 AM, with a great many places open (and busy) 24 hours a day, seven days a week. Credit card acceptance in bars and clubs is rare; if they do take plastic, this fact is prominently displayed.

Prices range from around $4 a drink in the best hotels to $1.50 or less in the neighborhood bars. Jazz clubs customarily have a two-drink minimum; annoyingly, some require you to order both drinks at once. Few Quarter clubs have a cover charge; bars in other sections of the city often prefer a cover to a drink minimum.

Music Venues

For a city of 600,000, New Orleans offers a vast selection of live music. To list every club and bar would be a massive undertaking. Many hotels, for example, feature piano bars. The most elegant, in the Royal Orleans main floor, is **The Esplanade**, a warm, moody lounge serving cocktails, desserts, and postprandial liqueurs. Open nightly in the evening until an hour or so after midnight. *621 St. Louis St., French Quarter, tel. 504/529–5333. Mon.–Sat. to 1 AM, Sun. to 11 PM. All major credit cards.*

Other hotels feature musical groups either on a seasonal basis or for weekend jazz brunches. New Orleans also has a good middle range of neighborhood restaurants or taverns that periodically feature music on weekends.

The heaviest concentration of music is found in the French Quarter. Most visitors discover the hot spots as they stroll through the old city. Hence, the descriptive sections on neighborhood clubs—those outside the Quarter and Downtown—in our listing are a bit longer, as these places are off the beaten track for most out-of-towners.

The clubs we have selected feature good bands on a regular basis, usually most nights of the week. This rundown is not a definitive list, only a reliable and reasonably thorough guide to the places best known for keeping the flames lit.

First, a few tips: Showtimes can vary greatly. Quarter clubs featuring Dixieland or traditional jazz get rolling early in the evening, usually by 8 PM; several clubs feature music in the afternoons as well, especially on weekends. The first set at most neighborhood clubs usually begins about 10 PM. Otherwise, it's advisable to call the club to double-check times and ask for directions if you need them.

Most clubs have a cover charge, which may or may not include a drink minimum. As a rule, the neighborhood clubs do not have a drink minimum and the entry fee is only for music.

Dixieland and traditional jazz performances take place primarily in the French Quarter and Downtown hotels. Dancing can be found in neighborhood clubs featuring R&B, Cajun, and rock 'n' roll.

Few nightclubs insist on a dress code. The French Quarter clubs tend to draw a well-dressed crowd by virtue of their proximity to hotels and major restaurants. Beyond the Quarter, it's a different story. New Orleanians tend to take in their music in casual garb.

There is no state law or city ordinance that governs closing times, but unless a club caters to a late-night crowd, the last set usually ends about 2 AM.

The most complete daily music calendar is broadcast every two hours (11:30 AM and 1:30, 3:30, 5:30, 7:30, and 9:30) on WWOZ, 90.7 FM, the community radio station devoted to New Orleans music. The most complete printed list is found in "Lagniappe," the Friday entertainment supplement to the *Times-Picayune*. The daily printed list is not as thorough. Never be shy about calling the clubs, even to find out what kind of music a given band plays.

French Quarter and Downtown

The Absinthe Bar is a late-night haunt given to hard-driving blues that rocks into the wee hours. *400 Bourbon St., tel. 504/525–8108. Open daily, noon–3 AM. AE.*

The Blue Room. In the Fairmont Hotel, this is the city's poshest music venue. Dining (excellent) is optional. Topflight performers like B.B. King, Lou Rawls, Stephan Grapelli. *Reservations recommended. University Pl., tel. 504/529–7111, Fri. and Sat. shows at 9 PM and 11 PM, Tues.–Thurs. and Sun. at 9:30 PM. Shows average 60 min. AE, CB, DC, MC, V.*

Bayou Bar and Cafe. Good Cajun music. *501 Bourbon St., tel. 504/529–4256. Open daily, 11 AM–until people are ready to stop partying. MC, V.*

Chris Owens Club. The lady, a Quarter icon, is a dancer-singer whose acts are slightly risqué, but always entertaining. *502 Bourbon St., tel. 504/523–6400. Doors open 9 PM, shows at 10 PM and midnight. Closed Sun.*

Creole Queen Riverboat. Scenic cruises with various jazz ensembles leave from the wharf by the Hilton. Buffet dinner optional. A nice outing for children and senior citizens. *Poydras St., at Riverwalk, tel. 504/524–0814. Boards nightly at 7 PM, cruises 8–10 PM. AE, MC, V.*

The Steamboat Natchez. *Toulouse Wharf Dock, tel. 504/587–0734; World Trade Center, tel. 504/586–7777. 11:30 AM and 2:30 PM year-round; evening jazz cruise seasonal. AE, MC, V.*

SS President. Saturday dinner dance; boards 8 PM, cruises 9 to 11 PM. Sunday brunch, board 11 AM, cruise noon to 2 PM, Oct.–May only. One to two concerts a month are also featured. *World Trade Center, tel. 504/522–3030. AE, MC, V.*

544 Club. A variety of traditional jazz nightly, and late-afternoon weekend sets. *544 Bourbon St., tel. 504/523–8611. AE, CB, DC, MC, V. Open 3:30 PM–3 AM.*

Mahogany Hall. Home of the famous Dukes of Dixieland, who perform nightly, except Sundays, starting at 9 PM. *309 Bourbon St., tel. 504/525–5595. CB, MC, V. Nightly 9 PM–12:30 AM.*

Maison Bourbon. When Wallace Davenport is not on tour, this is where you're likely to find the inimitable trumpeter. *641 Bourbon St., tel. 504/522–8818. No credit cards. Open till 12:15 AM.*

Mediterranean Cafe. Features afternoon jazz and piano music. Scotty Hill's French Market Jazz Band, one of the best brass bands in town, often performs here. Ask for their record. *1000 Decatur St., tel. 504/523–2302. AE, MC, V. Nightly till 11 PM.*

The New Storyville Jazz Hall. Traditional jazz with late night R&B. One of the best music halls in town. When Luther Kent sings, usually in the wee hours, the place really cooks. *1104 De-catur St., tel. 504/525–8199. Sets end anytime from midnight to 3 AM. AE.*

Pete Fountain's. The Dixieland clarinet maestro plays one show nightly at his club in the Hilton on Tuesday, Wednesday, Friday, and Saturday. Reservations necessary. Wear your good digs. *Poydras St., at the River, tel. 504/523–4374. Show at 10 PM runs till 11:15 PM. AE.*

Preservation Hall. A cultural landmark. The jazz tradition that flowered in the 1920s is devotedly enshrined here by a revolving calendar of distinguished New Orleans musicians, including the Humphreys Brothers, Harold Dejan and the Olympia Brass Band, Kid Sheik Colar, and Wendell Brunious, among others. Cover charge is a mere $2. A rustic environment; tight seating. No beverages are served, but you can BYO. *726 St. Peter St., tel. 504/523–8939. No credit cards. Nightly, 8:30 PM–12:30 AM. $2 per head.*

Seaport Cajun Cafe and Bar. Some of the hottest R&B-jazz fusions are played in late-night jam sessions at Sally Townes's home base. *424 Bourbon St., tel. 504/568–0981. 11:15 AM–midnight. AE, DC, MC.*

Snug Harbor. This club, located just outside the Quarter, is where the modern jazz idiom is enshrined. In a given month you're liable to find Tony Dagradi, Amasa Miller, Steve Masakowski, Kidd Jordan, or such returning luminaries as Henry Butler, Terence Blanchard, and Donald Harrison. The restaurant attached to the music space serves good blackened redfish. You can sit at the bar and listen to the music in the next room without paying the cover. *626 Frenchmen St., tel. 504/ 949–0696. Nightly sets, 10 PM–2 AM. AE, MC, V.*

Uptown Uptown means upriver from the French Quarter, but the area described by this generic term stretches from the Garden District past the university neighborhoods, all the way to the end of the St. Charles streetcar line, which stops at Carrollton and Claiborne avenues. The area runs the gamut from elegant residential blocks to middle- and lower-class neighborhoods. The difficulty is that it's often hard to tell where serene neighborhoods end and rougher ones begin.

Benny's Bar. Music really pops at Benny's (watch for a motley crowd on sizzling nights). Definitely not a place to dress up or seek the creature comforts. If you want down-home blues in a honky-tonk atmosphere, this is the ticket. As the owner himself proclaims: "There is never no cover charge at Benny's." *738 Valence St., tel. 504/895–9405. Nightly, till 4 AM. No credit cards.*

Jimmy's Music Club. On the cutting edge of rock, Jimmy's draws a college crowd and rockers in their 20s. New music and local bands perform regularly. *8200 Willow St., tel. 504/861–8200. Cash only.*

Maple Leaf. Down home and funky, this is the place to hear and dance to good Cajun music. Faded jeans are always the dress code of choice. In temperate months, there's a patio out back to enjoy when the main room overflows. Beausoleil and Rockin' Dopsie are among the great Cajun acts who perform here; weeknights the Leaf features a variety of local artists. Although the club is only a few blocks from the Oak and Carrollton streetcar stop, it's wise to take a cab. *8316 Oak St., tel. 504/866–5323. On earlier nights, sets stop at 2 AM; late one can run until 5 AM on weekends. No credit cards.*

Tipitina's. Arguably the best music club in town, this was home base for the late Professor Longhair, whose bust stands prominently between the bar and short-order grill. The home of New Orleans rhythm and blues, Tip's features a variety of local acts and big names passing through. The Neville Brothers perform here when they're not on the road, and they should be at the top of your list of things to see if there's any rock 'n' roll in your blood. *500 Napoleon Ave., tel. 504/897–3943. Sets end as early as 2 AM, as late as 5 AM. No credit cards.*

Tyler's. Each weekend the great saxophonist James Rivers leads his band, the Movement, at this night spot, which serves oysters and fried food. The nightly listings lean to jazz and R&B. This is one of the coziest and most colorful spots in town. *5234 Magazine St., tel. 504/891–4989. Sets usually run 10 PM–2 AM. AE, MC, V.*

Lakefront **Nexus.** Near the University of New Orleans campus, Nexus is an excellent club catering to modern jazz. Pianist David Torkanowsky plays frequently here. R&B is also featured at Nexus, though less frequently. There's a disco upstairs. *6200 Elysian Fields Ave., tel. 504/288–3440. Sets 10 PM–2 AM. AE, MC, V.*

Jefferson Parish **Spinagins.** This club is home to the jam session hosted by the
(Metairie/Kenner) New Orleans Jazz Club on the last Sunday of each month. *In the Landmark Hotel, 2601 Severn St., tel. 504/888–9500. Sets 12:30 PM–4 PM. AE, CB, DC, MC, V.*

Cabaret and Comedy

Can-Can Cabaret. Take a time trip back to Paris in the Gay '90s. Three shows nightly. A period and—dare we say—high-kicking routine. *The Royal Sonesta Hotel, 340 Bourbon St., tel. 504/524–9076. Reservations recommended. Last show at 12:15 AM. AE, MC, V.*

Marie Laveau's Restaurant. Features a Friday night "Hot Stuff New Orleans Style," starring Becky Allen, Fred Palmisano, and Wanda Rouza (who is also an accomplished pop singer). *329 Decatur St., tel. 504/525–9655. Shows at 11 PM and midnight. AE, DC, MC, V.*

Punchline Comedy Club. This magnet for laughter fans is located out in Jefferson Parish. The club features a rotating schedule of stand-up comics and comediennes Tuesday through Sunday nights. *1200 Clearview Pkwy., tel. 504/734–LAFF. 8:30 and 11 PM, Fri. and Sat.; other nights, 8:30 PM only. AE, DC, MC, V.*

Bars and Lounges

Many tourists seek atmosphere over music and the French Quarter has an abundance of establishments offering just that.

Napoleon House Bar and Cafe. Directly across from the Royal Orleans, this is a vintage hub, long popular with writers, artists, and locals of varying stripes. Murmuring ceiling fans, lovely patio, paintings, and soft lights convey a European mood. Sandwiches and cheese boards are also available. The waiters are unstintingly polite and will never rush you. The perfect place for either a late-afternoon people watching or an evening nightcap. *501 Chartres St., tel. 504/524–9752. 11 AM–1 AM. Closed Sun. AE, MC, V.*

Lafitte's Blacksmith Shop. Entertainment in this club is provided by a pianist named Miss Lilly, who plays show tunes and vintage hits like "As Time Goes By." Very popular with locals. *941 Bourbon St., tel. 504/523–0666. Open nightly, 10 PM–2 AM. No credit cards.*

ONLY ONE Hurricane per day or else! 8/89

Pat O'Brien's. One of the biggest tourist spots in town. Home of the Hurricane, an oversized alcoholic beverage (many people like to take their hurricane glass home as a souvenir). The bar on the left of the entrance is popular with Quarterites; the patio in the rear draws the young (and young-of-heart in temperate months), and the piano bar on the right side of the brick corridor packs in hearty celebrants during every season of the year. *718 St. Peter St., tel. 504/525–4823. Open daily, 10 AM–5 AM. No credit cards.*

The Old Absinthe House. A popular watering hole that draws folks from afternoons to late at night. Decor consists of hundreds of business cards pinned to one wall, money papering another, and absinthe jugs hanging from the ceiling for added character. *240 Bourbon St., tel. 504/523–0718. 11 AM–2 or 3 AM. AE, MC, V.*

Central Business District

Ernst Cafe. Serves complimentary hors d'oeuvres during happy hour on weeknights. A nice atmosphere and cordial clientele. *600 S. Peters St., tel. 504/525–8544.*

The Fairmont Hotel. The hotel has three distinctive lounges: **Fairmont Court** has large, lush murals on two sides of the seating area off the lobby. A bustling bar lines the third wall. Down the hall is the smaller, more elegant **Sazerac Bar**, adjoining the famous restaurant of the same name. *4 PM–midnight weekends; 9 PM–midnight during week.* Finally, **Bailey's** is a 24-hour bar and restaurant, a rarity in the CBD. *University Pl., tel. 504/529–7111. AE, DC, MC, V.*

Riverwalk

LeMoyne's Landing. A restaurant-oyster bar with a grand view of the Mississippi River. LeMoyne's sometimes features music. The outdoor cafe, adjacent to the Spanish Plaza, has a large fountain and circular seating area. Concerts are held here in warm months. Check the newspaper for details. *Riverwalk, tel. 504/524–4809. Open daily, 24 hours. AE, DC, MC, V.*

Uptown

4141. This classy avenue bar with a disco area, attached to Stephen & Martin's restaurant, is named for its address. Young professionals flock here in droves after work and linger into the night. The patio, with an oyster bar and cocktail-hour nachos, is lovely in summertime. This is a place where people dress well and go to be seen. *4141 St. Charles Ave., tel. 504/891–9873. Open till the wee hours. AE, DC, MC, V.*

Pontchartrain Hotel. The **Bayou Bar,** a lovely lounge, is just off the lobby as you enter. Popular with businessmen and Uptown residents, the bar is accessible to the streetcar line. *2031 St. Charles Ave., tel. 504/524–0581. Weekdays till midnight; Fri. and Sat. till 1 am. AE, CB, DC, MC, V.*

Restaurant de la Tour Eiffel. The bar is small but offers a commanding, elevated view of the neighborhood. An excellent place for late-night drinks. *2040 St. Charles Ave., tel. 504/524–2555. Restaurant stops serving at 10:30 PM; bar stays open until the last customer leaves. AE, DC, MC, V.*

11 Excursions

The Great River Road

by Honey Naylor

Freelance writer Honey Naylor's features have appeared in Travel & Leisure, New Orleans Magazine, USA Today, *and other national publications. She is also the author of* Fodor's Pocket Guide to New Orleans.

Although New Orleans has never been a typical Dixie city, the word "Dixieland" was coined here in the early 19th century. And you have but to look away, look away to the west of town to see that old times here are not forgotten. The Old South is in a state of grace along the Great River Road, between New Orleans and Baton Rouge, where elegant antebellum plantation homes have been carefully restored and furnished with period antiques.

Alas, the Great River Road itself is not as scenic as it once was. Along some stretches industrial plants mar the landscape on one side of the road, and on the other side the levee obstructs a view of the Mississippi. However, you can always park your car and climb up on the levee for a look at Old Man River. The Great River Road is also called, variously, LA 44 and 75 on the east bank of the river, and LA 18 on the west bank. All of the plantations described are listed in the National Register of Historic Places, and some of them are bed-and-breakfasts.

Getting Around

By Car Take I–10 west or U.S. 61 to Williams Boulevard. Drive toward the river and turn right on the Great River Road. Driving time to the nearest plantation is about 20 minutes from the airport. Plantation touring can take anywhere from an hour to two days, depending upon how many homes you want to see.

Escorted Tours

Tours by Isabelle (tel. 504/367–3963) takes you on a seven-hour plantation ramble through two antebellum homes, with lunch in Nottoway.
Gray Line (tel. 504/587–0861) does six-hour excursions to plantations, with stops at two homes and lunch (not included in the tour price) at The Cabin.

Exploring

The numbers in the margins correspond with the numbered points of interest on the Great River Road map.

① An appropriate place to begin a River Road ramble is **Destrehan Plantation.** The oldest plantation left intact in the lower Mississippi Valley, this simple West Indies–style house, built in 1787, is typical of the homes built by the earliest planters in the region. *9999 River Rd., 5 mi upriver from St. Rose, LA, tel. 504/ 764–9315. Admission: $4 adults, $2 children 6–11, $3 students and senior citizens. Open daily 10–4. Closed Thanksgiving, Christmas, New Year's Day, Mardi Gras Day, and Easter.*

② Twenty minutes and a million style miles away is **San Francisco.** Completed in 1856, the elaborate "Steamboat Gothic" house was once called St. Frusquin. The name is derived from a French slang term, *sans fruscins,* which means "without a penny in my pocket"—the condition the owner found himself in after paying exorbitant construction costs. Note the unusual louvered roof and the ornate millwork and ceiling frescoes. *LA 44 near Reserve, LA, 35 mi from New Orleans, tel. 504/535–2341. Admission: $5 adults, $3.50 students, $2.25 children 6–11. Open daily 10–4. Closed Thanksgiving, Christmas, New Year's Day, Mardi Gras Day, and Easter.*

3 The 28 gnarled oak trees that give **Oak Alley** its name were planted in the early 1700s; the house dates from 1839. If you're into trees, do take in the view from the upper gallery of the house. This was the setting for the TV remake of "The Long Hot Summer," which featured Don Johnson and Cybill Shepherd. *LA 18, 6 mi upriver of the Gramercy–Vacherie ferry, tel. 504/265–2151. Admission: $5 adults, $2.50 students, $1.50 children 6–12. Open daily 9–5. Closed Thanksgiving, Christmas, and New Year's Day.*

4 Built in 1835, **Tezcuco** is a graceful raised cottage with delicate wrought iron galleries, ornate friezes, and ceiling medallions. *LA 44, about 7 mi above Sunshine Bridge, tel. 504/562–3929. Admission: $5 adults, $2.50 children 4–12, $3.50 students and senior citizens. Open daily 10–5. Closed Thanksgiving, Christmas, and New Year's Day.*

5 Docents in antebellum garb guide you through **Houmas House,** a Greek Revival masterpiece famed for its three-story spiral staircase. *Hush Hush, Sweet Charlotte,* with Bette Davis and Olivia DeHavilland, was filmed here, as was the pilot for the TV series "Longstreet." The rear cottage, connected to the main house by a carriageway, was built in the late 18th century. *LA 942, ½ mi off LA 44 near Burnside, tel. 504/473–7841. Admission: $5 adults, $3 students, $2 children 6–12. Open daily Feb.–Oct. 5–10; Nov.–Jan. 10–4. Closed Christmas.*

6 Bayou Lafourche also boasts a movie star in **Madewood.** The galleried, 21-room, Greek Revival mansion with its massive white columns was the setting for "A Woman Called Moses," which starred Cicely Tyson. Noted 19th-century architect Henry Howard designed the house. *LA 308, 15 mi south of Donaldsonville, tel. 504/524–1988 or 504/396–7151. Admission: $4 adults, $3 students, $2 children under 12, 10% discount for senior citizens. Open daily 10–5. Closed Thanksgiving and Christmas.*

7 The South's largest plantation home, **Nottoway,** should not be missed. With 64 rooms, 53,000 square feet of space, 22 columns, and 200 windows, this gleaming white castle (the nearby town of White Castle was named for it) was the pièce de résistance of architect Henry Howard. Completed in 1859, the Greek Revival/Italianate mansion is famed in these parts for its white ballroom, which has its original crystal chandeliers and hand-carved Corinthian columns. *2 mi north of White Castle, tel. 504/545–2730. Admission: $6 adults, $2 children under 12. Open daily 9–5. Closed Christmas.*

River Road Plantations

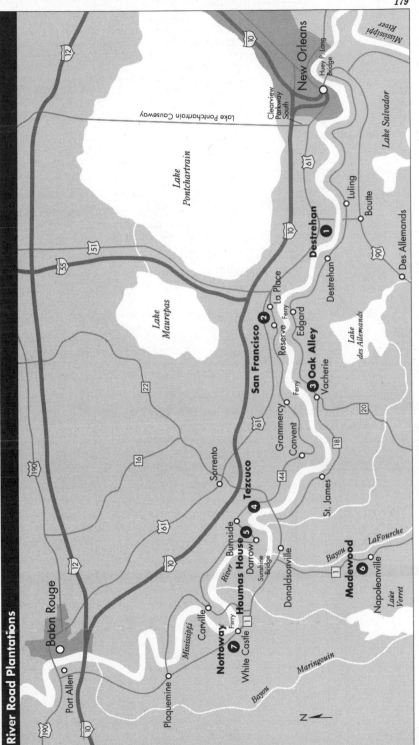

Dining

Burnside **The Cabin.** Yellowed newspapers cover the walls and ancient farm implements dangle here and there in a 150-year-old slave cabin-cum-restaurant. Crawfish stew and crawfish etouffee are specialties, but there are po-boys, burgers, and steaks, too. *Junction of LA 44 and 22, tel. 504/473-3007. Dress: informal. Reservations not required. AE, MC, V. Closed Thanksgiving, Christmas, New Year's Day. Inexpensive (under $15).*

Lodging

Napoleonville **Madewood.** Expect gracious Southern hospitality and pampering in either the Main Mansion, or the Charlet House and Elmfield Cabin, which are smaller houses on the plantation grounds. Accommodations in the latter are somewhat less cushy but considerably less pricey ($85 per couple). *New Orleans office: 420 Julia St., 70130, tel. 504/524-1988; Napoleonville office: Rte. 2, Box 478, 70390, tel. 504/369-7151. 5 rooms with bath in the main house, suites with bath in the smaller houses. No credit cards. Closed Thanksgiving and Christmas. Very Expensive ($85-$150).*

White Castle **Nottoway.** Ten antique-filled rooms, complete with a complimentary chilled bottle of champagne, are let to overnighters. Mornings begin with a Continental breakfast in bed, followed by a full breakfast in the dining room. *Box 160, 70788, tel. 504/545-2730. All rooms have private bath. AE, DC, MC, V. Closed Christmas Day. Expensive ($100-$125).*

Swamps and Bayous

Bayou is an Indian word meaning creek. The brackish, slow-moving waters of South Louisiana were once the highways and byways of the Choctaw, Chickasaw, and Chitimacha. Jean Lafitte and his freebooters easily hid in murky reaches of swamp, which were covered with thick canopies of subtropical vegetation. Pirate gold is said to be buried in the swamps. Ancient, gnarled cypresses with gray shawls of Spanish moss rise out of still waters. The state has an alligator population of about 500,000, and most of them laze around in the meandering tributaries and secluded sloughs of South Louisiana. Wild boars, snow-white egrets, bald eagles, and all manner of exotic creatures inhabit the swamps and marshlands. There are even rumors of a swamp monster, a critter said to be seven feet tall, weighing 350 pounds, with long orange locks and wild, wide eyes.

Unless you are a fur trapper, an alligator hunter, or a wild-eyed monster with orange hair in search of a mate, it is not recommended that you strike out into the swamps alone.

Guided Tours

The following tour operators are prepared to trek with you through the murky waters.

Honey Island Swamp Tours (tel. 504/641–1769). Dr. Paul Wagner, a wetland ecologist, guides flora and fauna tours of the 250-square-mile Honey Island Swamp on the Pearl River.

Tours by Isabelle (504/367–3963). A bilingual Cajun alligator hunter and fur trapper guides you through remote cypress swamps.

The Canoe and Trail Shop (tel. 504/833–9541). Canoeing on the Tangipahoa and Bogue Chitto rivers.

The Bayou Jean Lafitte (The New Orleans Steamboat Company, tel. 504/586–8777). Riverboat cruises to Barataria Bay, hideout of Lafitte and his pirates.

Cajun Country

The cradle of the Cajun craze rocks merrily away amid the bayous, rice paddies, and canebrakes to the west of New Orleans. Other parts of the country have only recently leapt on the Cajun bandwagon, but Southwestern Louisiana was Cajun long before red-hot Cajun was cool.

In Cajun Country (also called Acadiana), Cajun is not a trend— it's a tradition, dating from about 1604 when French settlers colonized a region they called *l'Acadie* in the present-day Canadian provinces of Nova Scotia and New Brunswick. The British seized control of the region in the early 18th century and the French were expelled. Their exile, called *le grand derangement*, was described by Henry Wadsworth Longfellow in his epic poem "Evangeline." Many Acadians eventually settled in 22 parishes of Southwestern Louisiana. Their descendants— "Cajun" is a corruption of "Acadian"—continue many of the traditions of the early French settlers of l'Acadie, living off the land as fur trappers and fisherfolk.

Lafayette, the largest city in Acadiana, offers a number of attractions, including art galleries and museums, devoted to the Acadian heritage. It is also a center for the performing arts and sports events, many of them presented with a Cajun flair.

The surrounding countryside is dotted with tiny towns and villages where antique-seekers and explorers can blissfully poke around. Centuries-old live oaks with ragged gray buntings of Spanish moss form canopies over the sightseeing paddle wheelers that kick up froth on the bayous. Country roads follow the contortions of the Teche (pronounced Tesh), the state's largest bayou, and meander through ancient Acadian villages where cypress cabins rise up out of the water on stilts and moored fishing boats and pirogues scarcely bob on the sluggish, bottle-green waters.

Louisiana is not called a sportsman's paradise for nothing. Laced as it is with waterways and wilds, this part of the state is largely responsible for that sobriquet. If fishing or boating is your thing, paradise lies 15 miles to the east of Lafayette in the Atchafalaya Basin, an 800,000-acre wilderness swamp. Saltwater fishing in the Gulf of Mexico is within easy reach of Lafayette. During winter months, hunters in search of waterfowl head for the coastal marshes to the south.

Food, music, and dancing are the very essence of Cajun life. Almost every hamlet has an annual festival of some sort, usually involving food, when townsfolk rouse themselves and raise the cypress rafters with foot-stomping music.

Cajun Mardi Gras in Lafayette is second only to its sister celebration in New Orleans. And in Acadia Parish, the *Courir du Mardi Gras*, or Mardi Gras run, is a wild affair with masked and costumed horseback riders following *le Capitaine* for a mad dash through the countryside.

Cajun French is an oral tradition, a 17th-century French that differs from modern-day French in much the same way that Elizabethan English differs from modern-day English. English is also spoken throughout Cajun Country, but you will hear Gallic accents and see many signs that read, *Ici on parle français*.

You'll also often hear the Cajun phrase, *Laissez les bon temps rouler*. It means, "Let the good times roll." Cajuns are fun-loving and friendly, and they love to show visitors *les bon temps*.

Getting Around

By Plane **Royale Airlines** (tel. 504/835–4154) has daily flights from New Orleans to Lafayette Regional Airport. The trip takes about 45 minutes.

By Car I–10 runs east-west from coast to coast and through New Orleans. Take I–10 west to the Lafayette exit, 128 miles from New Orleans. The interstate route will take an hour and 45 minutes. It is recommended that you return to New Orleans via U.S. 90 to take advantage of many scenic stopovers.

By Bus **Greyhound/Trailways** (tel. 504/525–4201) has numerous daily departures from New Orleans to Lafayette. The trip takes 3 to 3½ hours due to frequent stops along the way.

Guided Tours

Tours by Isabelle (tel. 504/367–3963). Customized, multilingual tours from New Orleans to Cajun Country.
Obscure Tours (tel. 504/944–1079). Customized bilingual tours for adventure travelers.
Allons à Lafayette (tel. 318/269–9607). Bilingual guides for escorted, customized tours.

Important Addresses and Numbers

Tourist Information The **Lafayette Convention and Visitors Commission** (Evangeline Thruway and 16th St., Box 52066, Lafayette 70505, tel. 318/232–3808). Open weekdays 8:30–5; weekends 9–5.

Emergencies Dial 911 for assistance. Or go to the emergency room, **Hamilton Medical Center** (2810 Ambassador Caffery Pkwy., Lafayette, tel. 318/981–2949).

24-Hour Pharmacy **Eckerd's** (3601 Johnston St., tel. 318/984–5220).

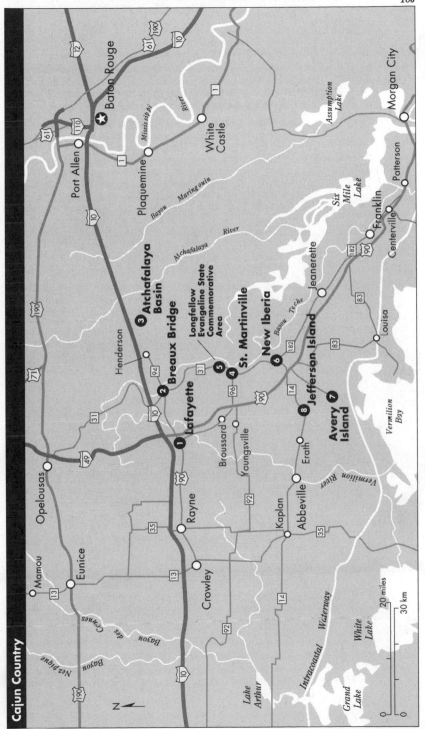

Cajun Country

Exploring

The numbers in the margins correspond with the numbered points of interest on the Cajun Country map.

❶ **Lafayette,** which calls itself the Capital of French Louisiana, is an appropriate place to get acquainted with Cajun lore and life. We'll take a look at that city first, and then tour the surrounding towns and villages.

The **Acadian Village** is a re-creation of an early 19th-century bayou settlement. The village nestles in 10 wooded acres complete with a meandering bayou crisscrossed by wooden footbridges. Each of the houses, which were built elsewhere in the 1800s and transferred to the site, represents a different style of Acadian architecture and is decorated with antique furnishings, utensils, and tools. The rustic general store, blacksmith shop, and chapel are all replicas of 19th-century buildings. *H. Mouton Rd., south of LA 342, tel. 318/981–2364. Admission: $4 adults, $1.50 children 6–14, $3 senior citizens. Open daily 10–5. Closed Thanksgiving, Christmas Eve, Christmas Day, New Year's Day, and Mardi Gras Day.*

In downtown Lafayette there are several buildings that played a part in Acadian history. A galleried town house, topped by a cupola, houses the **Lafayette Museum.** Built in the early 1800s, it was the *Maison Dimanche,* or Sunday House, of Jean Mouton, the city's founder. Later it served as home to Alexandre Mouton, ninth governor of Louisiana. The museum contains historical memorabilia and Carnival regalia. *1122 Lafayette St., tel. 318/235–4474 or 318/234–2208. Admission: $2 adults, $1 children under 12. Open Tues.–Sat. 9–5, Sun. 3–5; closed Mon.*

The **First City Hall** (217 Main St.) was home to the Bank of Lafayette until 1905, and the town's first public library. It now contains offices of the Council for the Development of French in Louisiana (CODOFIL). The Lafayette Artists Alliance is in the **Lafayette Hardware Store,** which has stood at the corner of Vermilion and Buchanan streets since before 1890. **Sans Souci,** the barn-red shotgun house at E. Vermilion and Congress streets, built in 1885, has been a post office, an inn, a tinsmith shop, and a saddle shop. It's now an art gallery, but for many years it was a well-known bookstore where book parties were held for the likes of Bennett Cerf, Frances Parkinson Keyes, and Irving Stone.

Time Out **Dwyer's Café** is a diner that's jammed with locals having breakfast at 5 AM. It features Cajun plate lunches, burgers, and sandwiches. *323 Jefferson St., tel. 318/235–9364. Open weekdays 4 AM–4 PM, Sat. 4 AM–2 PM. No credit cards. Inexpensive (under $20).*

As you stroll around Lafayette Centre, the downtown area, you'll see four colorful outdoor murals. Muralist Robert Dafford painted the Cajun accordion on the side of the Lee Furniture store, the Louisiana swamp scene across from Dwyer's Café, and the splashy cars on the Jefferson Tower Building. The microcosm of Lafayette at the Parc Auto du Centre Ville is the work of local artist Tanya Falgout.

The Louisiana Live Oak Society was founded in Lafayette more than 50 years ago, and a charter member of that silent but leafy set dominates the 900 block of St. John Street. The **St. John Oak** is 400 years old and has a matronly waistline of about 19 feet. Next to the tree is the **Cathedral of St. John the Evangelist** (914 St. John St.), a Romanesque church with Byzantine touches and an old cemetery behind the church. The cathedral began as a small mission of the St. Martin de Tours Church in St. Martinville. The church lawn was a campground for Union soldiers during the Civil War.

Changing exhibits at the **Lafayette Natural History Museum** examine the South Louisiana environment, and programs at the museum's planetarium explore the heavens. Workshops, movies, concerts, and light shows take place regularly at the museum as well as the annual Louisiana Native Crafts Festival, which is held in September. *637 Girard Park Dr., tel. 318/268–5544. Admission free. Open Mon., Wed., Thurs., and Fri. 9–5; Tues. 9–9; weekends 1–5.*

The museum's sister facility, **The Acadiana Park Nature Station,** is a three-story cypress pole structure that overlooks a 40-acre nature trail. Naturalists are on hand in the interpretive center, and discovery boxes help children get to know the wildflowers, birds, and other outdoorsy things they'll see on the 3½-mile nature trail. *E. Alexander St., tel. 318/235–6181. Admission free. Open weekdays 9–5, weekends 11–3.*

The Bayou Vermilion lazes through Lafayette, and the *Vermilion Queen* eases out on it for sightseeing, dinner, and moonlight cruises. *1604 Pinhook Rd., tel. 318/233–7700. Admission noon cruise: $7 adults, $4 children 4–12; dinner cruise: $19.50 adults, $11.50 children; moonlight cruise: $8 adults only.*

The towns described below can be explored in an easy day excursion from Lafayette. If your time in Cajun Country is limited, they may be seen as you return to New Orleans, in which case you can pick up U.S. 90 in New Iberia and continue on to the Crescent City.

② **Breaux Bridge** lies 10 miles northeast of Lafayette on LA 94. The tiny town calls itself the Crawfish Capital of the World, and the Crawfish Festival held in May of even-numbered years draws upwards of 100,000 people.

③ Pontoon boats at McGee's Landing take passengers for tours of the **Atchafalaya Basin.** You'll find McGee's on the levee road in Henderson, a 25-minute drive from Lafayette on I–10E. *Exit 115 at Henderson. Drive up onto the levee and turn right. McGee's Landing is 2 mi down the levee road on the left. Tel. 318/228–8519 or 318/228–2384. Admission: $7.50 adults, $4 children under 12. Daily tours.*

④ Following the writhings of Bayou Teche on LA 31 you'll come to **St. Martinville,** 15 miles south of Breaux Bridge, in the heart of Evangeline country.

Longfellow's poem about the star-crossed lovers Evangeline and Gabriel was based on a true story. According to the oft-told tale, the real-life lovers, Emmeline Labiche and Louis Arceneaux, met for the last time under the **Evangeline Oak** (Port St. and Bayou Teche). As in Longfellow's poem, the lovers were separated during the arduous Acadian exodus. Louis arrived in St. Martinville, a major debarkation port for the refugees, but it was many years before Emmeline came. The legend has it that the two saw each other by chance just as she stepped ashore. He turned deadly pale with shock and told her that having despaired of ever seeing her again, he was betrothed to another. *The Romance of Evangeline* was filmed in St. Martinville in 1929. Its star, Dolores Del Rio, posed for the bronze statue of Evangeline that the cast and crew donated to the town.

The statue of Evangeline is in the cemetery behind the church of **St. Martin de Tours** (123 S. Main St.), near the final resting place of Emmeline Labiche. St. Martin de Tours is the Mother Church of the Acadians, and one of the oldest Catholic churches in the country. Inside the church is a replica of the Lourdes grotto and a baptismal font said to have been a gift from Louis XVI.

St. Martinville was founded in 1761, and became a refuge for royalists who escaped the guillotine during the French Revolution. Known as Petit Paris, the little town was once the scene of lavish balls and operas.

The **Petit Paris Museum** on the church square contains historical records, Carnival costumes, a video history of Mardi Gras and of the Durand wedding of Oak and Pine Alley (which will be discussed at length below), and a chariot exhibit. *131 S. Main St., tel. 318/394–7334. Admission: $1 adults, 50 cents children under 12, 75 cents senior citizens. Open daily 9:30–4:30.*

In 1870, when the two daughters of Gerome Charles Durand decided to marry simultaneously, their father determined to make the double wedding an unforgettable occasion. Several days before the wedding giant spiders were released in the mile-long archway of trees leading to the house. On the wedding day the spiders' webs were sprayed with gold and silver dust to make a shimmering canopy for the wedding party. The Durand plantation is gone with the gold dust, but the Oak and Pine Alley remains two miles out of town on the Catahoula Road.

The chariots displayed in the museum are from an annual one-of-a-kind event, the **Chariot Parade,** which is a colorful procession of wagons, made by children, that depict anything from a streetcar to a castle. The children and their fanciful chariots circle the church square, beginning at dusk on the third Sunday of each August.

❺ North of the city limits on Highway 31 and Bayou Teche is the **Longfellow-Evangeline State Commemorative Area.** The 157-acre park, shaded by giant live oaks draped with Spanish moss, has picnic tables and pavilions, a boat launch, and early Acadian structures.

The Evangeline legend claims that Louis Arceneaux lived in the **Acadian House** on the park's grounds, but there is no evidence that he did. The house was built in the mid-18th century of handmade bricks, wooden pegs, and *bousillage* (an insulating mixture of mud, animal hair, and moss), and contains Louisiana antique furnishings. *Tel. 318/394–3754. Admission: $3 adults, $1.50 students, children under 6 free. Open Mon.– Sat. 9:30–4:30, Sun. 1–4.*

6 **New Iberia,** 14 miles south of St. Martinville, proudly calls itself the Queen City of the Teche and the capital of sugar-cane country. Several of the city's attractions are located relatively close to each other on Main Street.

Shadows-on-the-Teche, one of the South's most famous homes, was built for a wealthy planter more than a quarter of a century before the Civil War. Surrounded by lush gardens and towering oaks, the two-story rose-hued house has white columns, exterior staircases sheltered in *cabinets* (cabinet-like enclosures), and a pitched roof pierced by dormer windows. The Shadows is a museum property of the National Trust for Historic Preservation. *117 E. Main St., tel. 318/369–6446. Admission: $4 adults, $2 children 6–11, under 6 free. Open daily 9–4:30. Closed Thanksgiving, Christmas, and New Year's Day.*

Mintmere Plantation is a Greek Revival, galleried, raised cottage built eight feet off the ground and furnished with Louisiana antiques. The house dates from 1857, and was occupied by a Union general during the Civil War. Three suites are let to overnight guests, Yankee or otherwise. Also on the grounds is the **Armand Broussard Cottage,** which was built about 1790. *1400 E. Main St., tel. 318/364– 6210. Admission: $3.50 adults, $2.50 students, $3 senior citizens. Open daily Oct.–Apr. 10–4, May–Sept. 10–4:30. Closed Thanksgiving, Christmas, New Year's Day, and Easter.*

The **Gebert Oak** (541 E. Main St.) is a member in good standing of the Live Oak Society. Planted in 1831 and dripping with ferns and moss, the massive tree stretches over almost an entire lawn. At the corner of Weeks and St. Peter streets there is a seven-foot white marble statue of the **Emperor Hadrian** that was sculpted in Rome in AD 130.

The **Konriko Rice Mill** is the country's oldest rice mill, dating from 1912, and produces a distinctive wild pecan rice. Next to the mill is the Company Store, with Cajun crafts, foods, and a sight-and-sound show. *307 Ann St., tel. 318/367–6163. Admission to the mill: $1.50 adults, 75 cents children under 12, $1 senior citizens. Open daily 9–5.*

7 **8** **Avery Island** and **Jefferson Island,** to the south and southwest, respectively, of New Iberia, are not islands at all, but salt domes.

Avery Island, nine miles to the south, is the birthplace of Tabasco sauce, which pleases the Cajun palate and flavors many a Bloody Mary. The sauce was invented by Edmund McIlhenny in the mid-1800s, and the factory is presided over by the fourth generation of the McIlhenny family. Free tours of the factory are conducted daily. Avery Island's other attractions are its 200-acre Jungle Gardens, in which sits a 1,000-year-old Buddha, and Bird City, a bird sanctuary sometimes so thick with egrets that it appears to be blanketed with snow. *LA 329, tel. 318/369–6243. Admission to the gardens and sanctuary: $4 adults, $3 children 6–12, children under 6 free. Admission to the Tabasco factory is free. Open daily 9–5, including holidays.*

American actor Joseph Jefferson toured the country in the 19th century portraying Rip van Winkle. He became enamored of South Louisiana life and live oaks, and in 1870 he purchased 20 acres on Jefferson Island on which he built a winter home. In 1980, the salt dome beneath the house collapsed, draining Lake Peigneur (witnesses said it was like water running out of an unplugged bathtub) and causing severe damage to the property.

Live Oak Gardens has been restored to its former luxuriant state, with formal gardens and groves of oaks, crape myrtle, camellias, and azaleas. Jefferson's home is a three-story Southern Gothic house with Moorish flourishes, opulent furnishings, and rocking chairs on the wide veranda. A cafe in the reception area overlooks the lake. *284 Rip van Winkle Rd., off LA 14, tel. 318/367–3485. Admission: $5 adults, $2.50 children 5–16, $3.50 senior citizens. Open daily 9–5 during daylight saving time; 9–4 during winter.*

What to See and Do with Children

Atchafalaya Boat Basin Tours *(see* Exploring).
Avery Island *(see* Exploring).
Cajun Queen boat tours on Bayou Teche. *La Place d'Evangeline, St. Martinville, tel. 318/394–4010. Admission: $5 adults, $2.50 children.*
Jefferson Island *(see* Exploring).
Lafayette Natural History Museum and Nature Trail *(see* Exploring).
Lafayette Public Library. The Children's Department offers a variety of activities, including craft workshops, films, and puppet shows. *301 W. Congress St., tel. 318/261–5779. Admission free. Open Mon.–Thurs. 9–9, Fri.–Sat. 9–5.*
Longfellow-Evangeline State Commemorative Area *(see* Exploring).
Vermilion Queen (see Exploring).

Off the Beaten Track

"Factory" conjures up images of assembly lines and high-tech equipment, but **D. L. Menard's Chair Factory** (outside Erath) fits no such description, and the chairs made by Mr. Menard are very much in demand in this part of the country. In fact, Mr. Menard himself is very much in demand. Besides turning out chairs, he is a songwriter, a musician and performer (he plays the guitar, and some folks say he's Hank Williams reincarnate), a Cajun raconteur, and a *traiteur*, or healer.

Inside a garage that appears to be deserted, ladderbacks, old-fashioned rockers, stools, and Early American kitchen chairs are made by hand by Mr. Menard. The factory is a 20-year-old family business, with Mr. Menard's son making porch swings and his wife and daughter doing the weaving for the rush-bottom chairs.

Be sure to call before you go (tel. 318/937–5471). Mr. Menard is a very busy man. As he himself puts it, "Sometimes I'm too busy to work, I guaran*tee*." He's been touring professionally with his Cajun band since 1973, performing not only in more than 30 of these United States, but also in 17 foreign countries.

You'll have to keep a sharp eye out to spot his shop. *To reach D. L. Menard's from Lafayette, take U.S. 90 south to the junction of LA 89 and turn right. In the tiny town of Erath, make a left turn on LA 331, cross the railroad track, and drive 1 ½ mi. The shop is on the left next to a small frame house.*

A sign inside reads, Please Do Not Stand on Tables, Booths, Chairs, Jukebox, or Cigarette Machine. **Fred's Lounge** gets pretty lively during Mamou's Mardi Gras and Fourth of July celebrations. And every Saturday morning for more than 40 years live Cajun radio shows have been broadcast from Fred Tate's place. News, weather, sports, and, of course, lots of music emanate from the "studio," which is roped off like a boxing ring in the center of the small room. Cajuns who have chank-a-chanked (danced) late Friday night pack into Fred's on Saturday mornings, waltzing around the ropes and keeping the bartender busy. Things get revved up at 8 **AM** and keep going till 1 **PM**, and the show is aired on KVPI in Ville Platte.

Fred's Lounge is an hour's drive from Lafayette. *420 6th St., Mamou, tel. 318/468–5411. Take I–10 west, exit onto LA 13, and drive north through Eunice to Mamou, a town so small you can drive around for 5 minutes and find Fred's. Dress: Are you kidding? Admission free.*

Shopping

Gift Ideas   Restaurants all over the country serve their own versions of Cajun food, but you can take some of the real thing home with you. Among the shops that sell Cajun gift packages are **The Cajun Country Store** (211 Evangeline Thruway, Lafayette, tel. 318/233–7977), **Cajun Bayou Cuisine** (100 Normandy Rd., Lafayette, tel. 318/984–1493), and **B. F. Trappey's & Sons** (900 E. Main St., New Iberia, tel. 318/365–8281).

Flea Markets   Country crafts and collectibles are available at the **Antique Flea Market** (205 E. Louisiana Ave., Rayne, tel. 318/334–9520. Open the first and third weekends of each month), and you can browse indoors and out at **Jacques Square Flea Market** (623 Verot School Rd., Lafayette, tel. 318/232–4369. Open Wed.–Sun. 9–6).

Antiques   Antique-hunting is a favorite pastime in these parts. You can root around **Ruins & Relics** (1704 Jefferson & Taft Sts., Lafayette, tel. 318/233–9163. Open Tues.–Sat. 10–5), find books and magazines from the 1800s at **Le Magasin** (108 N. Polk St., Rayne, no phone. Open Sat. and Sun. 10–6), and deal with 10 dealers in the **Travel Treasures Antique Mall** (Hwy. 93 and W. Congress St., Lafayette, tel. 318/981–9414. Open Wed.–Sat. 10–5, Sun. noon–5).

Outdoor Activities and Participant Sports

Biking   Summer's high humidity can discourage rigorous exercise, but the flatlands offer easy riding. Bikes can be rented from

Pack and Paddle (601 E. Pinhook Rd., Lafayette, tel. 318/232–5854).

Bird-Watching Don Thornton takes small groups to his camp in the coastal marshes where 53 different species of birds can be seen (tel. 318/364–2752).

Boating and The 800,000-acre Atchafalaya Basin is 15 miles east of Lafa-
Fishing yette. Boat rentals, guides, and fishing gear can be rented at **McGee's Landing** (Levee Rd., Henderson, tel. 318/228–8519 or 318/228–2384).

Camping There are 6,000 acres with picnic areas, a boat ramp, cabins, and camping facilities at **Lake Fausse Point State Park** (Rte. 5, Box 4658, St. Martinville, 70502, tel. 318/229–4764).

Golf Birdies and eagles can be sought in **City Park** (Mudd Ave., Lafayette, tel. 318/261–8385) and **Vieux Chene Golf Course** (Youngsville Hwy., Broussard, tel. 318/837–1159).

Spectator Sports

Cajundome NBA exhibition and collegiate basketball, professional soccer exhibition games, wrestling, and other sports events take place here during the year (444 Cajundome Blvd., Lafayette, tel. 318/265–2100).

Horse Racing Thoroughbred racing April through Labor Day at **Evangeline Downs** (1 mi north of I-10 on I-49, Lafayette, tel. 318/896–6185), where each race begins, *Ils sont partis!*

Jousting The sport of knights was introduced here by early French settlers and revived in 1952. The **Tournoi,** with costumed knights on speedy steeds, takes place in mid-October during the annual Cotton Festival in Ville Platte (tel. 318/363–4521).

Dining and Lodging

Dining Cajun food is often described as the robust, hot-peppery country kin of Creole cuisine. Ubiquitous sea critters turn up in a wide variety of exotic concoctions, such as etouffees, bisques, and boulettes, and almost every Acadiana menu offers jambalaya, gumbo, and some blackened dish. Alligator meat is a great favorite, as are boudin and andouille, which are hot-hot sausages. Cajun food is very rich, and portions tend to be ample. Biscuits and grits are breakfast staples, and many an evening meal ends with bread pudding.

Category	Cost*
Very Expensive	$35 and up
Expensive	$25–$35
Moderate	$15–$20
Inexpensive	under $15

per person without tax (8%), service, or drinks

Lodging The greatest concentration of accommodations is in Lafayette, which has an abundance of chain motels and a few luxury hotels. In nearby towns there are antique-filled antebellum plantation homes that offer overnights complete with old-fashioned plantation breakfasts.

Category	Cost*
Very Expensive	Over $120
Expensive	$90–$120
Moderate	$50–$90
Inexpensive	under $50

double room; add 6% taxes or service

The following credit card abbreviations are used: AE, American Express; CB, Carte Blanche; DC, Diners Club; MC, MasterCard; and V, Visa.

Breaux Bridge
Dining

Mulate's. A roadhouse with flashing yellow lights outside and red-and-white plastic tablecloths inside, Mulate's is a Cajun eatery, a dance hall (live Cajun music every night except Mon.), an age-old family gathering place, and a celebrity that has been featured on "The Today Show" and "Good Morning, America," among other airings. A dressed-down crowd digs into the likes of stuffed crabs and the Super Seafood Platter. *325 Mills Ave. (Hwy. 94), tel. in LA 800/634–9880; elsewhere in USA 800/42–CAJUN. Dress: informal. Reservations not required. AE, MC, V. Closed Christmas Day. Inexpensive.*

Lafayette
Dining

Angelle's. A steep pitched roof and vaulted ceiling with cypress beams cover two dining rooms made cozy by old-brick fireplaces. Specialties include snapper Daniel (red snapper stuffed with crabmeat and shrimp topped with crab cream sauce) and broiled seafood platter of catfish, shrimp, frog legs, and crawfish in season. *U.S. 167N, across from Evangeline Downs, tel. 318/896–8416. Dress: informal. Reservations accepted but not required. AE, DC, MC, V. Closed Mon. and Christmas Day. Inexpensive.*

Cafe Vermilionville. A stately, two-story, white-columned house that was an inn in the 19th century. Casual elegance, with crisp white napery, old-brick fireplaces, and cocktails in a graceful gazebo. Among the specialties are redfish Anna, with lump crabmeat, artichoke hearts, and béarnaise sauce, and fried soft-shell crab with crawfish fettuccine. *1304 W. Pinhook Rd., tel. 318/237–0100. Dress: informal. Reservations advised. AE, DC, MC, V. Closed Christmas and New Year's Day. Inexpensive.*

Don's Seafood and Steakhouse. A local favorite since 1934, with specialties including stuffed red snapper and shrimp and oysters en brochette. The bread pudding is made by celestial beings. *301 E. Vermilion St., tel. 318/235–3551. Dress: informal. Reservations not necessary. AE, CB, DC, MC, V. Closed Christmas. Inexpensive.*

Prejean's. This restaurant is set in a small cypress house with a wide front porch and a 50-foot shrimp boat parked outside. Oyster shuckers work in a cozy bar, and locals gather at tables with red and white checked cloths to partake of Prejean's platter (seafood gumbo, fried shrimp, oysters, catfish, and seafood-stuffed bell peppers), and crawfish dinner, with the little critters etouffeed, bisqued, and fried. Live Cajun music every night. *3480 U.S. 167N, next to Evangeline Downs, tel. 318/896–3247. Dress: informal. Reservations not necessary. AE, CB, DC, MC, V. Closed Thanksgiving and Christmas. Inexpensive.*

Lodging **Evangeline Inn–Best Western.** You will surely not starve if you stay here: The motel is located in a long line of fast-food chains, five miles south of Evangeline Downs. The small, darkish lobby is done in an Early Motel motif; rooms are what you'd expect in a Best Western. *108 Frontage Rd., 70501, tel. 318/233–2090 or 800/528–1234. 194 rooms with bath. Facilities: restaurant, lounge, cable TV, pool. AE, CB, DC, MC, V. Inexpensive.*

Holiday Inn Central–Holidome. A huge complex sprawling over 17 acres, this motel-cum-indoor recreation center is like a streamlined small town designed by a hyperactive Yuppie planning committee. The split-level public areas are spacious, airy, and filled with lush plants. Guest rooms are a cut above the average Holiday Inn. *2032 N.E. Evangeline Thruway, 70509, tel. 318/233–6815 or 800/HOLIDAY. 250 rooms with bath. Facilities: restaurant, lounge, cable TV, airport shuttle, heated indoor pool with whirlpool and sauna, outdoor pool, 2 lighted tennis courts, 24-hr jogging track, game rooms, playgrounds and picnic areas, baby-sitting service. AE, CB, DC, MC, V. Moderate.*

Hotel Acadiana. The lobby is replete with cushy sofas, lots of gold leaf, and a huge chandelier. VIPs may opt for the Crown Service concierge floor, but all rooms have thick carpets, marble-top dressers, and wing chairs. Even-numbered rooms face the pool, and most rooms have wet bars and minirefrigerators. Built in 1980, the hotel is located across the road from the *Vermilion Queen* boat landing. *1801 W. Pinhook Rd., 70508, tel. 318/233–8120, in LA 800/874–4664, elsewhere in the United States 800/826–8386. 304 rooms with bath. Facilities: restaurant, lounge, cable TV with ESPN, 2 outdoor pools, facilities for handicapped, free parking. AE, DC, MC, V. Inexpensive.*

Lafayette Hilton & Towers. Mirrored pillars and medieval tapestries fill the ballroom-size lobby, and guest rooms are only slightly smaller. Traditional furnishings in standard rooms; rooms on concierge floors come with bathroom phones, Jacuzzis, and wet bars. Riverside rooms have a view of the Bayou Vermilion, upon whose bank this high rise rises. *1521 Pinhook Rd., 70508, tel. 318/235–6111 or 800/332–2586. 328 rooms with bath. Facilities: restaurant, lounge, heliport, airport limo, heated indoor pool, free parking, cable TV. AE, DC, MC, V. Moderate.*

Ti Frere's House. Built in 1880 of native cypress and handmade bricks, "little brother's house" has been a bed-and-breakfast since 1985. Located two miles from the Oil Center (an office and shopping complex), the Acadian-style house with Victorian trim is furnished with French and Louisiana antiques. Guests are greeted with a complimentary mint julep, and a plantation breakfast is served in the formal dining room. No pets, no children, no smoking (except in the galleries or in the gazebo). *1905 Verot School Rd., 70508, tel. 318/984–9347. 3 rooms with bath (1 double, 2 doubles). Facilities: washer/dryer. MC, V. Moderate.*

New Iberia **Patout's.** Ceiling fans whir overhead and stained-glass win-
Dining dows overlook luxuriant plants in the 1920s house. A third generation of Patouts oversees fresh Louisiana seafood specialties such as Ladyfish (redfish topped with shrimp and crabmeat) and seafood Patout (stuffed oysters and crawfish etouffee). *1846 Center St., tel. 318/365–5206. Dress: informal.*

Reservations not required. AE, DC, V. Closed Sun. Inexpensive.

Lodging **Mintmere Plantation.** A Greek Revival raised cottage on the banks of Bayou Teche. Built in 1857 and furnished with period antiques, it was occupied by a Union general during the Recent Unpleasantness (or, as it's more commonly known, the Civil War). On the grounds is an Acadian cottage, ca. 1790, also furnished with antiques. *1400 Main St., 70560, tel. 318/364–6210. 3 suites in the main house (1 with 2 bedrooms), 2 bedrooms in the cottage, all with private bath. No credit cards. Closed Thanksgiving, Christmas, New Year's Day, and Easter. Expensive.*

St. Martinville **La Place d'Evangeline.** In the late 18th century, the Castillo
Dining Hotel, a two-story, red-brick building next to the Evangeline Oak and Bayou Teche, was an inn for steamboat passengers and a gathering place for French Royalists. Since June of 1987, diners have feasted in the spacious, high-ceilinged rooms where the Royalists attended balls and operas. Steak Evangeline stuffed with lump crabmeat, redfish Gabriel topped with seafood sauce, and alligator boulettes are among the many offerings. *Port St. at Bayou Teche, tel. 318/394–4010. Dress: informal. Reservations not necessary. AE, MC, V. Open daily 8 AM–8 PM. Call for weekend closing times. Closed Christmas Day. Moderate.*

Lodging **Beno's Motel.** Large, well-lit public rooms. Each guest room is furnished with two twin, double, or king-size beds and separate dressing areas. *101 Clover Hill Rd., Hwy. 31, 70582, tel. 318/394–5523. All rooms with private bath. Facilities: restaurant, lounge, satellite TV, pool, free parking. DC, MC, V. Inexpensive.*

Arts, Festivals, and Nightlife

Theater The University of Southwestern Louisiana's Performing Arts Department presents contemporary plays and dance concerts from early fall until late spring. Performances are in USL's Burke Hall. *For tickets and information contact the Performing Arts Department, Box 43850, Lafayette, 70504, tel. 318/231–6357.*

Théâtre 'Cadien performs plays in French in conjunction with the local Abbey Players. *200 S. State St., Abbeville, 70510, tel. 318/893–2936.*

Lafayette Community Theatre *(529 Jefferson St., Lafayette, 70501, tel. 318/235–1532).* Presents contemporary plays with Cajun flair.

Concerts Internationally renowned guest artists perform with the **Acadiana Symphony Orchestra** (tel. 318/233–7060) during its November through April season.

The **Lafayette Concert Band's** season includes both classical and pop, with appearances by guest artists. *For information write to Box 53762, Lafayette, 70505, tel. 318/233–7060.*

Major concert attractions are featured at Lafayette's **Cajundome.** *For information and tickets contact the Dome at 444 Cajundome Blvd., Lafayette, 70506, tel. 318/265–2100.*

Choral music is performed during the fall and spring by **Chorale Acadienne.** *For information write to 704 Lee Ave., Lafayette, 70501, tel. 318/233–7060.*

International symphony orchestras and dance companies are presented by **Lafayette Community Concerts,** *Box 2465, Lafayette, 70502, tel. 318/233–7060.*

Festivals Each year, during the third weekend of September, Lafayette hosts **Festival Acadiens.** Cajun music and Cajun food are showcased. For details contact the Lafayette Convention and Visitors Commission. Other festival events include the **Louisiana Native Crafts Festival** at the Natural History Museum (*see* Exploring), the **Deep South Writers' Conference,** and the **Louisiana Film/Video Festival** at the University Art Museum (101 Girard Park Dr.).

Lafayette's newest festival was inaugurated in July 1987. **Festival International de Louisiane** is a blend of local and international entertainers, artisans, and chefs. Opening ceremonies for the premier event included a 400-voice chorus and hundreds of musicians and dancers in native costume. *Les Chefs de Cuisine d'Acadiana* prepared a food fest; poets, mimes, musicians, storytellers, and stilt-walkers performed in the street; and **La Place des Enfants** provided puppets, folk tales, music, and dance for children. *For information contact Festival International de Louisiane, Box 4008, Lafayette, 70502, tel. 318/232–8086.*

Nightlife While you're deep in the heart of Cajun Country you'll have a chance to chank-a-chank at a *fais-do-do.* Chank-a-chank? Fais-do-do? The little iron triangles played in Cajun bands make a rhythmic chank-a-chank sound, and dancing to the beat is chank-a-chanking. A fais-do-do (pronounced fay-doh-doh, meaning go to sleep) is a country dance. The term comes from words mothers murmured to put their babies to sleep while the fiddlers tuned up before a dance.

Rock, R&B, country/western, and reggae are all alive and well in Cajun Country, and there are nightclubs and lounges that feature golden oldies and cheek-to-cheek dancing. But Cajun music is unique and this is where it all began, so we'll focus on it in this section.

Fais-do-dos are family affairs, with young and old two-stepping and waltzing together to the fiddles, accordions, and chank-a-chanking triangles. They're held either in dance halls or outdoors in the square throughout the region. Attire is very informal, and so is the ambience.

Pick up a copy of *The Times of Acadiana* and check the "On the Town" listings for fais-do-dos, as well as for other forms of nighttime fun. The newspaper is free and available in hotels, restaurants, and shops.

The places listed below regularly feature Cajun music and dancing.

Mulate's (*see* Dining).
Prejean's (*see* Dining).
Randol's. Cajun cuisine in a greenhouse setting, with music and dancing nightly. *2320 Kaliste Saloom Rd., Lafayette, tel. 318/981–7080.*

La Poussiere. An age-old Cajun dance hall. *1212 Grand Point Rd., Breaux Bridge, tel. 318/332–1721.*

Belizaire's. Alligator meat and two-stepping feet are what you'll find in this Cajun joint. *2307 N. Parkerson St., Crowley, tel. 318/788–2501.*

Cajun Music Show. A live radio broadcast, mostly in French, that has been described as a combination of the Louisiana Hayride, the Grand Ol' Opry, and the *Prairie Home Companion. Saturday nights at 6 in the Liberty Theatre, Park Ave. in downtown Eunice. Admission: $1.*

Index

Personal Itinerary

Departure *Date*

Time

Transportation

Arrival *Date*   *Time*

Departure *Date*   *Time*

Transportation

Accommodations

Arrival *Date*   *Time*

Departure *Date*   *Time*

Transportation

Accommodations

Arrival *Date*   *Time*

Departure *Date*   *Time*

Transportation

Accommodations

Personal Itinerary

Arrival *Date*   *Time*

Departure *Date*   *Time*

Transportation

Accommodations

Arrival *Date*   *Time*

Departure *Date*   *Time*

Transportation

Accommodations

Arrival *Date*   *Time*

Departure *Date*   *Time*

Transportation

Accommodations

Arrival *Date*   *Time*

Departure *Date*   *Time*

Transportation

Accommodations

Personal Itinerary

Arrival *Date*   *Time*

Departure *Date*   *Time*

Transportation

Accommodations

Arrival *Date*   *Time*

Departure *Date*   *Time*

Transportation

Accommodations

Arrival *Date*   *Time*

Departure *Date*   *Time*

Transportation

Accommodations

Arrival *Date*   *Time*

Departure *Date*   *Time*

Transportation

Accommodations

Personal Itinerary

Arrival *Date*   *Time*

Departure *Date*   *Time*

Transportation

Accommodations

Arrival *Date*   *Time*

Departure *Date*   *Time*

Transportation

Accommodations

Arrival *Date*   *Time*

Departure *Date*   *Time*

Transportation

Accommodations

Arrival *Date*   *Time*

Departure *Date*   *Time*

Transportation

Accommodations

Personal Itinerary

Arrival *Date*   *Time*

Departure *Date*   *Time*

Transportation

Accommodations

Arrival *Date*   *Time*

Departure *Date*   *Time*

Transportation

Accommodations

Arrival *Date*   *Time*

Departure *Date*   *Time*

Transportation

Accommodations

Arrival *Date*   *Time*

Departure *Date*   *Time*

Transportation

Accommodations

Addresses

Name

Address

Telephone

Name

Address

Telephone

Name

Address

Telephone

Name

Address

Telephone

Name

Address

Telephone

Name

Address

Telephone

Name

Address

Telephone

Name

Address

Telephone

Name

Address

Telephone

Name

Address

Telephone

Name

Address

Telephone

Name

Address

Telephone

Name

Address

Telephone

Name

Address

Telephone

Name

Address

Telephone

Name

Address

Telephone

Addresses

Name	*Name*
Address	*Address*
Telephone	*Telephone*
Name	*Name*
Address	*Address*
Telephone	*Telephone*
Name	*Name*
Address	*Address*
Telephone	*Telephone*
Name	*Name*
Address	*Address*
Telephone	*Telephone*
Name	*Name*
Address	*Address*
Telephone	*Telephone*
Name	*Name*
Address	*Address*
Telephone	*Telephone*
Name	*Name*
Address	*Address*
Telephone	*Telephone*
Name	*Name*
Address	*Address*
Telephone	*Telephone*

Addresses

Name	*Name*
Address	*Address*
Telephone	*Telephone*
Name	*Name*
Address	*Address*
Telephone	*Telephone*
Name	*Name*
Address	*Address*
Telephone	*Telephone*
Name	*Name*
Address	*Address*
Telephone	*Telephone*
Name	*Name*
Address	*Address*
Telephone	*Telephone*
Name	*Name*
Address	*Address*
Telephone	*Telephone*
Name	*Name*
Address	*Address*
Telephone	*Telephone*

Addresses

Name	*Name*
Address	*Address*
Telephone	*Telephone*
Name	*Name*
Address	*Address*
Telephone	*Telephone*
Name	*Name*
Address	*Address*
Telephone	*Telephone*
Name	*Name*
Address	*Address*
Telephone	*Telephone*
Name	*Name*
Address	*Address*
Telephone	*Telephone*
Name	*Name*
Address	*Address*
Telephone	*Telephone*
Name	*Name*
Address	*Address*
Telephone	*Telephone*
Name	*Name*
Address	*Address*
Telephone	*Telephone*

Addresses

Name	*Name*
Address	*Address*
Telephone	*Telephone*
Name	*Name*
Address	*Address*
Telephone	*Telephone*
Name	*Name*
Address	*Address*
Telephone	*Telephone*
Name	*Name*
Address	*Address*
Telephone	*Telephone*
Name	*Name*
Address	*Address*
Telephone	*Telephone*
Name	*Name*
Address	*Address*
Telephone	*Telephone*
Name	*Name*
Address	*Address*
Telephone	*Telephone*
Name	*Name*
Address	*Address*
Telephone	*Telephone*

Addresses

Name	*Name*
Address	*Address*
Telephone	*Telephone*
Name	*Name*
Address	*Address*
Telephone	*Telephone*
Name	*Name*
Address	*Address*
Telephone	*Telephone*
Name	*Name*
Address	*Address*
Telephone	*Telephone*
Name	*Name*
Address	*Address*
Telephone	*Telephone*
Name	*Name*
Address	*Address*
Telephone	*Telephone*
Name	*Name*
Address	*Address*
Telephone	*Telephone*
Name	*Name*
Address	*Address*
Telephone	*Telephone*

Fodor's Travel Guides

U.S. Guides

Alaska
American Cities
The American South
Arizona
Atlantic City & the
  New Jersey Shore
Boston
California
Cape Cod
Carolinas & the
  Georgia Coast
Chesapeake
Chicago
Colorado
Dallas & Fort Worth
Disney World & the
  Orlando Area

The Far West
Florida
Greater Miami,
  Fort Lauderdale,
  Palm Beach
Hawaii
Hawaii *(Great Travel
  Values)*
Houston & Galveston
I-10: California to
  Florida
I-55: Chicago to New
  Orleans
I-75: Michigan to
  Florida
I-80: San Francisco to
  New York

I-95: Maine to Miami
Las Vegas
Los Angeles, Orange
  County, Palm Springs
Maui
New England
New Mexico
New Orleans
New Orleans *(Pocket
  Guide)*
New York City
New York City *(Pocket
  Guide)*
New York State
Pacific North Coast
Philadelphia
Puerto Rico *(Fun in)*

Rockies
San Diego
San Francisco
San Francisco *(Pocket
  Guide)*
Texas
United States of
  America
Virgin Islands
  (U.S. & British)
Virginia
Waikiki
Washington, DC
Williamsburg,
  Jamestown &
  Yorktown

Foreign Guides

Acapulco
Amsterdam
Australia, New Zealand
  & the South Pacific
Austria
The Bahamas
The Bahamas *(Pocket
  Guide)*
Barbados *(Fun in)*
Beijing, Guangzhou &
  Shanghai
Belgium & Luxembourg
Bermuda
Brazil
Britain *(Great Travel
  Values)*
Canada
Canada *(Great Travel
  Values)*
Canada's Maritime
  Provinces
Cancún, Cozumel,
  Mérida, The
  Yucatán
Caribbean
Caribbean *(Great
  Travel Values)*

Central America
Copenhagen,
  Stockholm, Oslo,
  Helsinki, Reykjavik
Eastern Europe
Egypt
Europe
Europe *(Budget)*
Florence & Venice
France
France *(Great Travel
  Values)*
Germany
Germany *(Great Travel
  Values)*
Great Britain
Greece
Holland
Hong Kong & Macau
Hungary
India
Ireland
Israel
Italy
Italy *(Great Travel
  Values)*
Jamaica *(Fun in)*

Japan
Japan *(Great Travel
  Values)*
Jordan & the Holy Land
Kenya
Korea
Lisbon
Loire Valley
London
London *(Pocket Guide)*
London *(Great Travel
  Values)*
Madrid
Mexico
Mexico *(Great Travel
  Values)*
Mexico City & Acapulco
Mexico's Baja & Puerto
  Vallarta, Mazatlán,
  Manzanillo, Copper
  Canyon
Montreal
Munich
New Zealand
North Africa
Paris
Paris *(Pocket Guide)*

People's Republic of
  China
Portugal
Province of Quebec
Rio de Janeiro
The Riviera *(Fun on)*
Rome
St. Martin/St. Maarten
Scandinavia
Scotland
Singapore
South America
South Pacific
Southeast Asia
Soviet Union
Spain
Spain *(Great Travel
  Values)*
Sweden
Switzerland
Sydney
Tokyo
Toronto
Turkey
Vienna
Yugoslavia

Special-Interest Guides

Bed & Breakfast
  Guide: North America
  1936...On the
  Continent

Royalty Watching
Selected Hotels of
  Europe

Selected Resorts
  and Hotels of the U.S.
Ski Resorts of North
  America

Views to Dine by
  around the World

Join us in updating the next edition of your Fodor's guide

Title of Guide:

1 Hotel ☐ Restaurant ☐ *(check one)*

Name

Number/Street

City/State/Country

Comments

2 Hotel ☐ Restaurant ☐ *(check one)*

Name

Number/Street

City/State/Country

Comments

3 Hotel ☐ Restaurant ☐ *(check one)*

Name

Number/Street

City/State/Country

Comments

Your Name *(optional)*

Address

General Comments

Business Reply Mail

First Class   Permit Nº 7775   New York, NY

Postage will be paid by addressee

Fodor's Travel Publications

201 East 50th Street

New York, NY 10022